IMAGES
of America

OLD SAN CARLOS

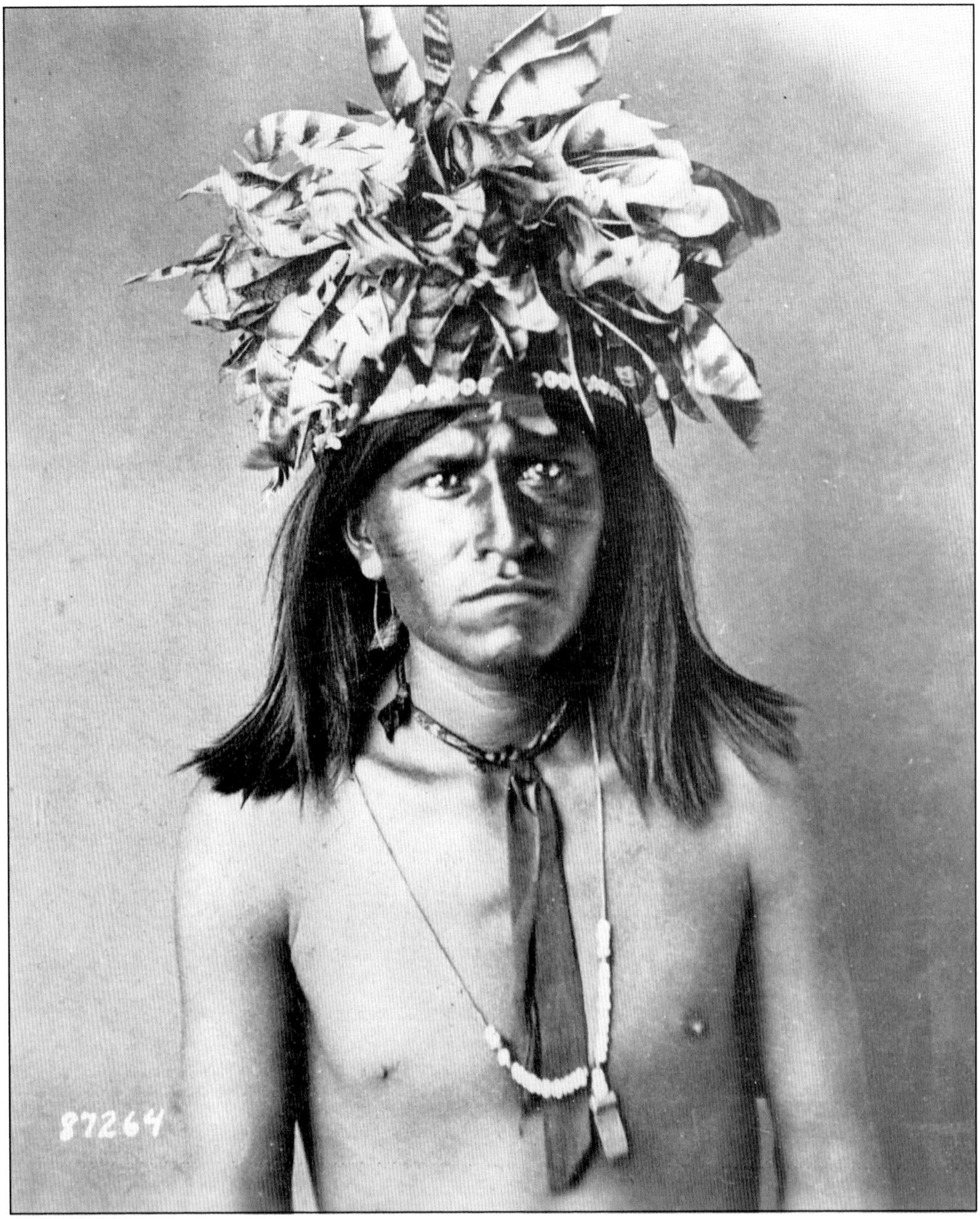

This man is identified as Ya-va-ki-shi, an Apache scout, in the photograph caption. Other sources tentatively identify him as possibly being Yavapai, photographed in the late 1870s by G. H. Rothrock. Regardless of tribal affiliation, he was probably enlisted at San Carlos following the removal of the Yavapai to that agency. He wears the traditional turkey-feather war cap and tweezers around his neck. (Courtesy National Archives and Records Administration [NARA], RG 111, Signal Corps Collection, No. 87264.)

ON THE COVER: Members of Troop C, 1st Cavalry, are posed alongside their frame barrack building at San Carlos in 1894. (Courtesy NARA, RG 111, Signal Corps Collection, No. 107683.)

IMAGES
of America

OLD SAN CARLOS

Paul and Kathleen Nickens

Arizona Historical Foundation

ARCADIA
PUBLISHING

ISBN 978-0-7385-5891-2

Published by Arcadia Publishing
Charleston, South Carolina

Printed in the United States of America

Library of Congress Catalog Card Number: 2008928327

For all general information contact Arcadia Publishing at:
Telephone 843-853-2070
Fax 843-853-0044
E-mail sales@arcadiapublishing.com
For customer service and orders:
Toll-Free 1-888-313-2665

Visit us on the Internet at www.arcadiapublishing.com

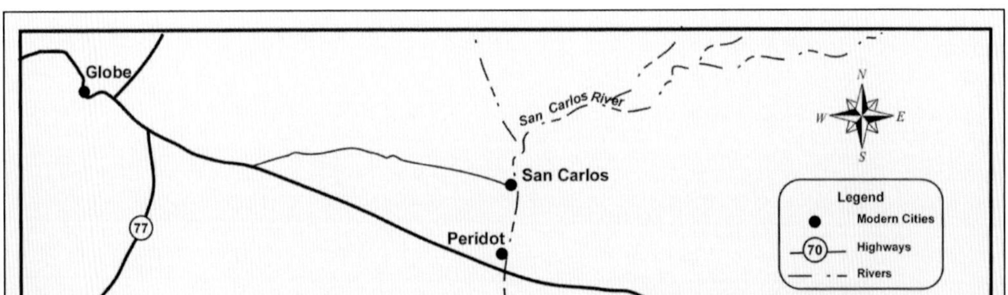

This map shows the location of Old San Carlos (1873–1929) in relation to the Coolidge Dam and San Carlos Reservoir, as well as present-day San Carlos, the headquarters of the San Carlos Indian Agency since 1929. Before 1929, three reservation population districts were identified: San Carlos, Bylas, and Rice (now "new" San Carlos). (Courtesy Lisa A. Nickens.)

Contents

Acknowledgments		6
Introduction		7
1.	Apache and Yavapai Groups	11
2.	San Carlos Agency to 1900	33
3.	Post of San Carlos	47
4.	Apache and Yavapai Police and Scouts	67
5.	San Carlos Agency after 1900	87
6.	Schools and Missions	107
7.	The End of Old San Carlos	117

Acknowledgments

The authors would like to first and foremost express appreciation to our editor at Arcadia Publishing, Jared Jackson, along with other staff at Arcadia, for vital assistance and guidance in the preparation of this book.

The impetus for this volume in the Images of America series originated several years ago when the senior author was contracted to the Phoenix Area Office of the Bureau of Indian Affairs for archaeological studies at San Carlos Reservoir. Gratitude is extended to that office for initial support and encouragement.

Since that time, photographic images and other information have been acquired from a number of offices and archives that help chronicle the incredible history of Old San Carlos. We sincerely appreciate the assistance received from the skilled staffs at each of the following locations. Places visited in search of information and images include the following: Arizona Historical Foundation (AHF); Arizona Historical Society; Arizona State University Libraries (ASUL), Archives and Special Collections; Cumberland County Historical Society (CCHS), Carlisle, Pennsylvania; Gila County Historical Society (GCHS); National Archives and Records Administration (NARA), College Park, Maryland, Laguna Niguel, California, and Washington, D.C.; University of Arizona Libraries, Special Collections; and the U.S. Army, Military History Institute, Carlisle, Pennsylvania. We would also like to thank Diane Drobka for her generosity, allowing access to and use of her photograph collection of the San Carlos area. Photographic illustrations included herein came from the collections of those archives listed above with acronyms added.

The maps in the book were prepared by our daughter, Lisa A. Nickens. Her skill and eye for detail have enhanced our book by providing meaningful information to the reader. We sincerely thank her for her important contribution.

Introduction

At the beginning of the 19th century, much of the region that would eventually become New Mexico and Arizona was still in the hands of Spain. The Spaniards called the area "Apachería," a designation that also included thousands of square miles in northern Mexico. The native occupants of the area included the widely distributed Athapaskan-speaking groups that came to be known collectively as the Apaches. Their neighbors were the various Pueblo villages to the east along the Rio Grande Valley, the linguistically related Navajo to the north, the Piman-speaking groups of the Arizona desert lands to the west, and the Pai groups to the northwest. By the middle of that century, the region had become part of the United States by virtue of negotiated agreements with Mexico.

The Apaches were not a cohesive tribe but were gathered in several somewhat large regional groupings and local bands as varied as the expansive physiographic province they inhabited. The various Apache groups were confusingly identified at times in the late 19th and early 20th centuries because of their cultural and geographic diversity, and the highly mobile nature of their way of life—characteristics that became only more complex and confounding over time as they adapted to and were forced to comply with the vagaries of U.S. government Native American affairs policies.

For the purposes of this book, two larger Apache groupings are important. The first is the Western Apache, originally located over a large part of east central Arizona, including the Aravaipas, Pinalenos, Coyoteros, White Mountain, and Tonto Apaches, and other local bands. Today these groups occupy the adjacent Fort Apache and San Carlos Indian Reservations in east central Arizona and the much smaller Tonto Apache Indian Reservation near Payson, Arizona. The second cluster of bands includes those generally referred to as the Chiricahua Apaches, residing in what is now southeastern Arizona, southern New Mexico, and parts of northern Mexico. The Chiricahua, along with their closely related neighbors, the Warm Springs Apaches of south central New Mexico, were at various times sent to the San Carlos Reservation in the late 1800s, but several times, factions broke from the confinement. Because of their primary role in the well-known Apache wars of the late 19th century, the Chiricahua people were designated by the federal government as prisoners of war and sent first to Florida and then to Alabama in the late 1880s. Their descendents eventually landed at Fort Sill, Oklahoma, and later some went on to the Mescalero Apache Reservation in New Mexico.

As the westward expansion of American settlement entered Apache lands in the 1860s, inevitable conflicts arose. Initially, the U.S. authorities embarked on a campaign to essentially eliminate the local native population. Faced with the quick realization that this approach was not practical, the U.S. government then undertook a "peace policy," involving the creation of bounded reservations for the various tribes and bands on which they could become self-sufficient in due time. Thus, an executive order, dated December 14, 1872, created a reservation for all of the Western Apache bands, with the agency to be located at the confluence of the Gila and San Carlos Rivers. Initially known as the White Mountain Reserve, it became more commonly called the San Carlos Indian

Reservation after the agency headquarters. The same executive order set aside a reserve for the Chiricahuas in southeastern Arizona, but it was cancelled four years later.

The San Carlos Agency was first occupied in February 1873 and immediately became the seat of unrest since many Apaches preferred to remain where they had lived for centuries and not be forced to the new agency. Coupled with these cultural preferences were other important considerations in that the site for the agency was considered a somewhat inhospitable locale, and since it was a new undertaking, there were no accommodations for either the agency personnel or native people. Furthermore, there was no immediate way to feed such a large concentration of people. This lack of preparation led to the staffing of a temporary encampment of U.S. Army troops next to the agency to exert control and policing actions as needed.

To add fuel to a rapidly growing firestorm, the federal government soon initiated a "concentration policy," a strategy that was ultimately proven to be misguided and tragic. Under this approach, all the Western Apache groups were required to physically move to the agency, angering those living in the more attractive northern part of the reserve. In 1874, about 1,500 Yavapai people and Tonto Apaches were also forcefully marched to San Carlos from their reservation to the northwest. Two years later, the Chiricahua Reservation was dissolved and its occupants, at least those that did not escape to Mexico, were removed to San Carlos. The following year, members of the Warm Springs Apache Reservation in New Mexico were similarly sent to San Carlos. By 1877, there were more than 5,000 Apaches and Yavapais located at the San Carlos Agency, making it the largest population center in the Territory of Arizona at the time.

During the next 10 years or more, the San Carlos Agency remained in near constant strife. The concentration of several tribes and bands in one place proved to be a mistake. Long-standing rivalries between groups came to the forefront as they dealt with proximity to one another, and others, particularly the Chiricahuas, chafed at having been forced from their former homelands to San Carlos. This unhappiness led to several breakouts, in which various groups bolted from the reservation, resulting in the well-known, decade-long series of Indian wars in the Southwest. During the same period, ongoing arguments ensued between military and civilian authorities over who could best manage the agency and wield control over the unhappy occupants. Based in part on the failure of either the military or civilian personnel to exercise effective control over the rebellious Apaches, and partly because of widespread graft and other improprieties on the part of some civilian agents and contractors, the army was given exclusive authority over the agency in 1884, a role it would keep until the military post was closed in 1901.

The pervasive unhappiness of Apaches and non-Apaches alike associated with San Carlos is adequately expressed in the following first person descriptions of the locale:

> San Carlos! That was the worst place in all the great territory stolen from the Apaches. If anybody had ever lived there permanently, no Apache knew of it. Where there is no grass there is no game. Nearly all of the vegetation was cacti; and though in season a little cactus fruit was produced, the rest of the year food was lacking. The heat was terrible. The insects were terrible. The water was terrible. What there was in the sluggish river was brackish and warm. Pools along side the channel afforded places for insects to hatch. They served, as I know now, as breeding places for clouds of mosquitoes. Insects and rattlesnakes seemed to thrive there; and no White Eye could possibly fear and dislike snakes more than do Apaches. There were tarantulas, Gila monsters, and centipedes. At times it was so hot that I am sure the thermometer would have registered well above 120 degrees. At San Carlos, for the first time within the memory of any of my people, the Apaches experienced the shaking sickness [malaria]. (Chiricahua Apache man, exiled to Florida and later educated at Carlisle Industrial School.)

> San Carlos won unanimously our designation "Hells Forty Acres." A gravelly flat in the confluence of two rivers rose some thirty feet or so above the river bottoms and was dotted here and there by drab adobe buildings of the Agency. Scrawny, dejected lines of scattered

> cottonwoods, shrunken, almost leafless, marked the course of the streams. Rain was so infrequent that it took on the semblance of a phenomenon when it came at all. Almost continuously dry, hot, dust and gravel-laden winds swept the plain, denuding it of almost every vestige of vegetation. In the summer a temperature of 110 degrees in the shade was cool weather. At all other times of the year flies, gnats, and unnamable bugs swarmed in the millions. (3rd Cavalry officer stationed at Camp San Carlos 1883–1884.)

> Perhaps the rudest and poorest accommodations for officers and men to be found in the Army are met with on the Indian reservation at San Carlos. San Carlos is afflicted with many severe dust storms, each usually lasting about three days. During one of these the men in their quarters, with canvas sides and numerous cracks and holes in the walls, are literally covered with dust and remain so during the whole storm. (U.S. Army report on "Sanitary Condition of the Army," 1893.)

The final surrender of the last Chiricahua hostiles, led by Geronimo, occurred in 1886, and, along with the deportation of that tribe to Florida soon thereafter, ended the Native American campaigns in the region. By 1900, other groups that had been compelled to go to San Carlos in the 1870s, including the Apache bands from the White Mountain area, the Tonto Apaches, and the Yavapais, were allowed to leave San Carlos and return to reservations in their former homelands. The Fort Apache Reservation, including a separate agency for the White Mountain Apache Tribe, was set aside from the larger reservation in 1897. All remaining army troops and supplies were withdrawn from San Carlos in November 1901, and the buildings were turned over to the Interior Department.

Those Apaches that remained at San Carlos, known collectively as the San Carlos Apaches, continued to farm and develop the area around the agency in the early 20th century. Their travails were, however, far from over. Following years of study, some 22,000 acres of land were withdrawn from the reservation in 1924 for the construction of Coolidge Dam and reservoir. When completed in 1928, the dam's pool would inundate the San Carlos Agency and the old military camp, along with nearly 200 Apache homes and farms. Consequently, in 1929, the agency was moved about 12 miles north up the San Carlos River, keeping the same name. Some of the old agency buildings were dismantled and moved to the new location; others were dynamited in place. The original agency location, now called "Old San Carlos," remains in the reservoir pool and occasionally emerges when the water level is drawn down for irrigation water needed downstream on the Gila River. The Apache name for the old agency locale is *ni-te-gu-chi*, loosely translated as "bare land extending to the river."

Although briefly mentioned in all the written sources relating the early history of the Apaches, the state of Arizona, and the voluminous literature devoted to the Apache wars of the late 19th century, the considerable role that the San Carlos Agency and adjacent army camp played in the march of events has not been told in detail. This book partially remedies this oversight by offering a visual overview of the place and, more importantly, the people of Old San Carlos.

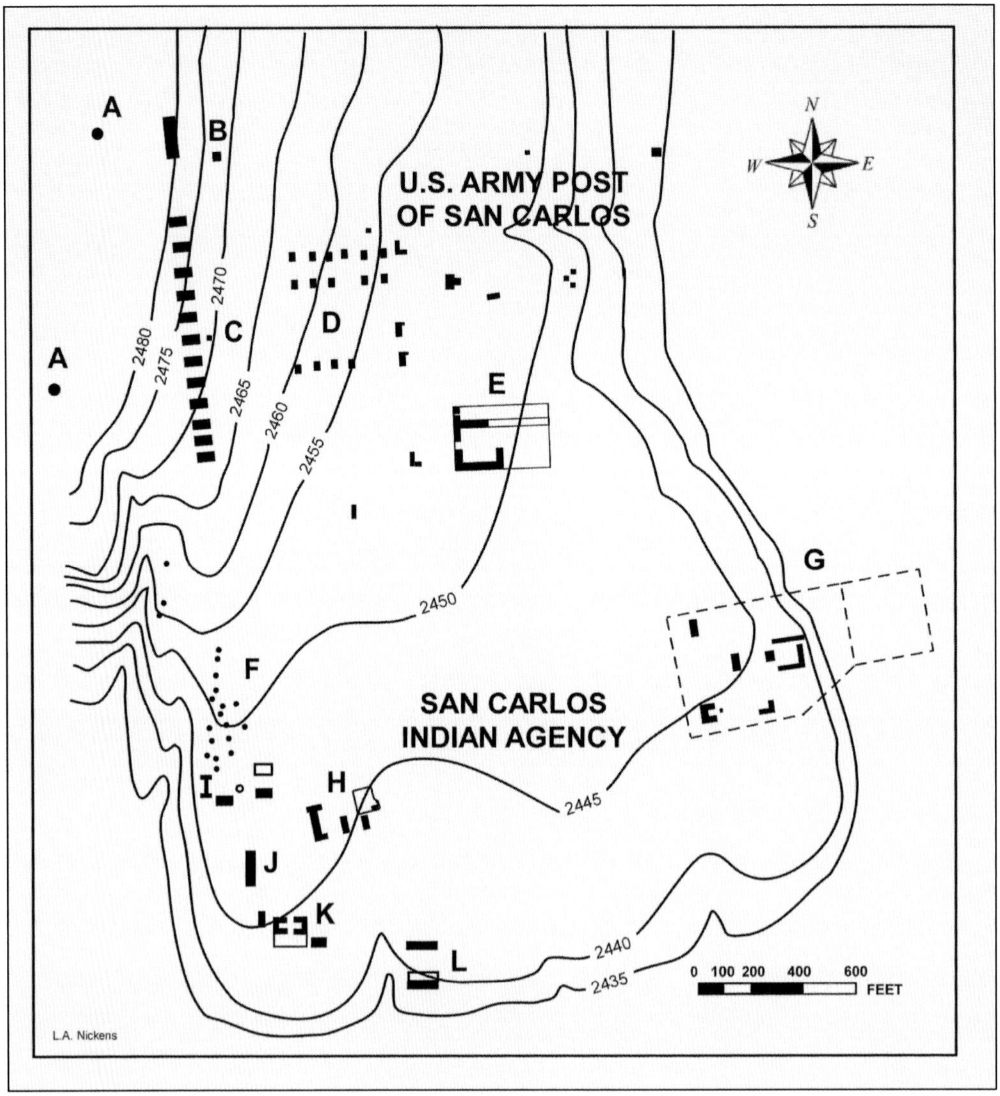

This map shows the layout of the San Carlos Indian Agency and military post, as mapped in 1899: A) water tanks, B) hospital, C) officers' housing, D) enlisted barracks, E) stables, F) Indian police wickiups, G) school grounds, H) trader's store complex, I) guardhouse, J) stone warehouses, K) U.S. Indian Agency offices, and L) shops and stables. (Courtesy Lisa A. Nickens.)

One

Apache and Yavapai Groups

The policy adopted by the federal government following the creation of the San Carlos Indian Agency in 1873 involved the relocating and intermingling of many Apache and Yavapai groups and bands who had formerly lived autonomously over a wide geographic expanse. Following a series of extremely difficult and, more often than not, tragic events during the next 25 years, all of the native groups were finally settled on reserves by the turn of the 20th century, where they exist today.

The Chiricahua Apaches bands were most severely impacted. After being removed to San Carlos in 1876, both insurgents and those who had peacefully remained on the reservation were exiled to Florida in 1886, never to return to their homelands. Today their descendents live on the Fort Sill Apache Reservation in Oklahoma and the Mescalero Apache Reservation in southeastern New Mexico.

Four separate groups of Yuman-speaking Yavapais (Tolkepaya, Kwevkepaya, Yavape, and Wikupeya) were sent from their reservation at Fort Verde to San Carlos in 1875. Not being Apaches, they greatly resented their stay at San Carlos. After years of requests to return home, they were finally resettled just after 1900 to reservations at Fort McDowell, Camp Verde, and Prescott.

The Tonto Apache, who had been sent to San Carlos with the Yavapais, now occupy a small reservation near Payson. The other Western Apaches continue to occupy the reservation that was originally set aside for them in 1872, although the larger reserve was divided into the San Carlos Reservation and the Fort Apache Reservation to the north in 1897.

Throughout the years from 1873 to 1900, all of the above groups were subjected to a multitude of social and physical hardships, all the while attempting to adapt to the changing conditions of reservation life. The history of cultural survival in each case is nothing short of extraordinary. Both the Apache and Yavapai groups survived the invasion of their aboriginal homelands, conquest by an experienced military adversary, removal, and assimilation. This chapter pays tribute to all of these peoples as shown in images from their collective time at the San Carlos Indian Agency.

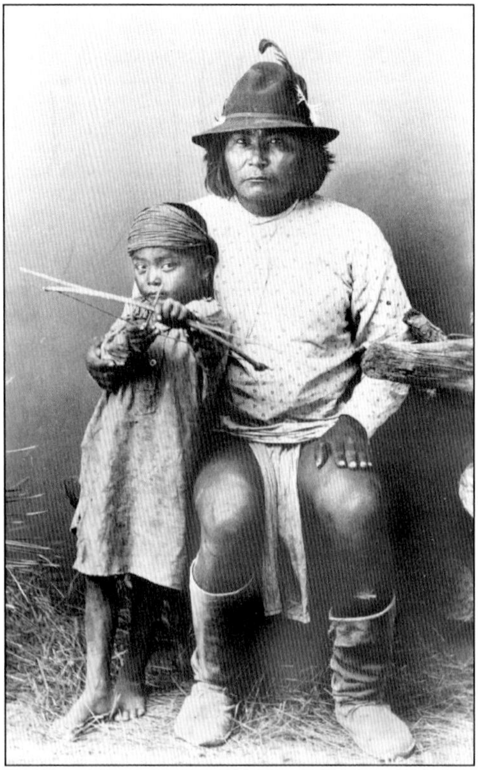

This posed studio view of a man, identified as Apache Joe, and his son was produced in the Arizona Territory in the 1880s. The man's attire shows a combination of traditional and Anglo clothing. (Courtesy NARA, RG 111, Signal Corps Collection, No. 107516.)

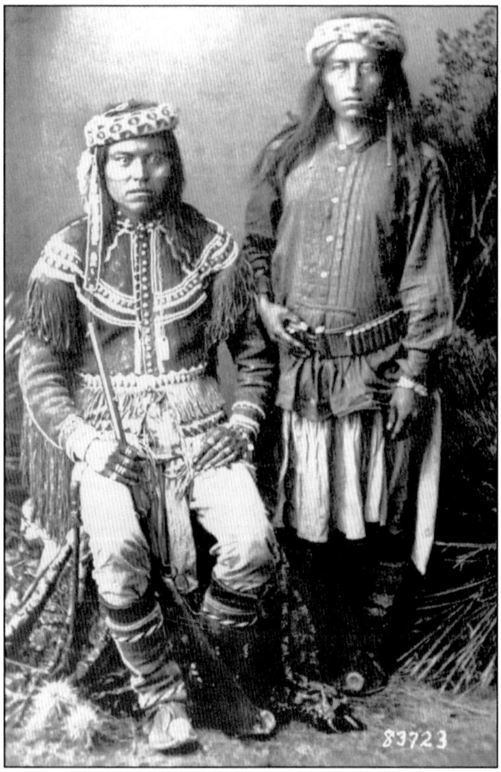

These two men, identified as Gud-i-ze-eh (left) and Malte (right), White Mountain Apaches, were members of Lt. John B. McDonald's scout company at San Carlos, 1885–1887. Gud-i-ze-eh wears a buckskin shirt decorated with beadwork and metal disks. (Courtesy AHF, Sacks Collection, SCS No. 167; photograph by Ben Wittick.)

This unidentified Apache girl, wrapped in a print cloth shawl, was photographed about 1878 at the San Carlos Agency by George Rothrock. (Courtesy AHF, Rothrock Collection, No. 184; stereograph by George H. Rothrock.)

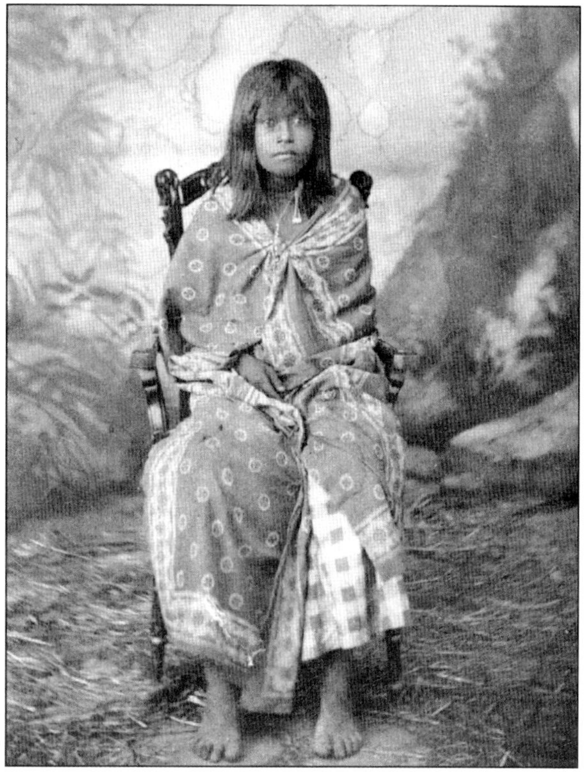

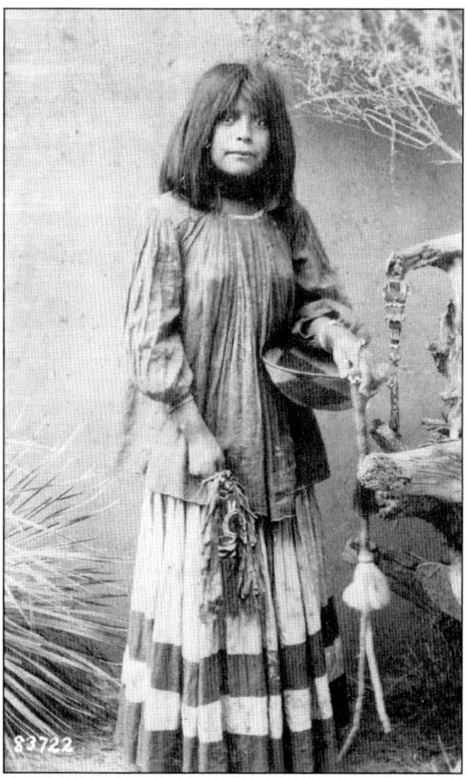

This 1885 photograph is identified as a Yuma Indian girl at the San Carlos Indian Agency. Tolkepaya people at San Carlos were often incorrectly referred to at the time as Apache Yumas. In fact, they were not Apaches but Yavapais. (Courtesy NARA, RG 111, Signal Corps Collection, No. 83722.)

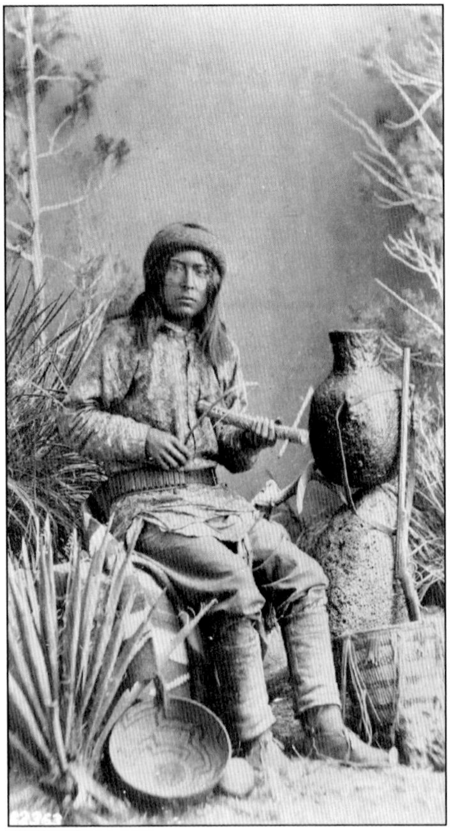

This young man is identified as Chasi-ta, the son of Bonito, a leader of the Warm Springs Chiricahua Apache. He wears face paint, leggings, moccasins, and an empty military ammunition belt, and holds a traditional Apache stringed fiddle. (Courtesy NARA, RG 111, Signal Corps Collection, No. 82363; photograph by Ben Wittick or A. Frank Randall.)

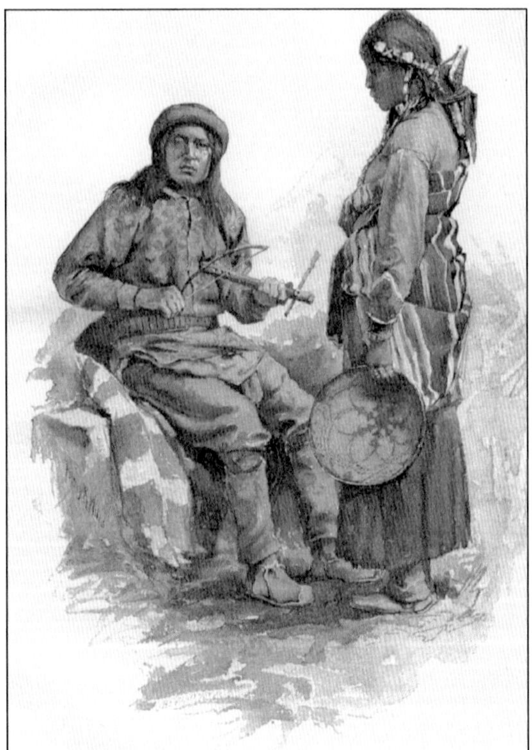

APACHE FIDDLER AND MAIDEN.

This drawing of an Apache fiddler and maiden by I. R. Miles appeared in an 1887 *Century Magazine* article by Frederick Schwatka entitled, "Among the Apaches." Note the incorporation of the previous image of Chasi-ta in the drawing. Schwatka was an army lieutenant stationed in the San Carlos area in the early 1880s. (Courtesy authors' collection.)

An Apache man is shown painting his face in this image from the mid-1880s. A war amulet is worn in the man's hair on the left side. Decorated with shells, silver ornaments, and beads, the string amulets were considered necessary for warding off blows and missiles during battles. (Courtesy NARA, RG 111, Signal Corps Collection, No. 85765.)

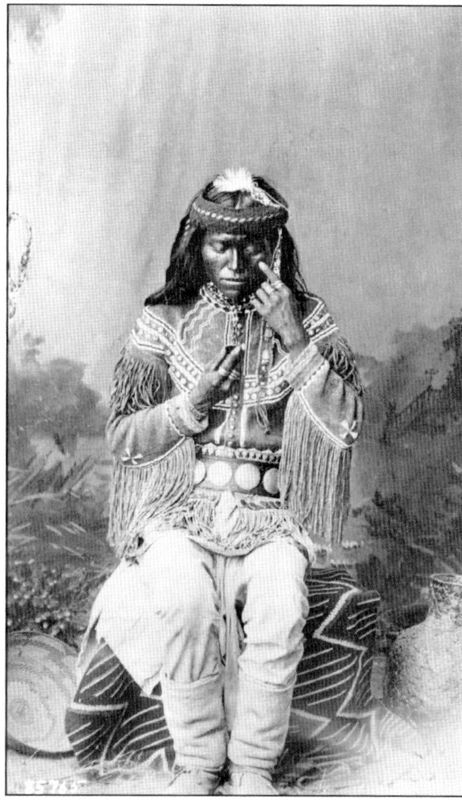

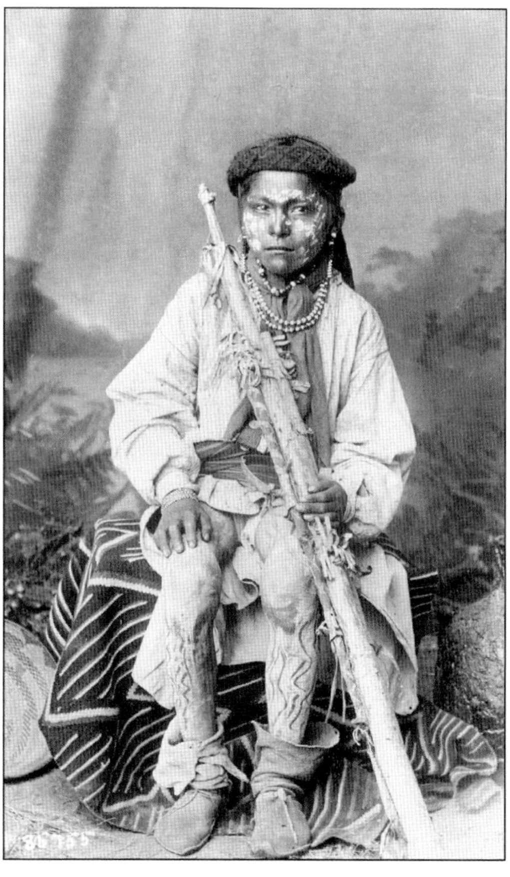

A young Apache warrior is posed in this studio photograph wearing facial and body paint. Younger novices might be taken along on less hazardous raids so that they would correctly learn the conduct of the adult fighter. (Courtesy NARA, RG 111, Signal Corps Collection, No. 85755.)

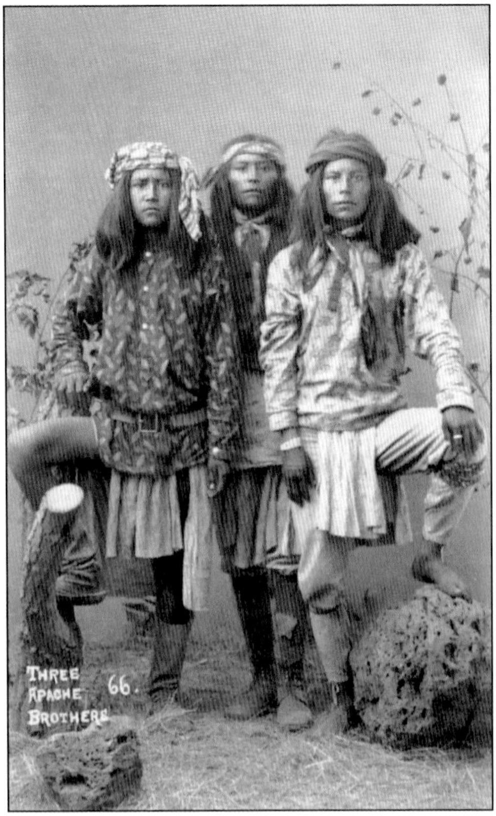

Three Apache brothers are shown in this studio image, probably from the late 1880s. An interesting assortment of footwear is evident. The man on the left has on the traditional Apache moccasins, the one in the center is wearing leather lace-up shoes, and the man at the right is barefooted. (Courtesy ASUL, Sammy Jones Collection, No. SJ-162.)

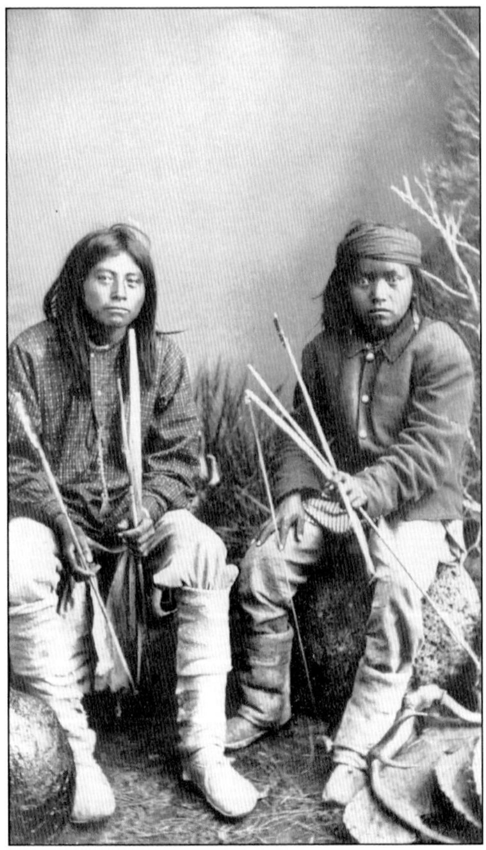

Young Apache boys in the 19th century were taught skills they would need in adult life at an early age. Usually a grandfather was available to help his grandson fashion smaller and cruder bows and arrows than those of the adults. As he matured, he learned to make better bows and arrows. (Courtesy NARA, RG 111, Signal Corps Collection, No. 85766.)

Three generations of a Tolkepaya Yavapai family are shown in this photograph. Erroneously referred to in earlier times by Anglos as Yuma Apaches or Apache Yumas, the Tolkepaya ranged over a large area of southwest Arizona before being concentrated with other Yavapai groups at Camp Verde and then at San Carlos. (Courtesy NARA, RG 111, Signal Corps Collection, No. 82329.)

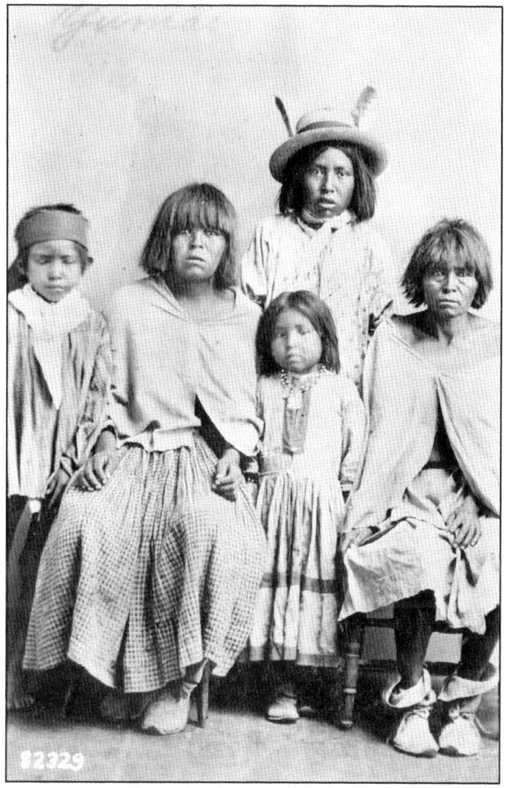

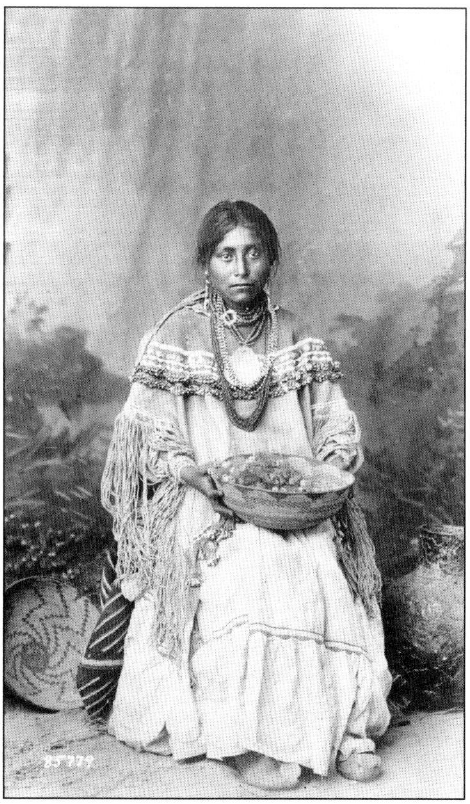

The caption for this 1880s photograph reads, "Coyetena, an Apache bride." Western Apache women usually entered marriage before the age of 18 and men in their early 20s. Nearly all marriages were between members of unrelated clans within the bands, thereby creating reciprocal obligations between persons of different groups. (Courtesy NARA, RG 111, Signal Corps Collection, No. 85779.)

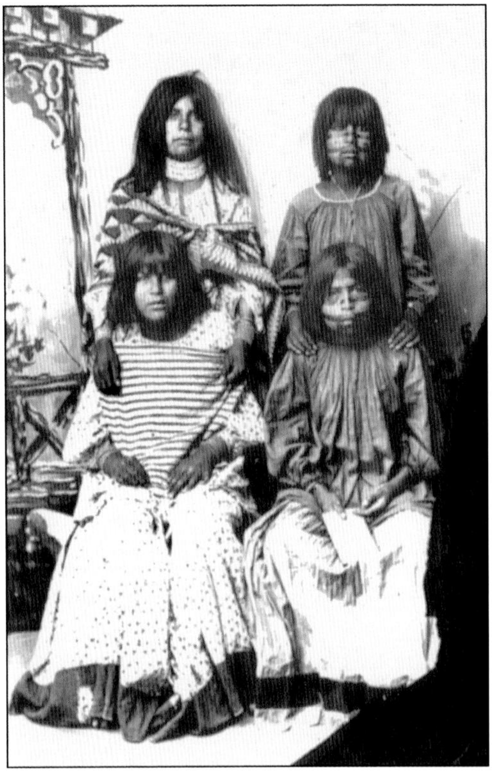

Four San Carlos Apache women are seen in this 1880 photograph. The two on the right have their faces painted, a trait practiced by some of the Apache groups at the San Carlos Agency. (Courtesy ASUL, Ryder Ridgeway Collection, RR-75.)

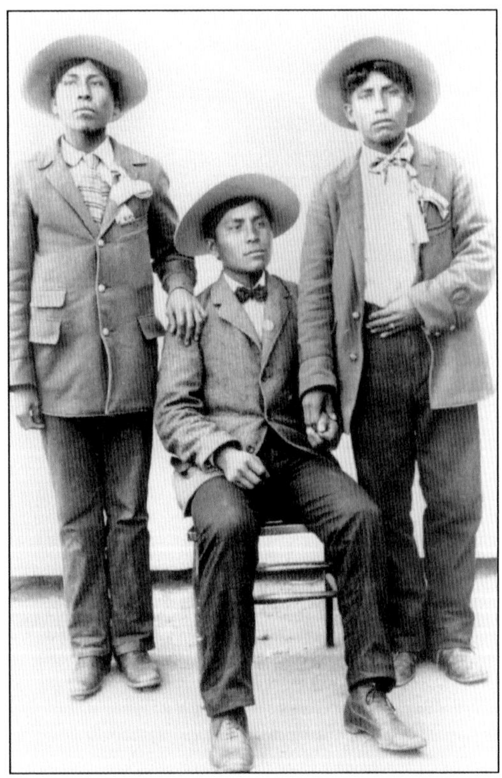

The three young San Carlos men in this photograph from around 1900 are decked out in their finest clothing. The occasion is unknown but may be associated with either heading off to or returning from an off-reservation boarding school. At that time, older students were sent to both the Indian Industrial School at Carlisle and the Phoenix Training School. (Courtesy GCHS, GM 27-130.)

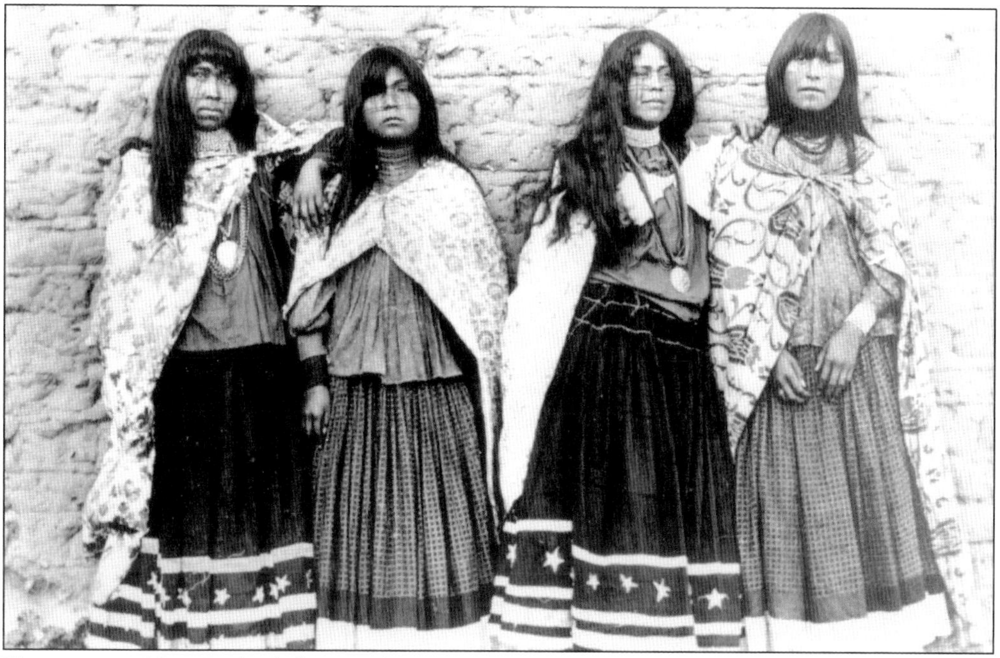

Two groups of San Carlos ladies are shown in these two photographs, both taken about 1900. In the image above, younger women each have identically painted facial designs. They are wearing the traditional camp dress with commercial cloth shawls. Use of the same cloth for the skirts may indicate that two sets of sisters are included. The older women below exhibit more diversity in their clothing, including heavier blankets for some of the shawls. Use of the two-piece skirt and blouse camp dress became common as everyday attire in the 1870s, replacing the earlier buckskin garments. The transition in material coincided with the availability of cloth issued at the government agency. (Above, courtesy GCHS, GM 27-121; below, courtesy GCHS, GM 27-122.)

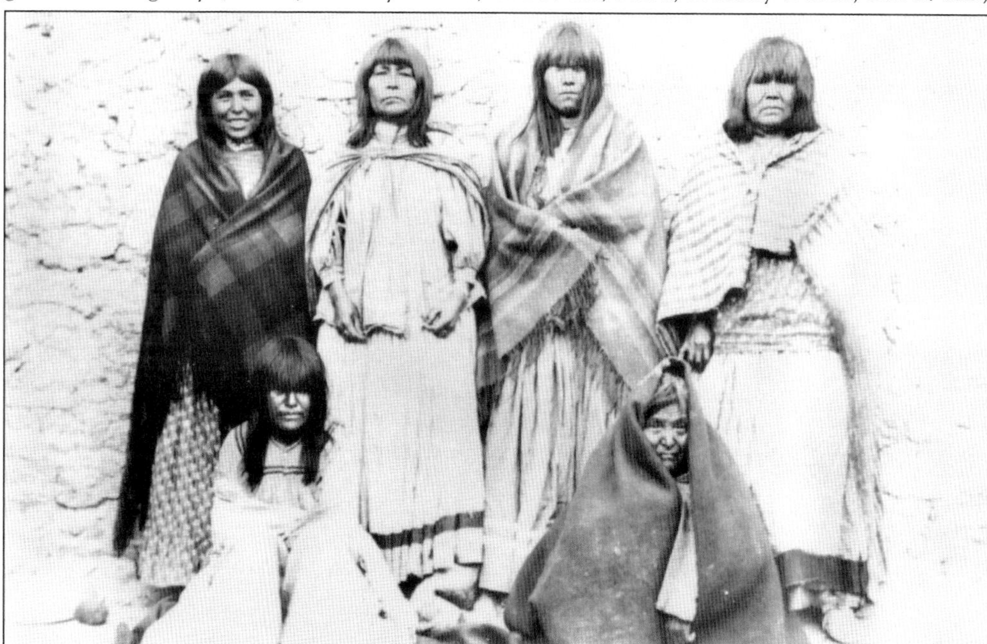

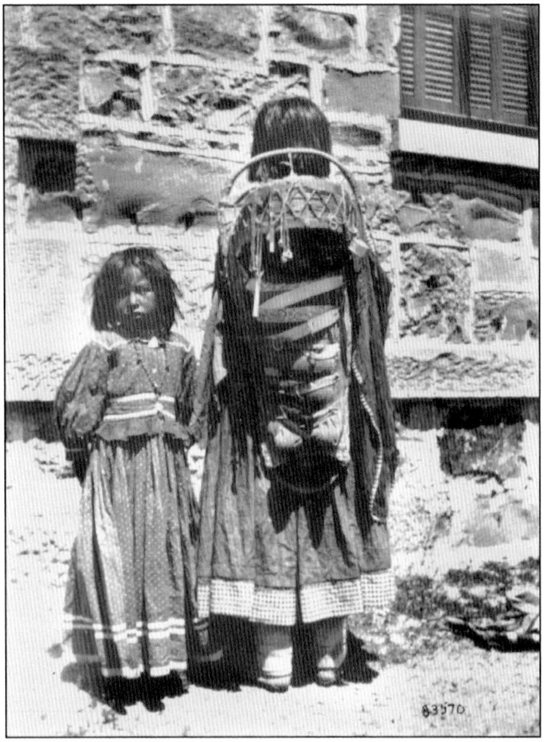

An Apache mother with her daughter and infant in cradleboard are pictured in this 1895 photograph at the San Carlos Indian Agency. The photographer was obviously more interested in depicting the manner of carrying the baby rather than showing the mother. (Courtesy NARA, RG 111, Signal Corps Collection, No. 83570.)

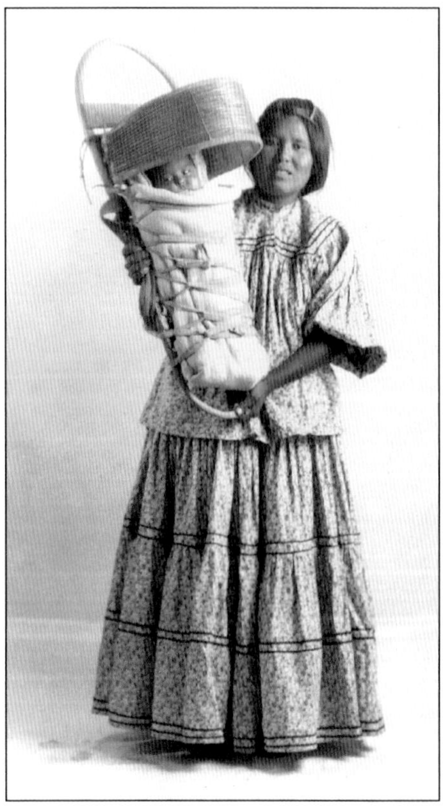

The distinctive Western Apache cradleboard could be carried on the back or hung on the side of the mother's horse saddle. The cradleboard was made with either yucca or sotol (Desert Spoon) leaves woven onto an elongated wooden hoop. At the head, a canopy roof was attached to protect the infant from rain and sunlight, and another cloth could be laid on top of that for additional protection. (Courtesy GCHC, GM 27-135.)

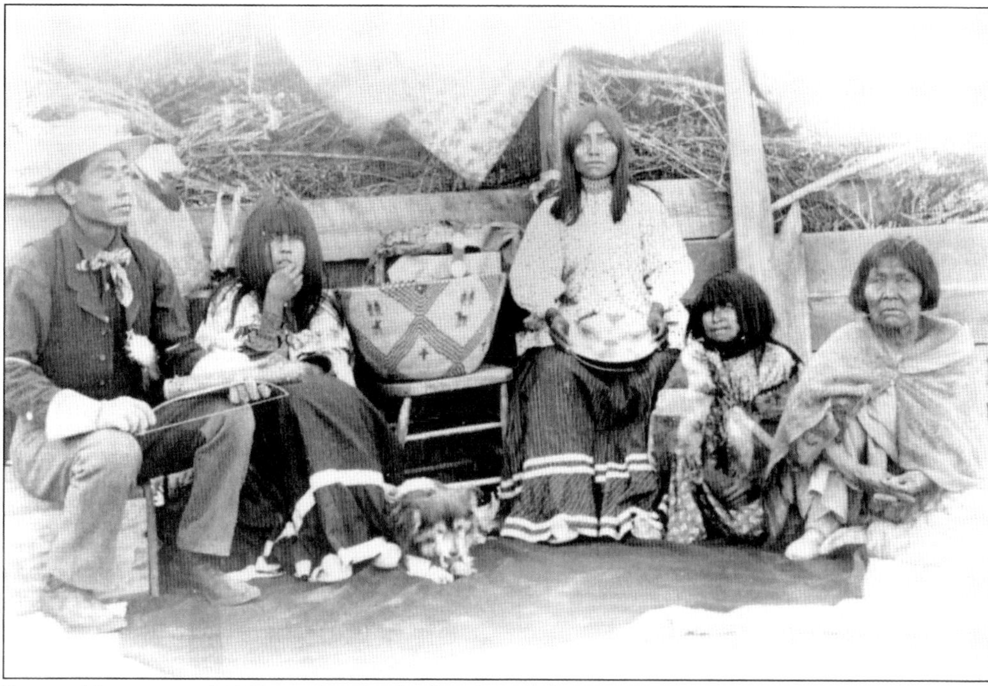

Pictured here around 1900 is a San Carlos family and their pet. The man holds an Apache stringed fiddle while his wife shows off her basketry. (Courtesy GCHS, GM 27-123.)

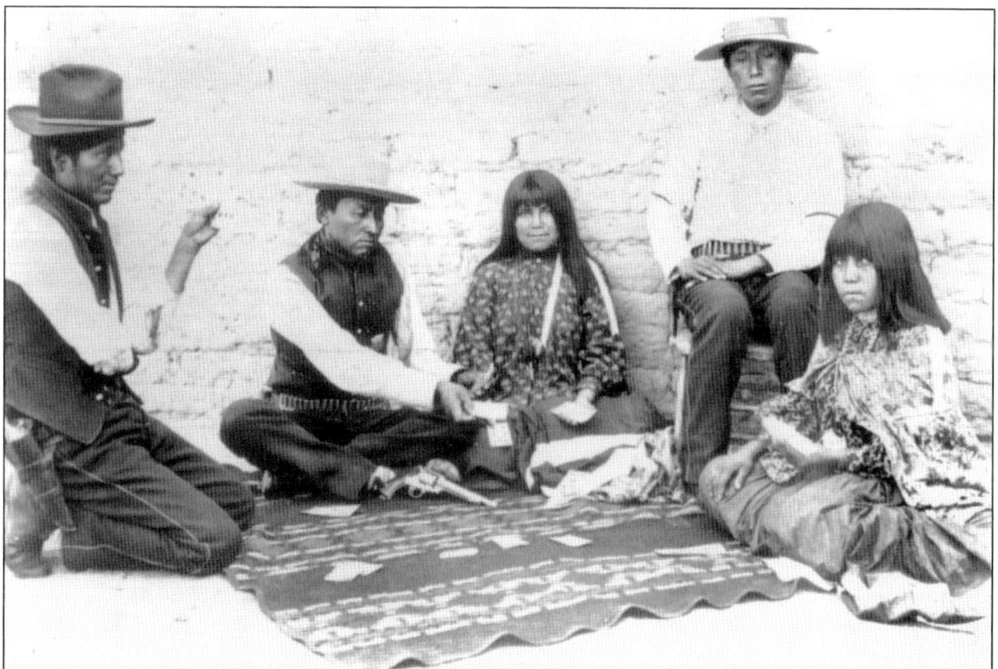

A group of San Carlos Apaches is playing cards around 1900. Gambling with cards, a favorite form of recreation among the Apaches, especially women, was prohibited and punished by tribal courts in the early 1900s. Reservation traders were barred from selling decks of cards. (Courtesy GCHS, GM 27-124.)

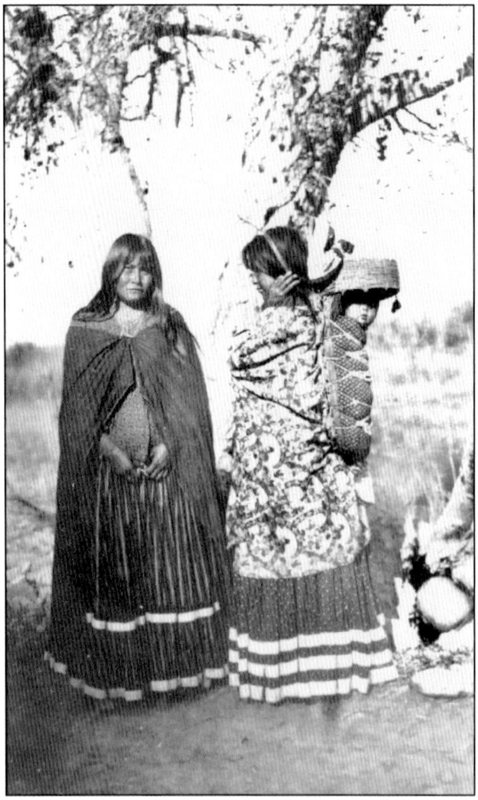

Two Apache women, one with an infant in a cradleboard, are pictured here around 1900. Also visible is a medicine amulet hanging from the front of the cradleboard's hood, which was commonly attached to cradles for luck and good health. (Courtesy GCHS, GM 27-53.)

From the bags and blanket roll on the horse, it appears that this San Carlos woman may have been engaged in the gathering of plant subsistence resources at the time of the photograph. Gathering of undomesticated plants supplemented the generally inadequate agricultural yield and rations issued at the government agency. (Courtesy AHF, Apache Collection, IA-36; photograph by Putnam Studios.)

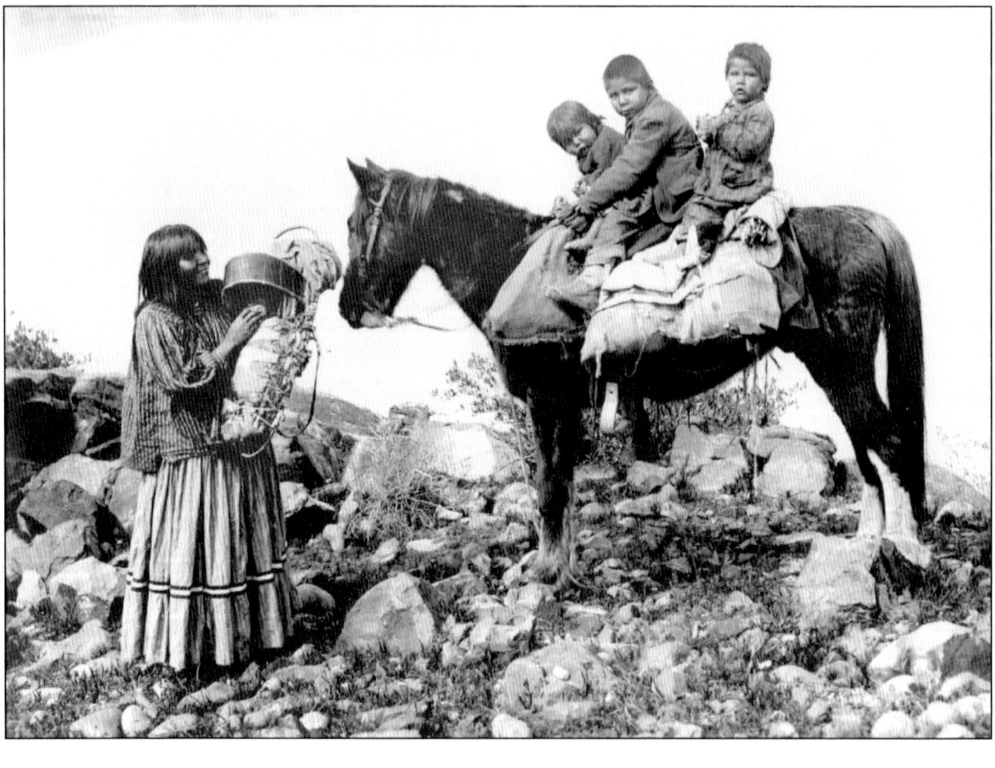

This unidentified San Carlos man, possibly a scout, has the typical traditional haircut and headband of the late 19th century, combined with an Anglo corduroy-vest overshirt. Apache men of the time used metal tweezers, often made from splitting and hammering flat brass rifle cartridges, to pluck facial hair. (Courtesy GCHS, GM 27-5.)

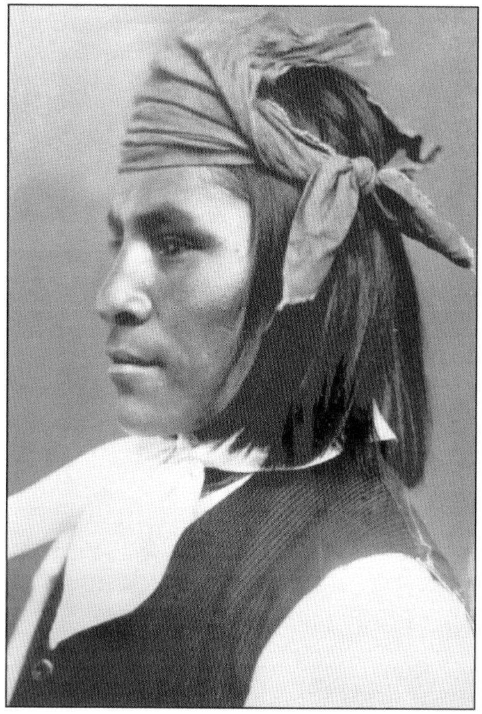

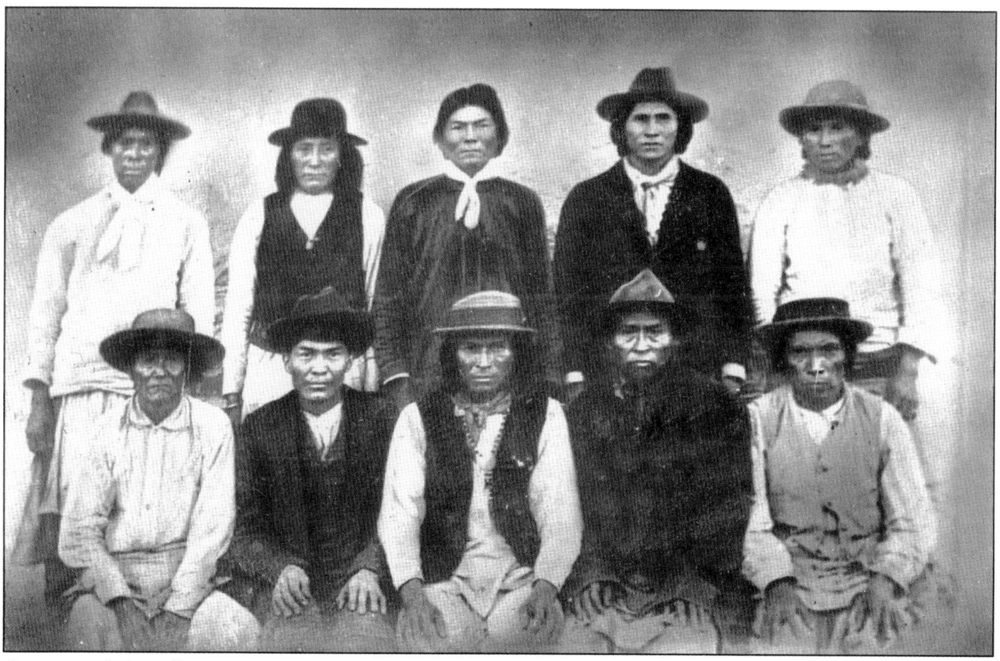

Convicted Apache prisoners in Globe, Arizona, are pictured here in October 1889. From left to right are (first row) Has-tin-tu-do-dy (San Carlos Apache), Nah-diz-az (Tonto-Yavapai), Wash-lan-ta-ha (San Carlos Apache), Joe-klissy-an (San Carlos Apache), and Miguel (Yaqui Indian adopted by San Carlos Apaches); (second row) Lac-gon (San Carlos Apache), Has-kay-ah-yah (Tonto Apache), Say-es (San Carlos Apache), Es-ki-bi-nadel (Apache Kid, San Carlos Apache), and Bob McIntosh (San Carlos Apache). (Courtesy GCHS, GM 27-136.)

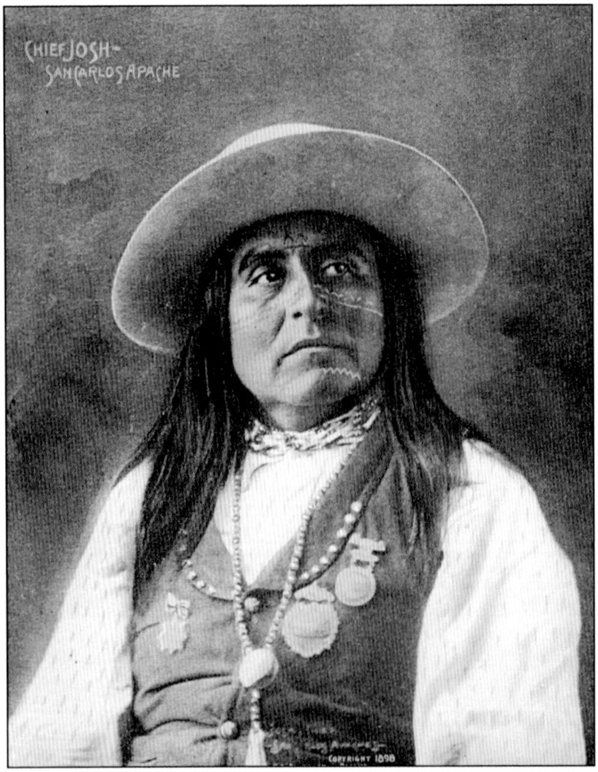

Known as "Chief Josh" to Anglos, Go-zhah was the leader of a delegation of 21 San Carlos Apaches and Yavapais that attended the 1898 Trans-Mississippi and International Exposition in Omaha, Nebraska. Earlier in the 1890s, Go-zhah had been both a fugitive and a scout enlisted to help capture the Apache Kid. Geronimo, Naichi, and 20 other Chiricahuas from Fort Sill were also in attendance at Omaha. (Courtesy authors' collection.)

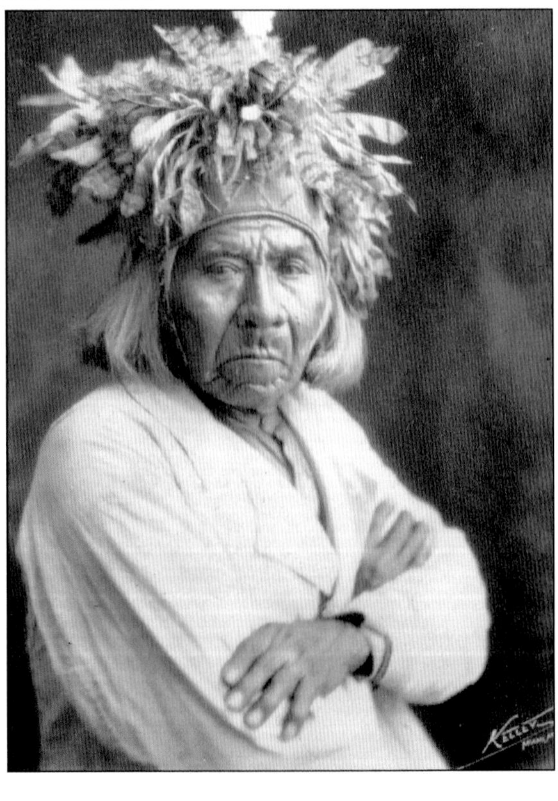

A former army scout, San Carlos policeman, and friend of agent John Clum, Talkalai (1817–1930) was born about 20 miles north of Globe. As an adult, he was the leader of the Apache Peaks band. He lived most of his later years in the town of Miami and died on the same day that the Coolidge Dam was dedicated. (Courtesy GCHS, GM 27-68; photograph by Roy Kelley.)

Eskiminzin (c. 1828–1895), leader of the Aravaipa Apaches, was photographed here in Washington, D.C., in 1876 while on a visit to the East with agent John Clum. He lived much of his life on his farm on the San Pedro River, off the reservation. (Courtesy NARA, RG 111, Signal Corps Collection, No. 89537.)

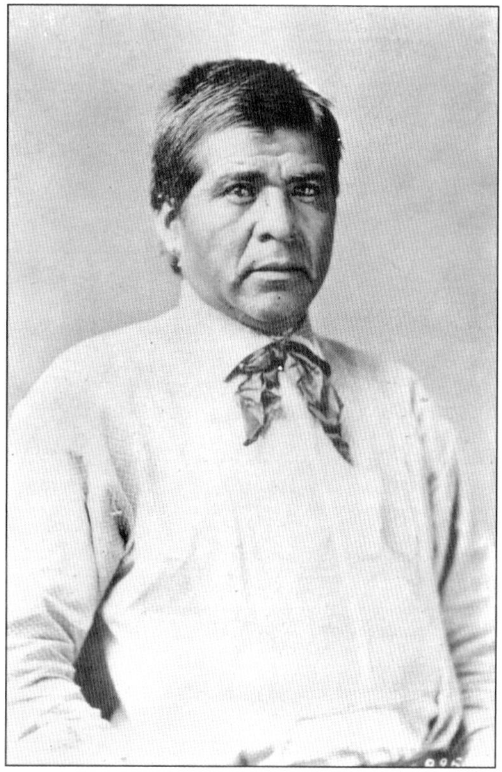

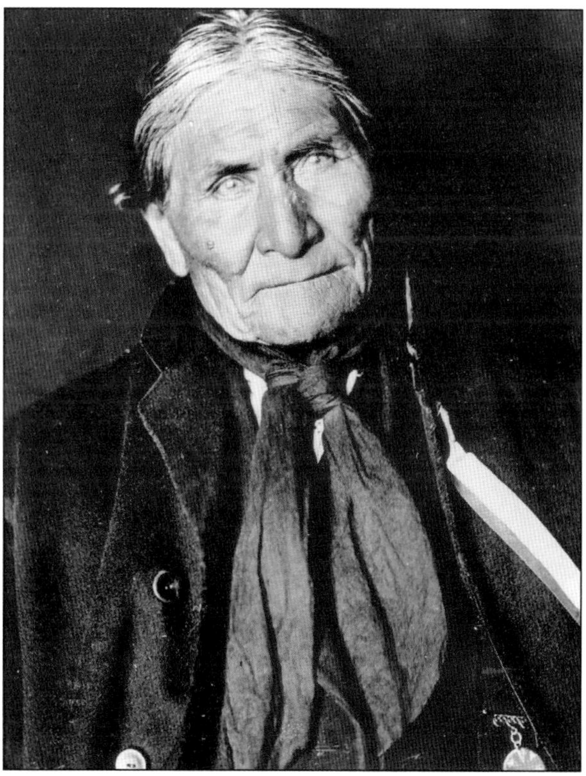

Geronimo (Goyathlay, 1829–1909) is pictured here during a 1905 visit to Washington, D.C., for Theodore Roosevelt's inauguration. Geronimo was at San Carlos several times between 1876 and 1886. Leader of the Chiricahua insurgents in the 1880s, Geronimo surrendered in 1886 and was sent to Fort Pickens, Florida, then to Mount Vernon, Alabama, and finally ended up at Fort Sill, Oklahoma. (Courtesy NARA, RG 111, Signal Corps Collection, No. 89505.)

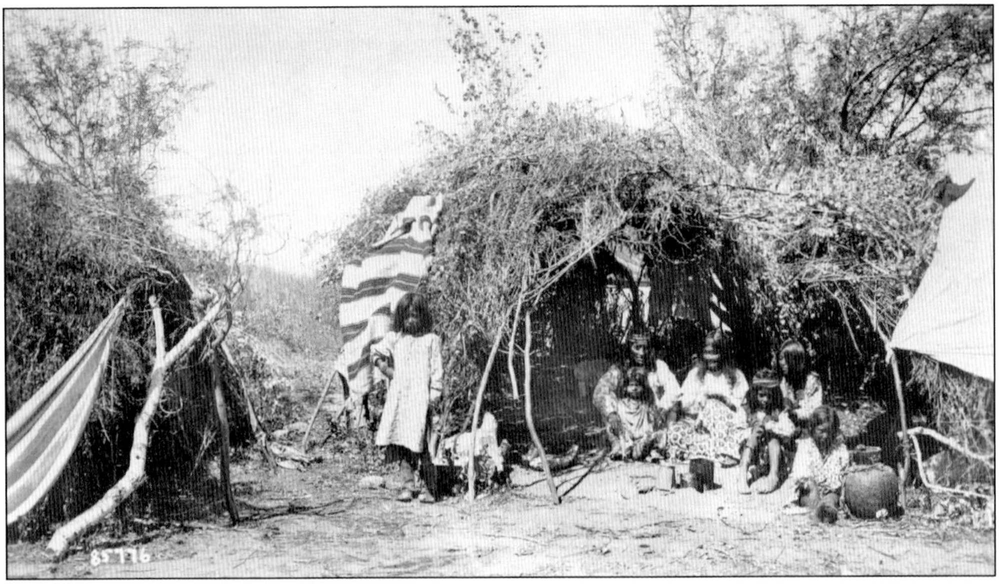

Pictured here is a Tolkepaya Yavapai family in camp at San Carlos, probably in the 1880s. After being forced to San Carlos in 1875, the Yavapai groups were settled on the south side of the Gila River, opposite the agency. (Courtesy NARA, RG 111, Signal Corps Collection, No. 85776.)

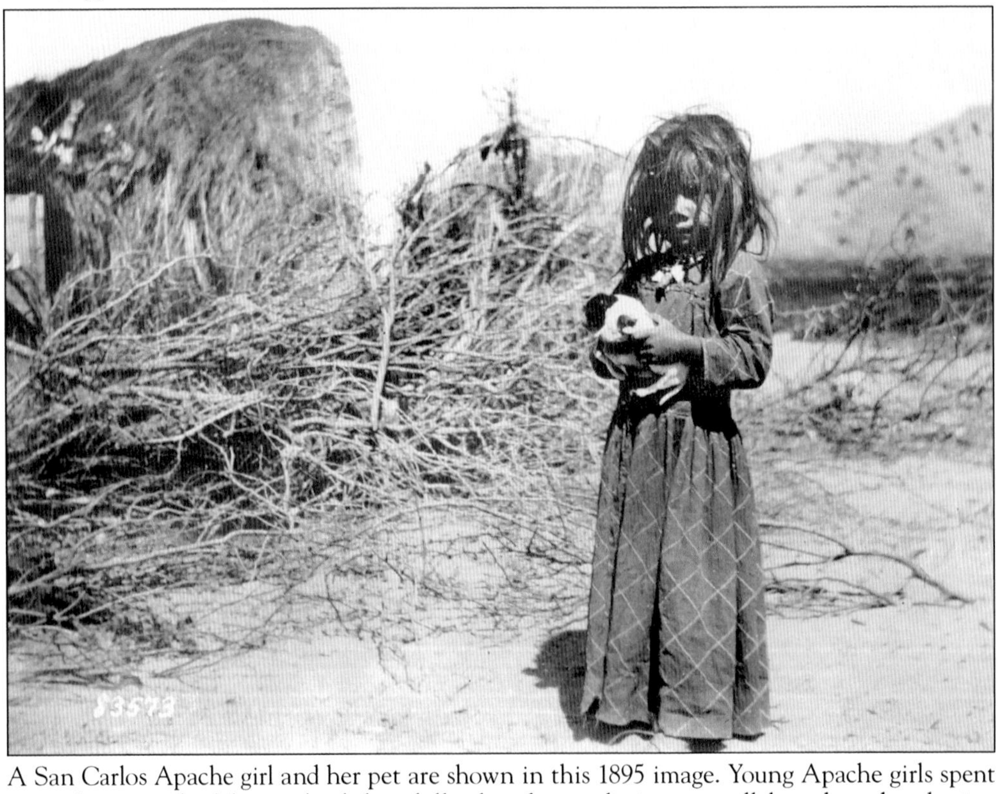

A San Carlos Apache girl and her pet are shown in this 1895 image. Young Apache girls spent time playing with elaborate buckskin dolls placed in realistic toy cradleboards and gathering food near the camp. Pet puppies and rabbits were common. (Courtesy NARA, RG 111, Signal Corps Collection, No. 83573.)

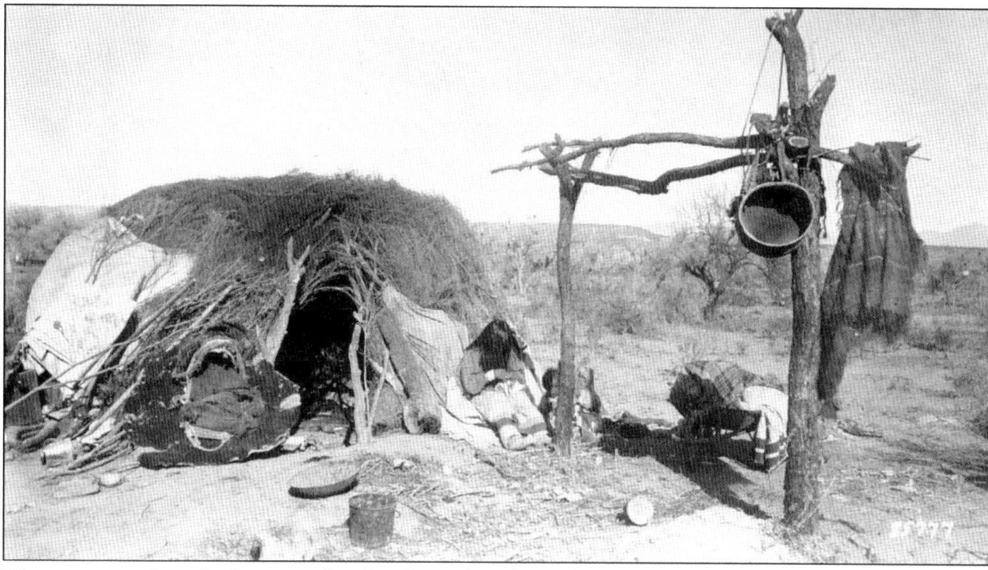

This camp at San Carlos is said to be that of a Chiricahua medicine man. The role of medicine men was important to all of the Apache groups. Men accorded this status were involved in several types of ceremonies, especially associated with the curing of sicknesses and during use of the sweat bath. (Courtesy NARA, RG 111, Signal Corps Collection, No. 85777.)

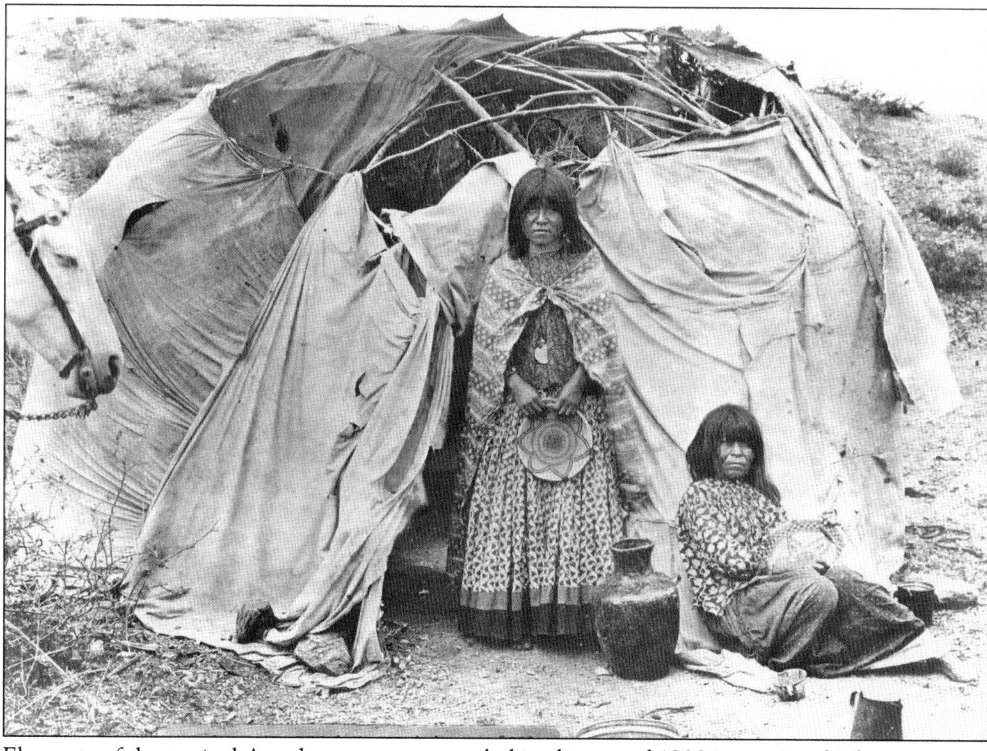

Elements of the typical Apache camp are revealed in this posed 1880 image in which two women in camp dresses are shown in front of a canvas-covered wickiup home. Containers in the view include the coiled bowl forms in their hands and the twined, pitched water jar on the ground. Metal containers are also shown. (Courtesy AHF, Apache Collection, IA-10.)

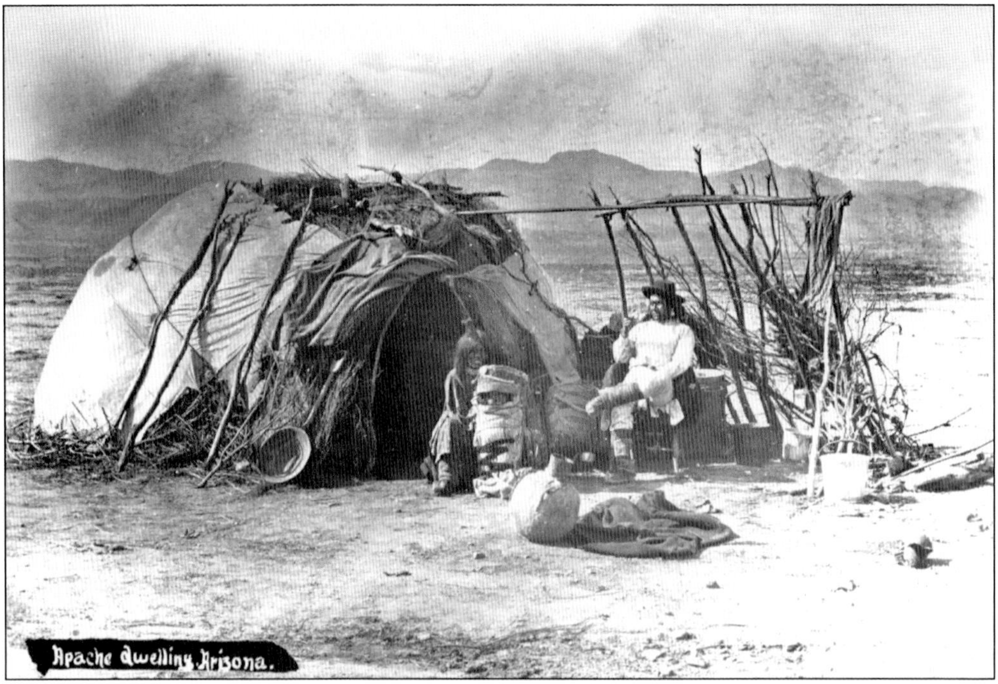

A Chiricahua Apache camp on the San Carlos River is shown in this Ben Wittick photograph from the 1880s. The seemingly obligatory basketry props of the time have been conspicuously positioned in the image. (Courtesy AHF, Zonta Collection, Z0-65; photograph by Ben Wittick.)

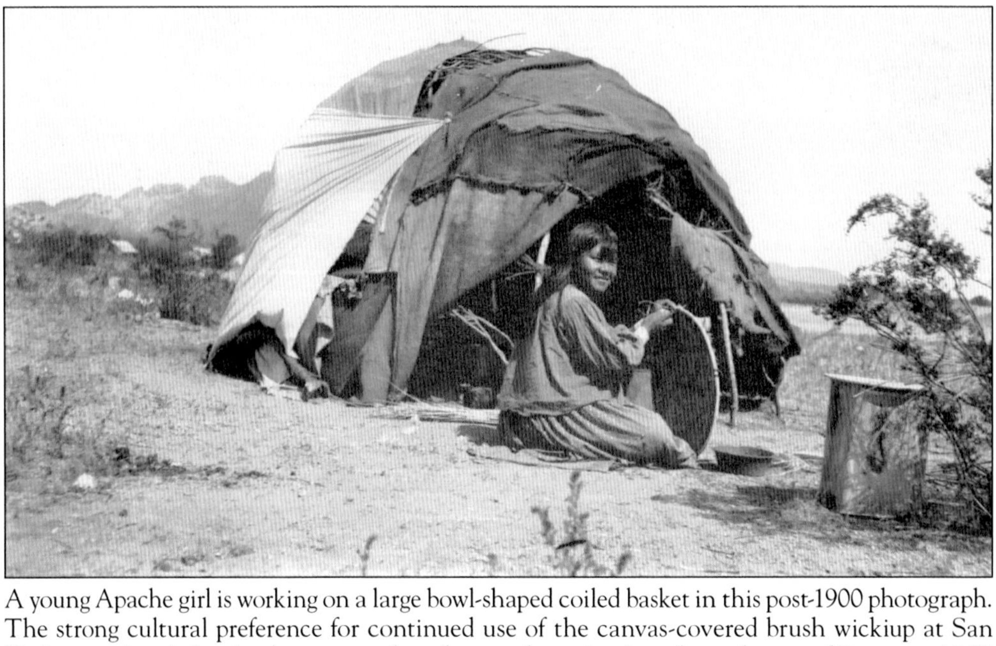

A young Apache girl is working on a large bowl-shaped coiled basket in this post-1900 photograph. The strong cultural preference for continued use of the canvas-covered brush wickiup at San Carlos perplexed the Anglo agents, who advocated moving into frame houses. (Courtesy AHF, Apache Collection, IA-35.)

This young Bylas Apache woman of the 1920s wears the traditional beadwork T-necklace, in this case decorated with mirrors. Since about 1900, the T-necklace has been commonly worn by the bride at Western Apache weddings and by girls at their puberty ceremony. (Courtesy ASUL, Francis J. Uplegger Collection, CPSPC 187:4.8; photograph by Gracie Taylor.)

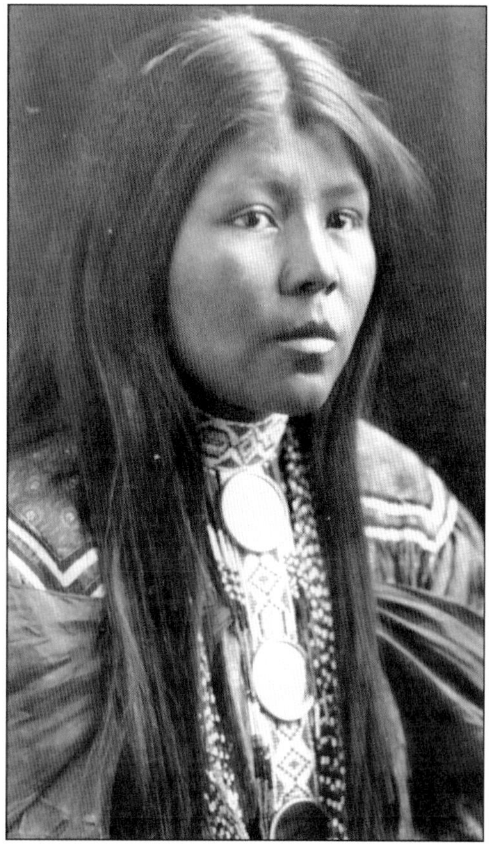

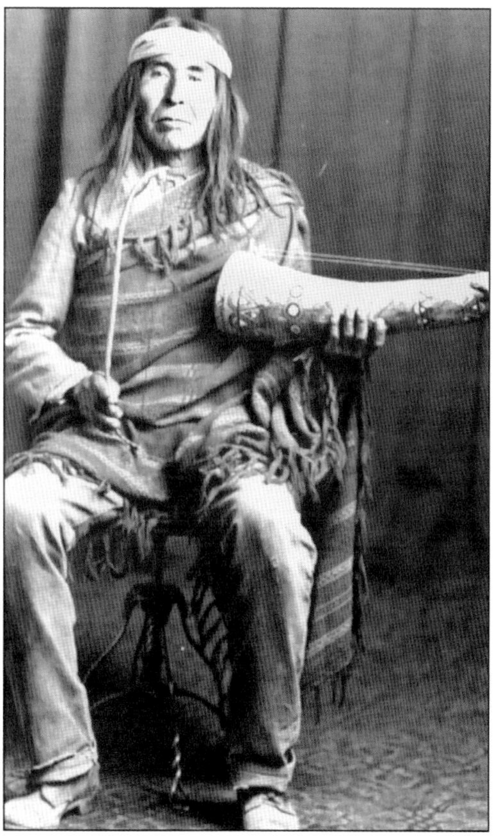

Fiddles made from century plant flower stalks were used by the Apaches to play a variety of ceremonial songs, social dance songs, love songs, and corn-beer (*tiswin*) drinking songs. This man was photographed at Bylas in the 1920s. (Courtesy ASUL, Francis J. Uplegger Collection, CPSPC 187:4.42; photograph by Gracie Taylor.)

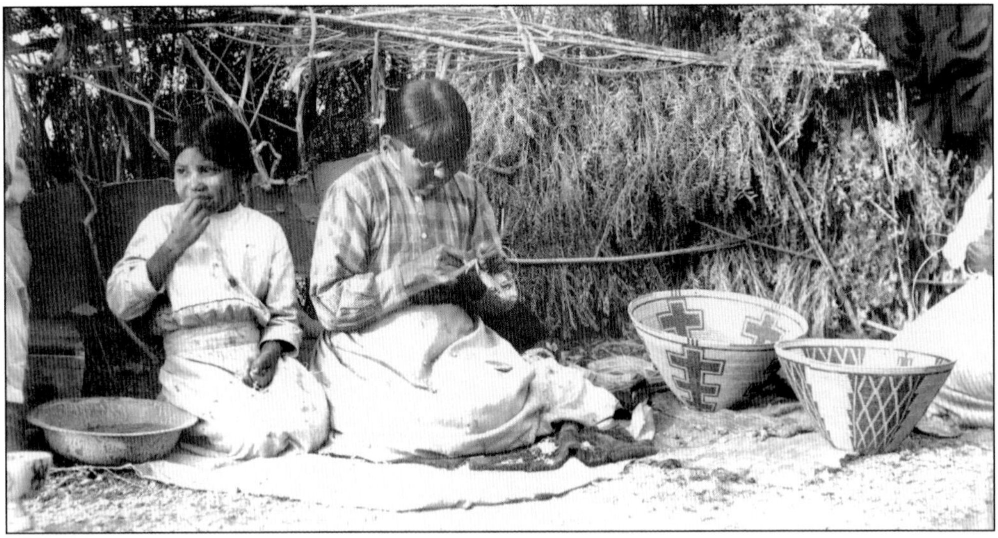

Western Apache baskets were by far the most elaborate of those made by all the Apache groups. A three-rod foundation was fashioned of slender willow, cottonwood, or sumac twigs. The coil was small and round, providing rigidity for the basket. The most common form produced was the open bowl and the storage jar, with intricate designs woven into the form to express the weaver's individuality. Both of the weavers in these two photographs are working on coiled bowl-shaped baskets. A finished *tus*, or pitched water jar, with a carrying strap attached, can be seen to the left of the weaver in the image below. (Above, courtesy AHF, Dane Coolidge Collection, COO No. 110; below, courtesy GCHS, GM 27-147.)

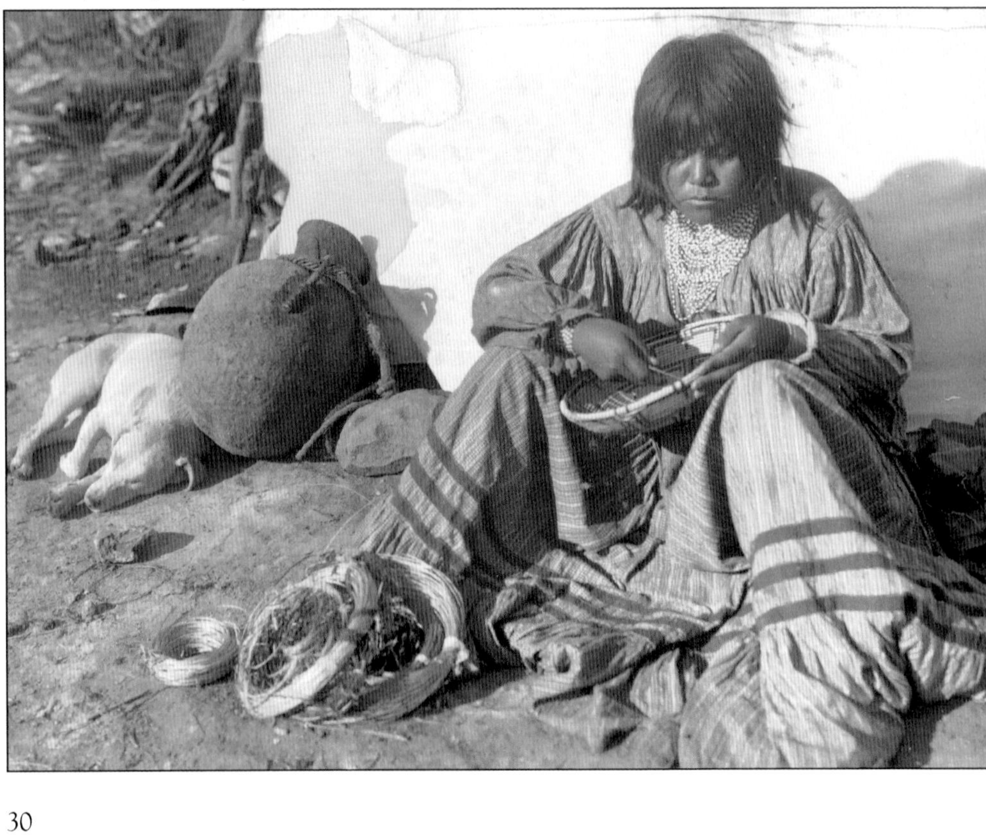

The San Carlos Apaches have long been celebrated for their tightly woven coiled basketry. In 1904, San Carlos agent Luther Kelly observed that women at the agency netted about $3,000 from selling baskets. This 1920s photograph shows a selection of baskets from the collection of Dan R. Williamson of Globe. (Courtesy GCHS, GM 27-37.)

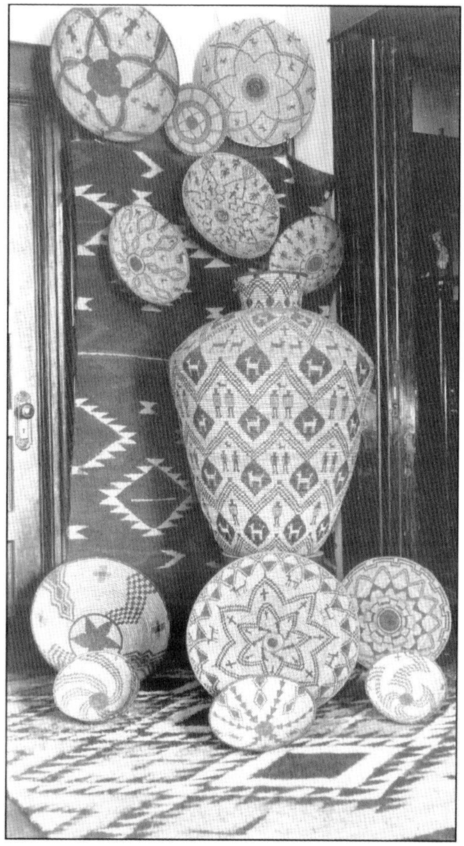

A San Carlos basket weaver is pictured below with several specimens of her handiwork. This type of twined basket (*tus*), usually made with squawberry or sumac twigs, was first caulked with a paste of ground juniper leaves, then covered with melted pine pitch to create a watertight vessel. Handles were added to allow easy carrying. (Courtesy GCHS, GM 27-147; Norman's Studio, Globe.)

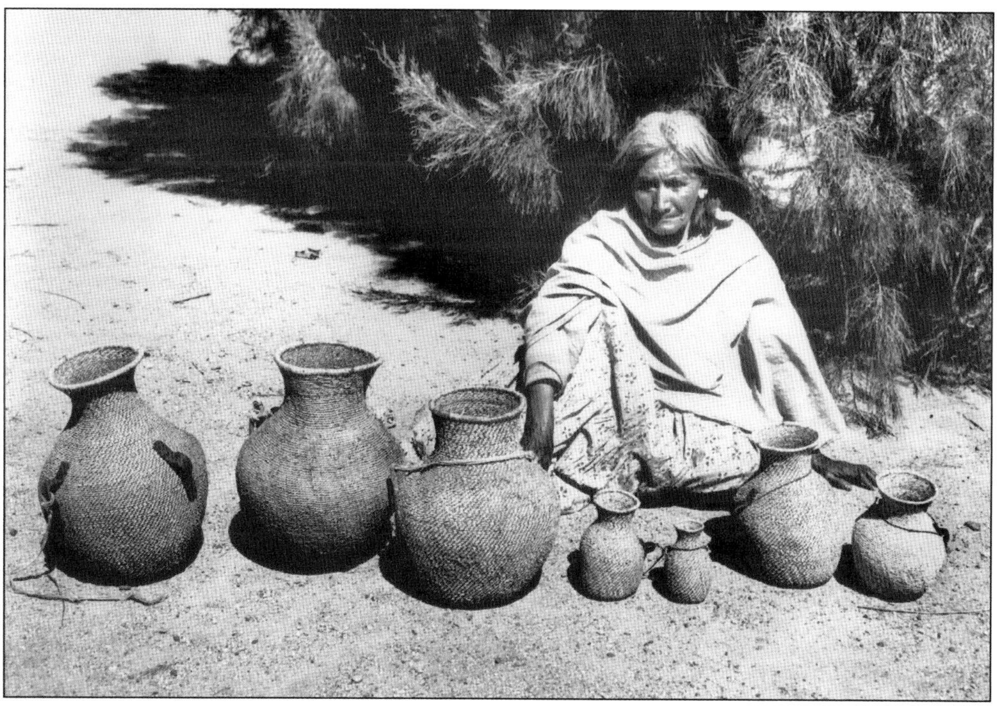

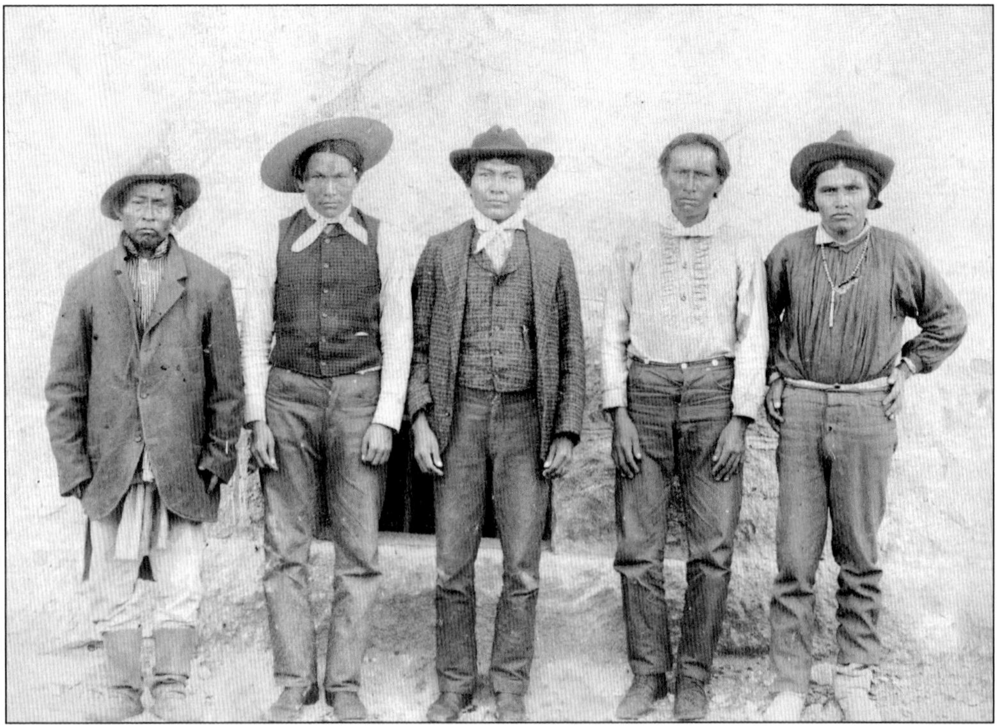

Five San Carlos Apache men were photographed at the agency, probably around 1900. The mixing of Anglo and traditional clothing attire is evident. Two of the men are wearing the Apache buckskin moccasins. (Courtesy GCHS, GM 27-63; photograph by James Anderson.)

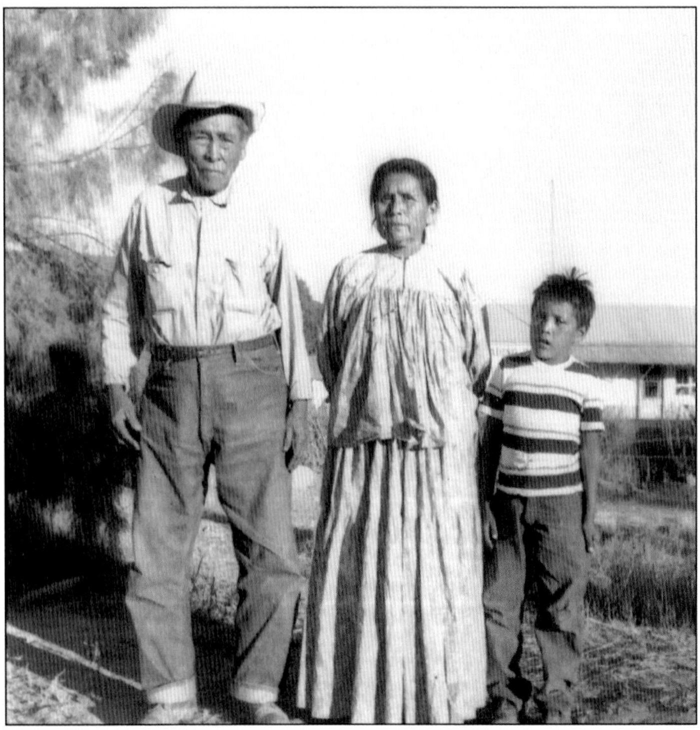

Educated at the Carlisle Indian School in the 1890s, Donald McIntosh Sr. (1880–1967) was a former tribal judge and councilman at San Carlos. He is pictured here in the 1940s. His father was Archie McIntosh (1843–1902), a Scotsman who married a Chippewa woman. Archie McIntosh came to Arizona in 1871 as a scout with Gen. George Crook and served as a scout and guide for the army at San Carlos until 1883. (Courtesy GCHS, GM 27-64.)

Two

San Carlos Agency to 1900

In late February 1873, some 1,200 Apaches arrived at the junction of the San Carlos and Gila Rivers to begin a new way of life. They had, over nearly a three-week period, marched from their previous home at the just-abandoned Camp Grant military post, located about 50 miles to the southwest. Federal authorities had recently selected the San Carlos locale for a permanent agency, replacing the temporary one that had existed at Camp Grant, a place where malaria had been rampant among the native population.

The new agency got off to an inauspicious beginning, one that was only a harbinger of things to come over the next few decades. The site was located on a large gravel terrace overlooking the Gila River, about a mile west of the San Carlos River. There was little topsoil, scant vegetation, and no on-site source of water. The move was accompanied by little if any planning and supervisory ineptitude. No shelter, provisions, or other necessary supplies would be available to the new arrivals for weeks to come.

In a testament to perseverance on the part of all involved, the San Carlos Indian Agency would continue to overcome a seemingly never-ending string of obstacles, including mismanagement and, at times, outright bitter arguments over whether the civilian Indian Service or the military should have authority; internal strife among native groups brought to the reservation; and dealing with disgruntled groups of Apaches periodically taking unauthorized leaves of absence. Moreover, the place proved to be only a little healthier for the native population than the Camp Grant vicinity. San Carlos was characterized by an inhospitable climate and sporadic flooding of the rivers that destroyed not only parts of the agency itself, but also irrigation facilities designed to make the Apaches self-sufficient farmers.

Because of these ongoing conditions, rationing of foodstuffs and other supplies became an indispensable way of life for the native people at San Carlos, lasting into the early 20th century. The importance of this weekly event is reflected in many of the images in this chapter.

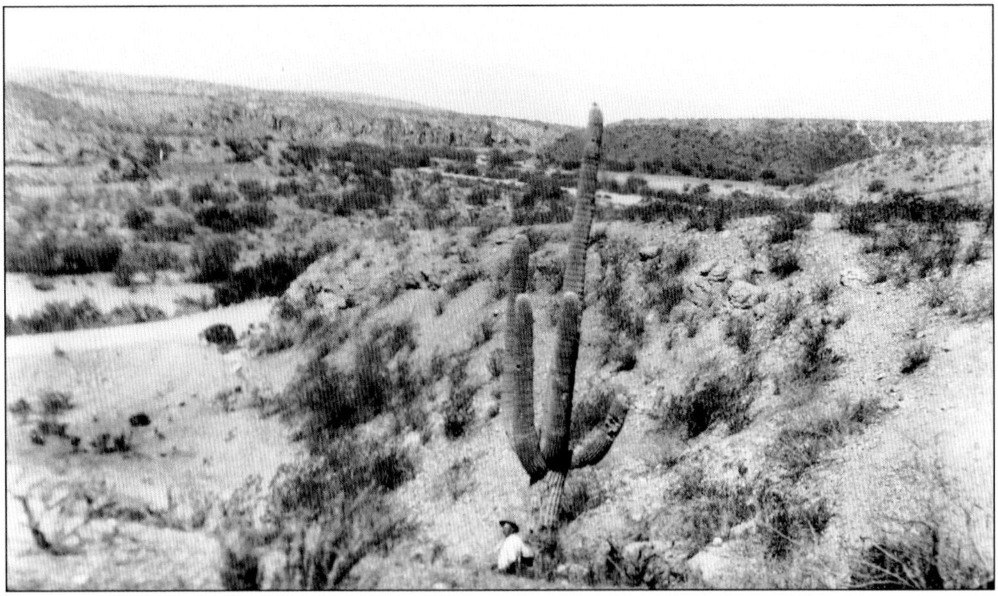

The general character of the environmental setting around the San Carlos Indian Agency is evident in this 1920s photograph. The view appears to be along the San Carlos River valley, just above the agency location. (Courtesy NARA, RG 14.)

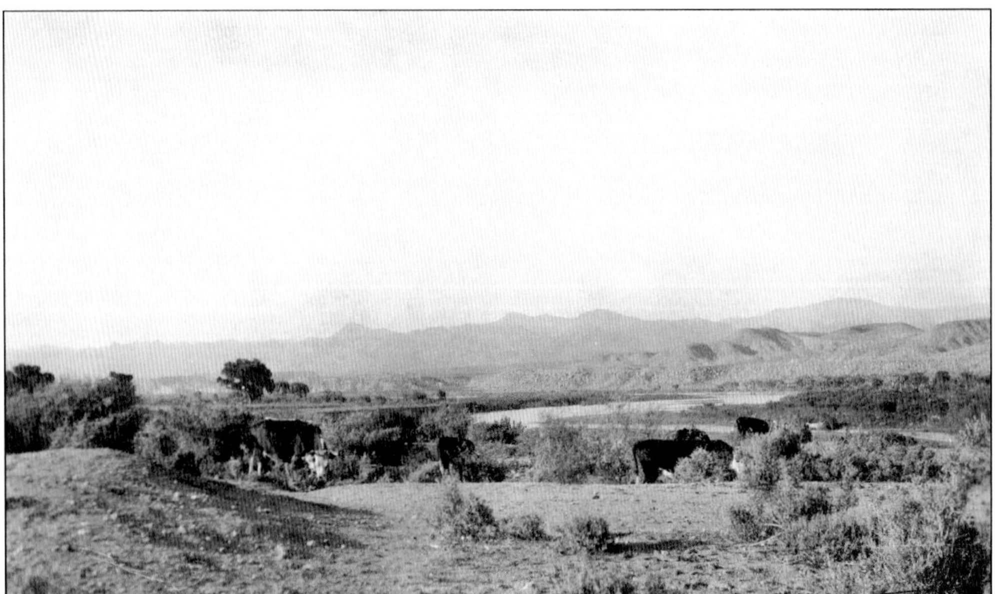

This 1920s view of the Gila River valley, looking to the west, was most likely taken in the vicinity of Bylas, about 15 miles east of the agency site. (Courtesy Diane Drobka collection; photograph probably by Gracie Taylor.)

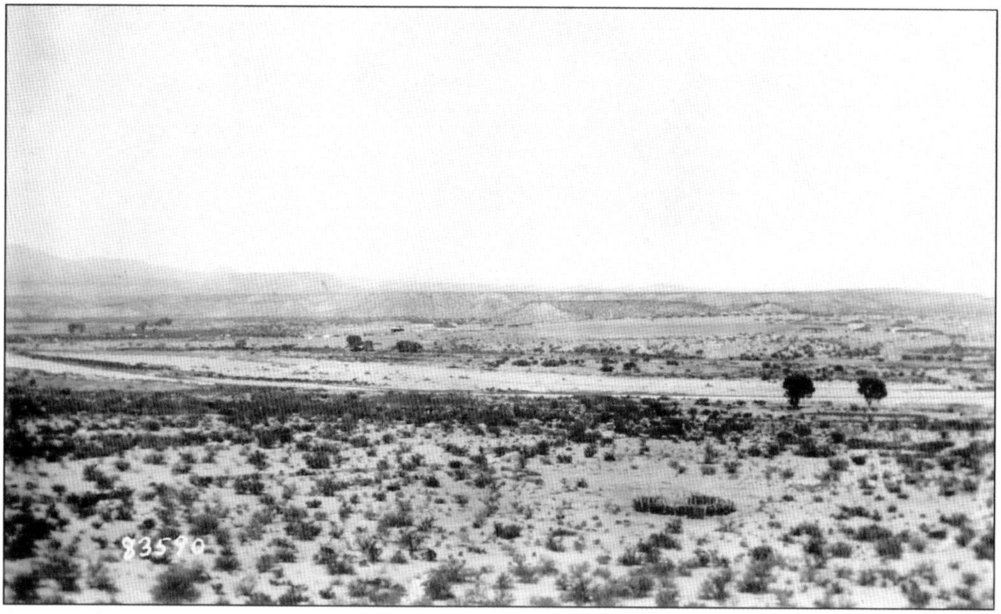

A general view of the territory, in the vicinity of San Carlos, is seen in this April 1895 photograph, looking northwest across the Gila River. The agency and military post are spread across the flat at the base of the hills. Barely visible are the agency buildings (left center) and the schoolhouse complex (far right) with the military structures behind. (Courtesy NARA, RG 111, Signal Corps Collection, No. 83590.)

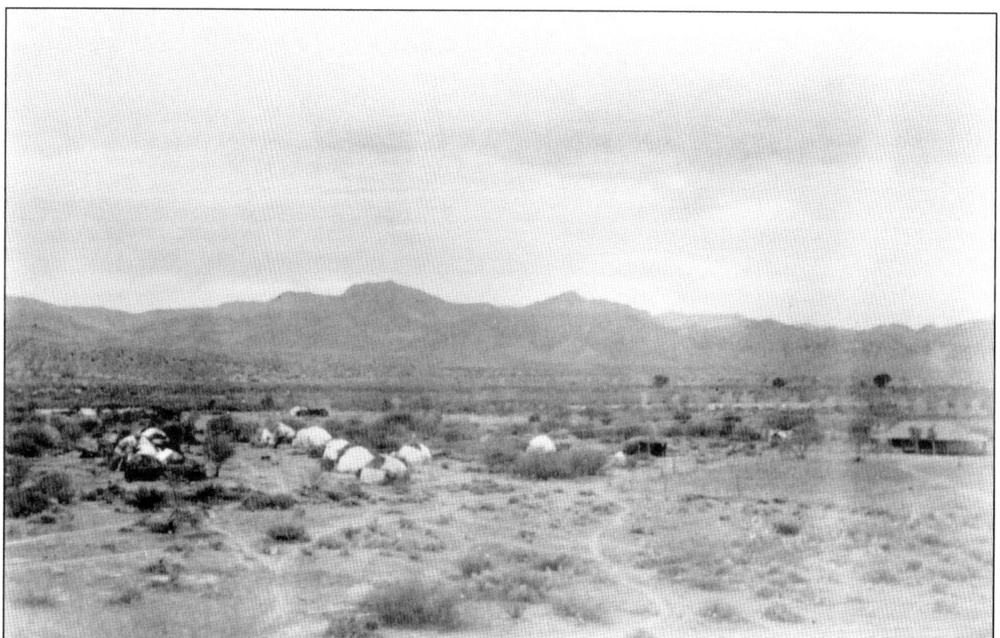

A typical Apache camp with a cluster of canvas-covered brush wickiup homes is shown in this undated, south-looking picture of the San Carlos Indian Agency. A frame building associated with the agency can be seen at the far right. (Courtesy GCHS, GM 27-14.)

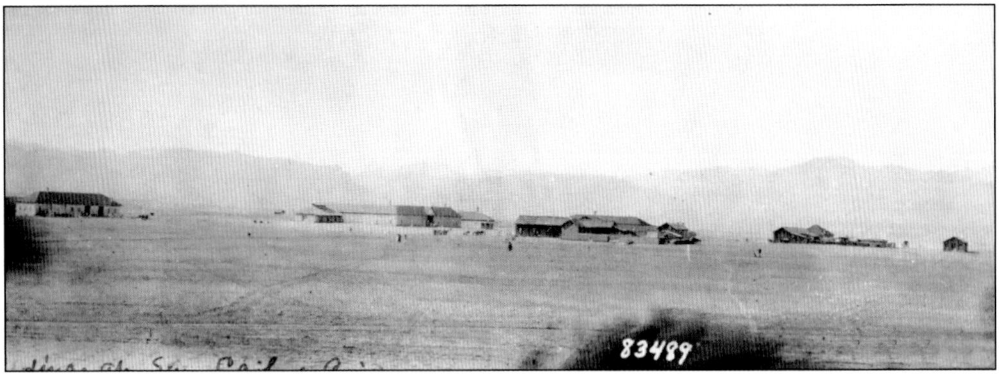

The desolate character of the locale selected for the San Carlos Agency is clearly evident in this 1893 view of the agency buildings. The buildings at the far left are the shops. Moving right in the view are the agency office building and warehouse, the trader's store complex, and the guardhouse at far right. (Courtesy NARA, RG 111, Signal Corps Collection, No. 83489.)

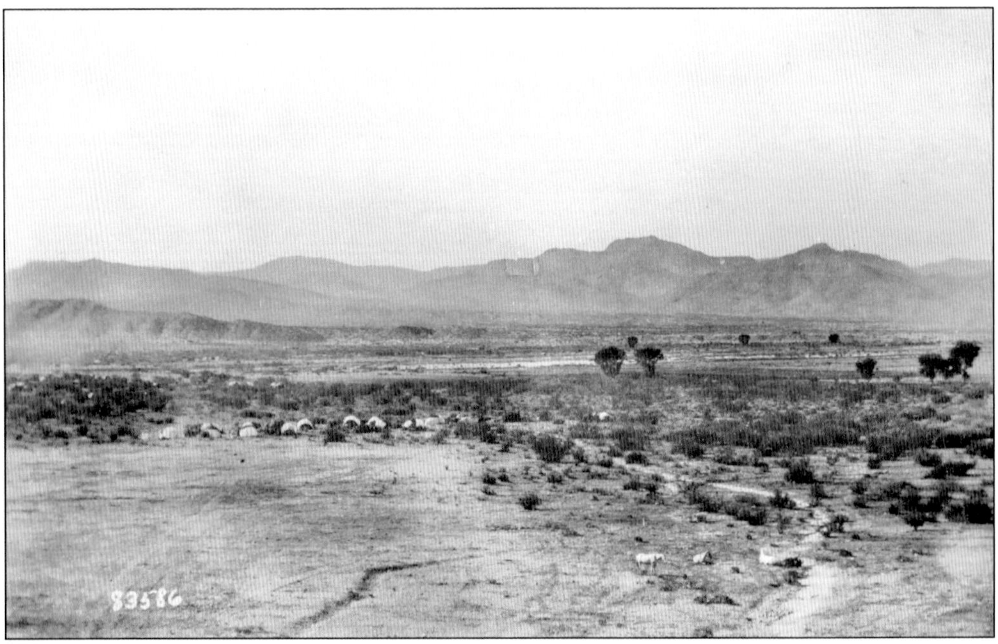

Apache and Yavapai camps were spread along the San Carlos and Gila Rivers for several miles, as reflected in this 1892 photograph. As new groups arrived in the mid-1870s, agent John Clum was mindful to geographically separate the different Western Apache and Yavapai groups in an attempt to secure peaceful relations. (Courtesy NARA, RG 111, Signal Corps Collection, No. 83586.)

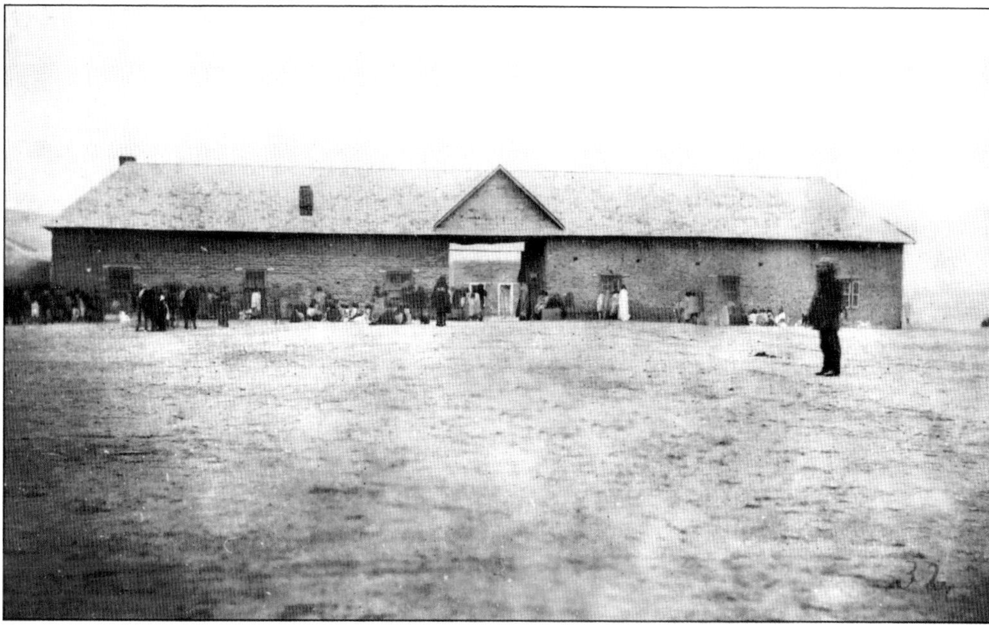

Construction of the agency office building was started under the supervision of agent John Clum in August 1874. Built by a mason and eight Apache laborers, who were paid at a rate of 50¢ per day, the structure was laid out in a hollow square with an office, council room, dispensary, dining room, kitchen, storeroom, and seven large dwelling rooms. (Courtesy NARA, RG 75, No. 75-IP-2-1.)

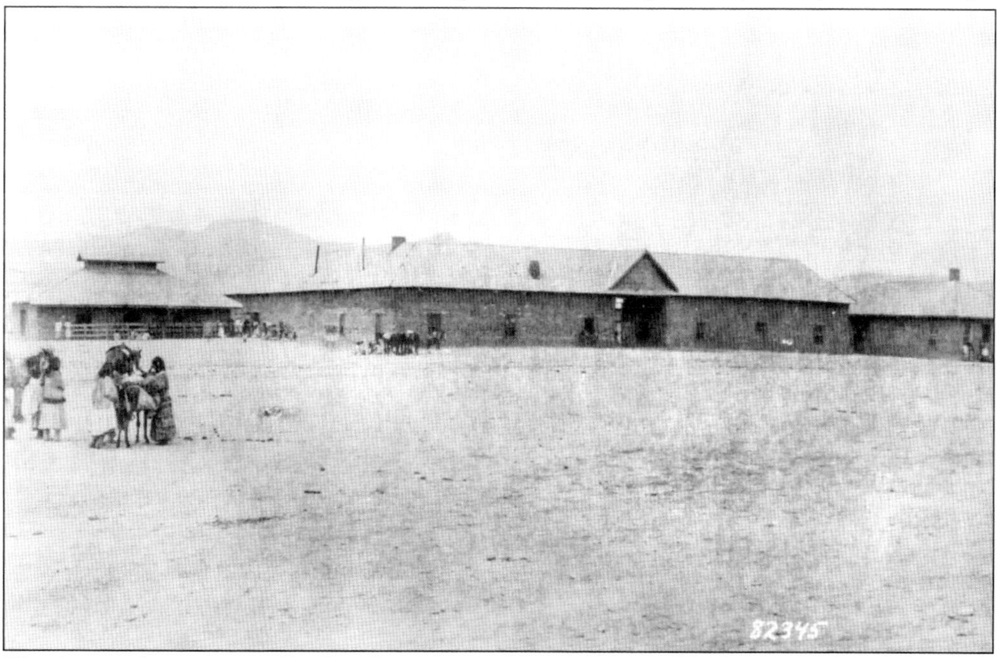

The San Carlos Agency office building, along with the smaller warehouse at left where rations were issued, is seen in this 1883 image. The agency buildings were located on a wide gravelly terrace about 30 feet above the Gila River floodplain. The lack of water on the flat meant that it was barren of trees and nearly all kinds of plants. (Courtesy NARA, RG 111, Signal Corps Collection, No. 82345.)

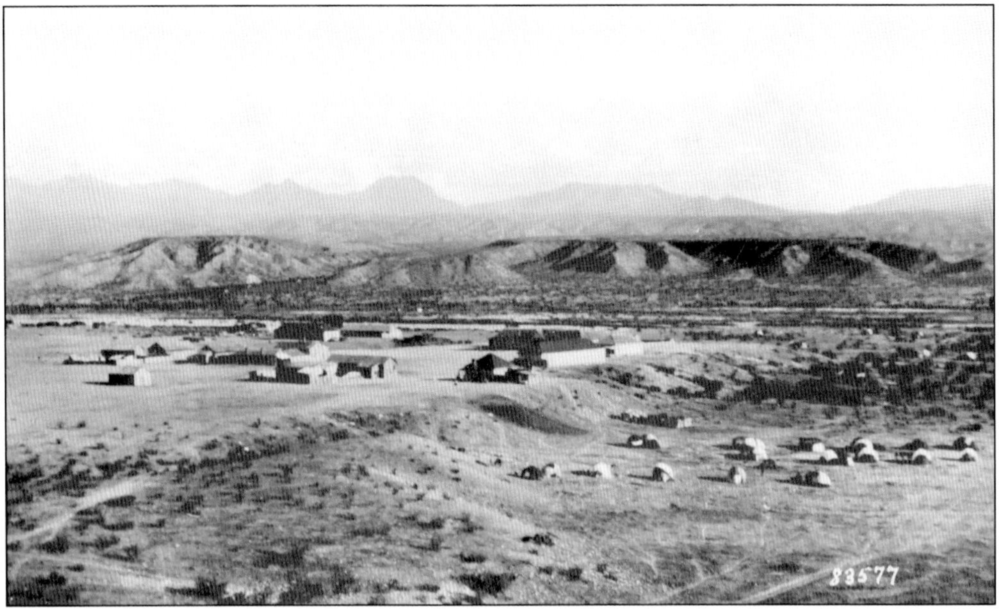

This 1895 view provides a nice overview of the San Carlos Indian Agency, looking south across the Gila River valley toward the Mescal Mountains. Clusters of canvas-covered wickiup Apache homes can be seen distributed about the lower level of the river floodplain. (Courtesy NARA, RG 111, Signal Corps Collection, No. 83577.)

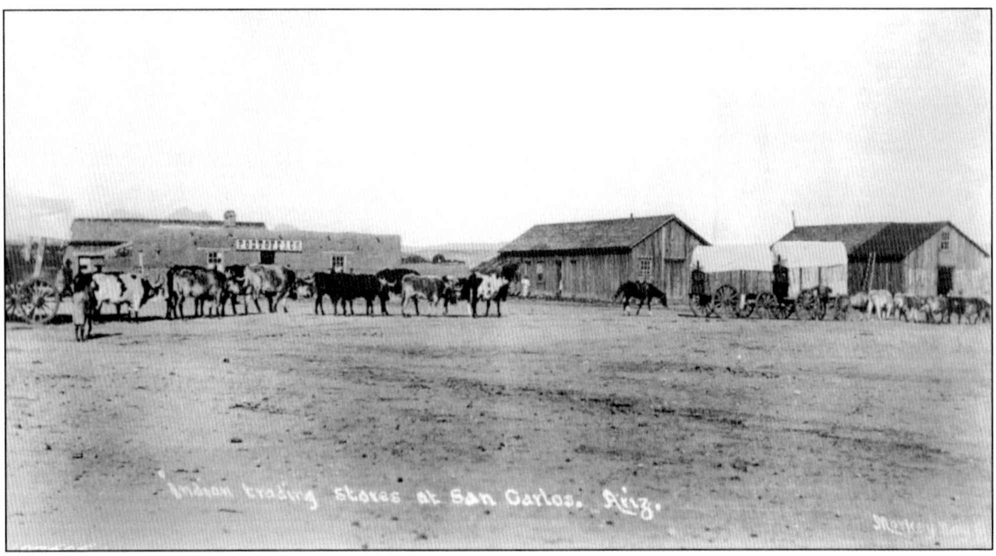

This late-1880s view of the trading post complex at San Carlos is looking to the north-northeast. The trading post, left, also functioned as the San Carlos Post Office between 1875 and 1929. Along with the trader's storehouses at right, two oxen wagon teams are visible. (Courtesy NARA, RG 111, Signal Corps Collection, No. 107505; photograph by Daniel Markey.)

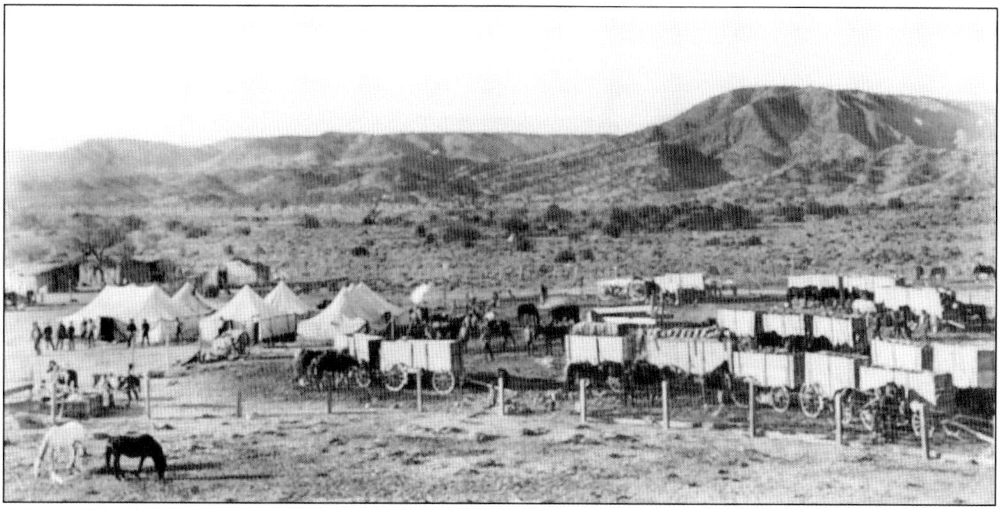

About 15 miles east of the agency was the hamlet of Geronimo, so named because the Chiricahua people, including Geronimo and his family, were settled in this vicinity in the late 1870s. The site of a subagency from 1875 to 1883, Geronimo later served as a stop for wagon teams and later as a short-term railhead for the railroad in 1895. (Courtesy ASUL Forrest Doucette Collection, No. RR-74.)

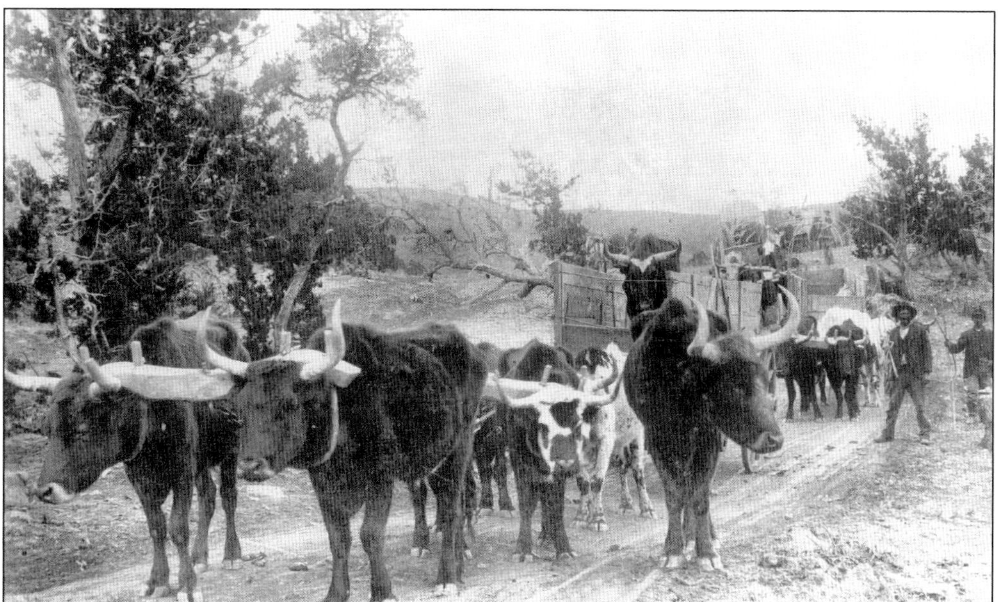

Bull teams were used to transport critical supplies from Willcox to the San Carlos Reservation for both civilian and military needs. An ox team is on the wagon road near Fort Thomas in this 1882–1883 photograph. (Courtesy NARA, RG 111, Signal Corps Collection, No. 89099.)

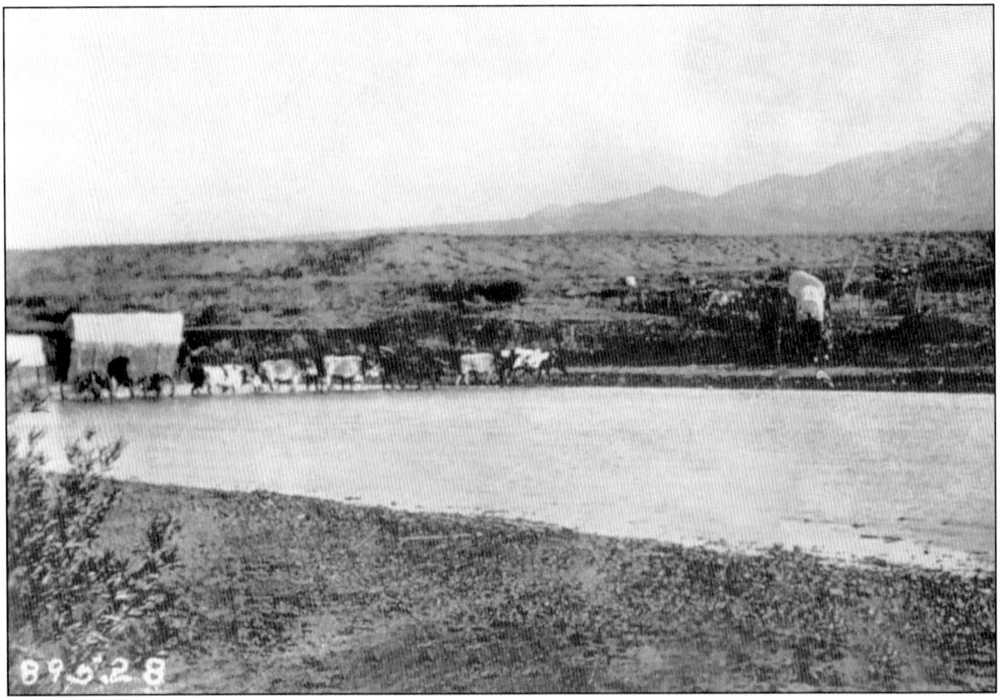

Ox teams with wagons and trailers are leaving the San Carlos Indian Agency in 1880. The wagon caravan is headed east along the Gila River toward Fort Thomas and on to Willcox. Issuance of badly needed weekly rations to several thousand Apaches and Yavapais required a reliable flow of supplies along the wagon road. (Courtesy NARA, RG 111, Signal Corps Collection, No. 107516.)

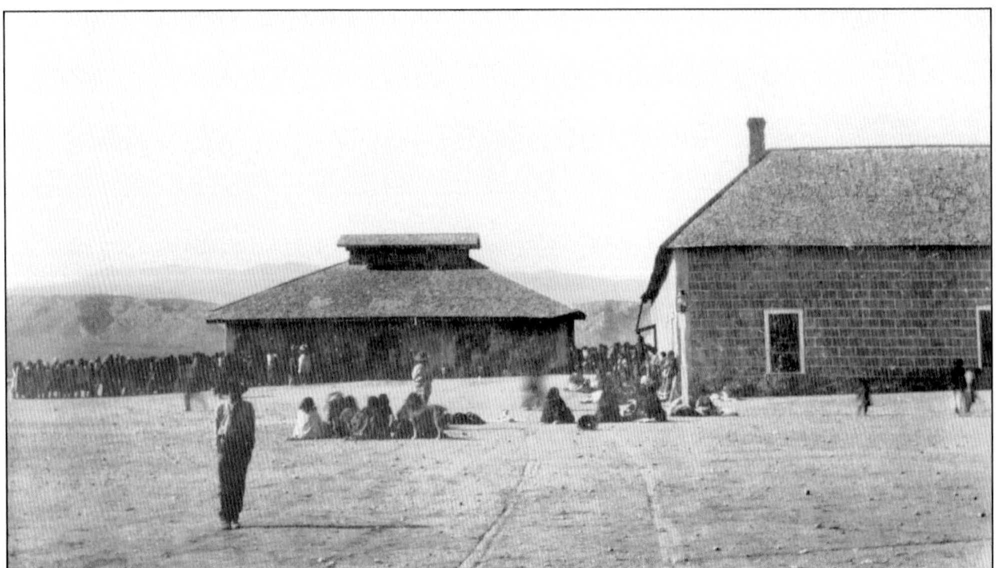

The issuing of rations started immediately after the agency was established in 1873 and would continue for about 50 years. In 1886, fifty percent of the native population still subsisted on government rations. This undated image shows a ration line at the warehouse and the corner of the agency office building at right. (Courtesy GCHS, GM-27-31.)

In 1880, rations issued every Thursday to each person included five-and-a-half pounds of flour, four ounces of beans, eight pounds of sugar per 100 rations, four pounds of coffee per 100 rations, one pound of salt per 100 rations, and one small cake of soap. On Fridays, 10 pounds of beef were issued to each person. (Courtesy AHF, Rothrock Collection IA-27; stereograph by George Rothrock, late 1870s.)

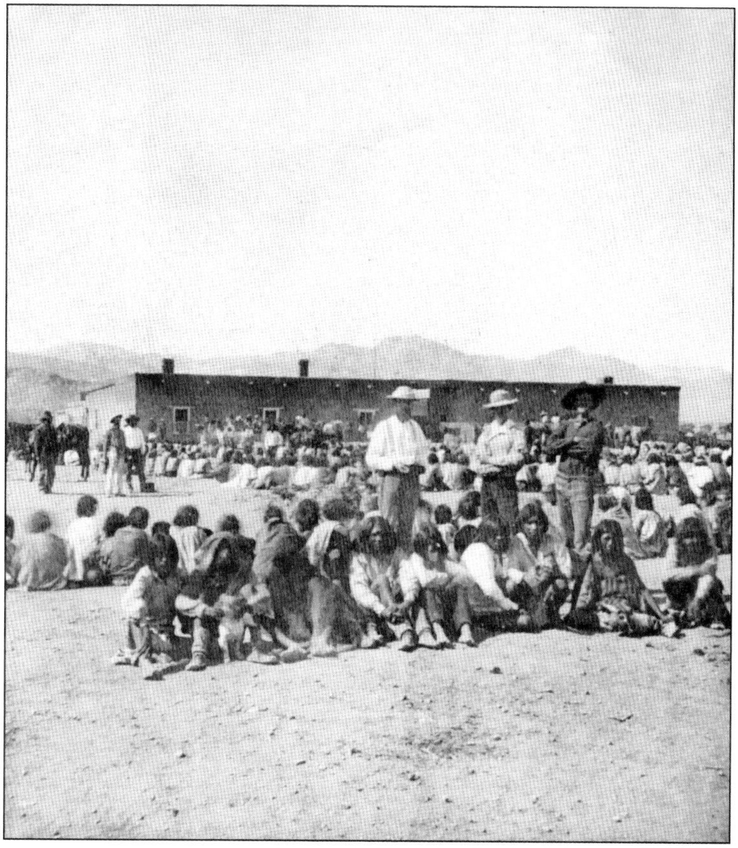

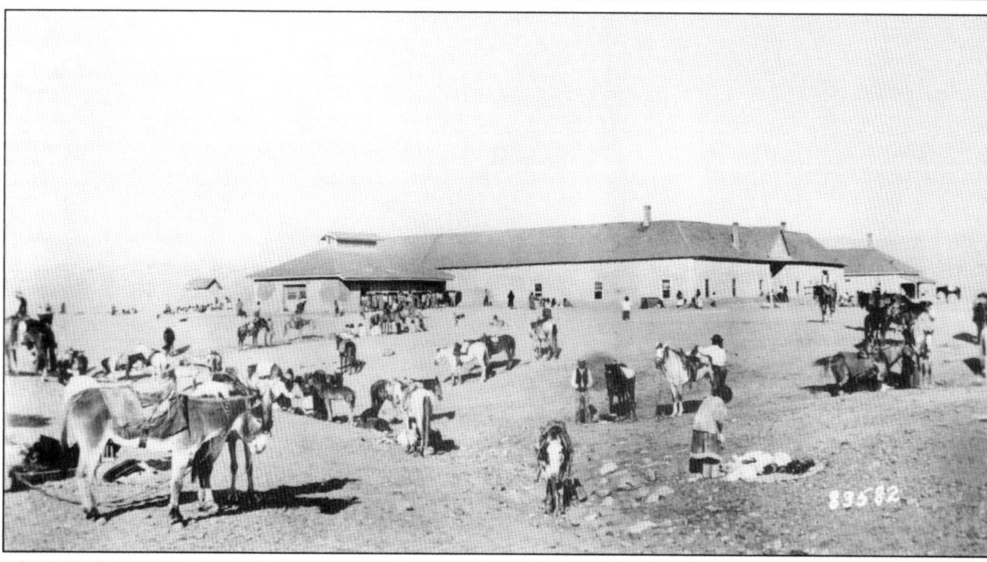

This 1895 scene shows the activity of ration day at the San Carlos Agency as people came in from the outlying camps to receive supplies. In 1888, agent Capt. John Bullis observed that rations were issued to 3,396 of the reservation's population and that government-issued rations constituted one-third of their annual food supply. (Courtesy NARA, RG 111, Signal Corps Collection, No. 83582.)

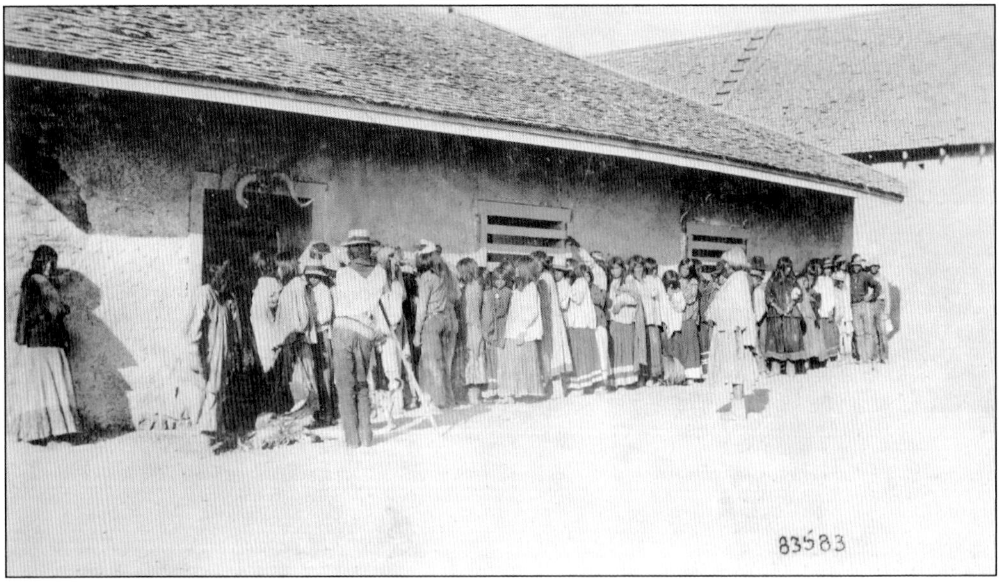

This photograph, taken between 1892 and 1897, shows a close-up of the ration line. In 1880, agent J. C. Tiffany noted that ration day was a gala event for the many tribes, identified by their dress, cut of hair, paint upon the face, style of clothing, and actions. (Courtesy NARA, RG 111, Signal Corps Collection, No. 83583.)

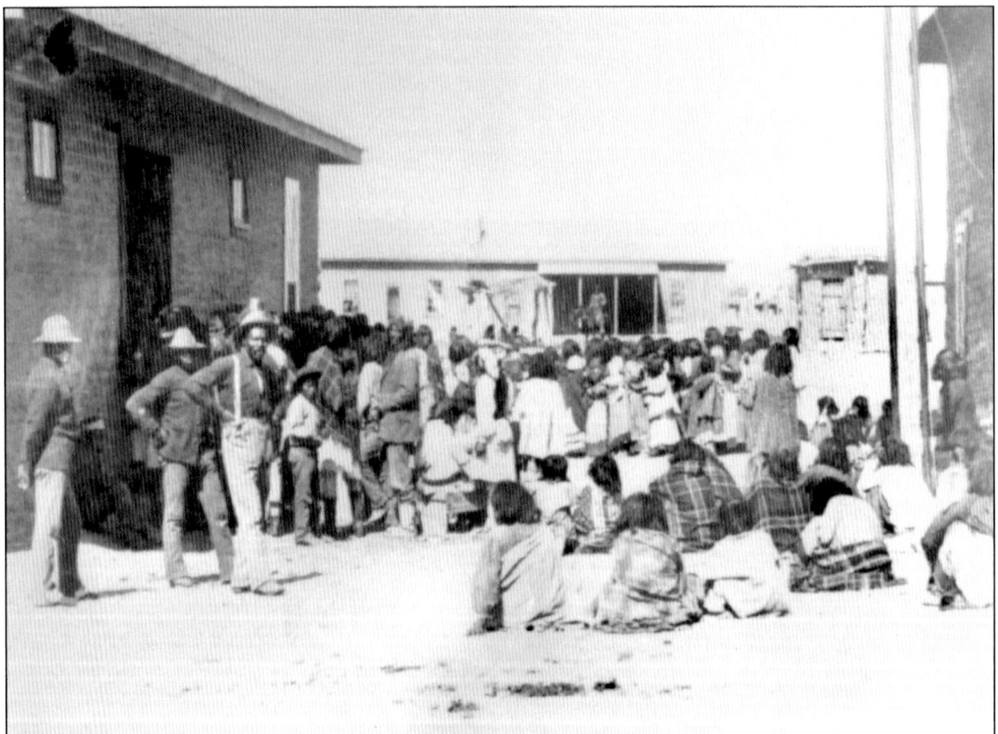

In addition to foodstuffs, other supplies of necessity were issued to the population. Here clothing is being passed out during the early 1890s under the watchful eye of buffalo soldiers of the 24th Infantry, seen at left. (Courtesy GCHS, GM 27-100.)

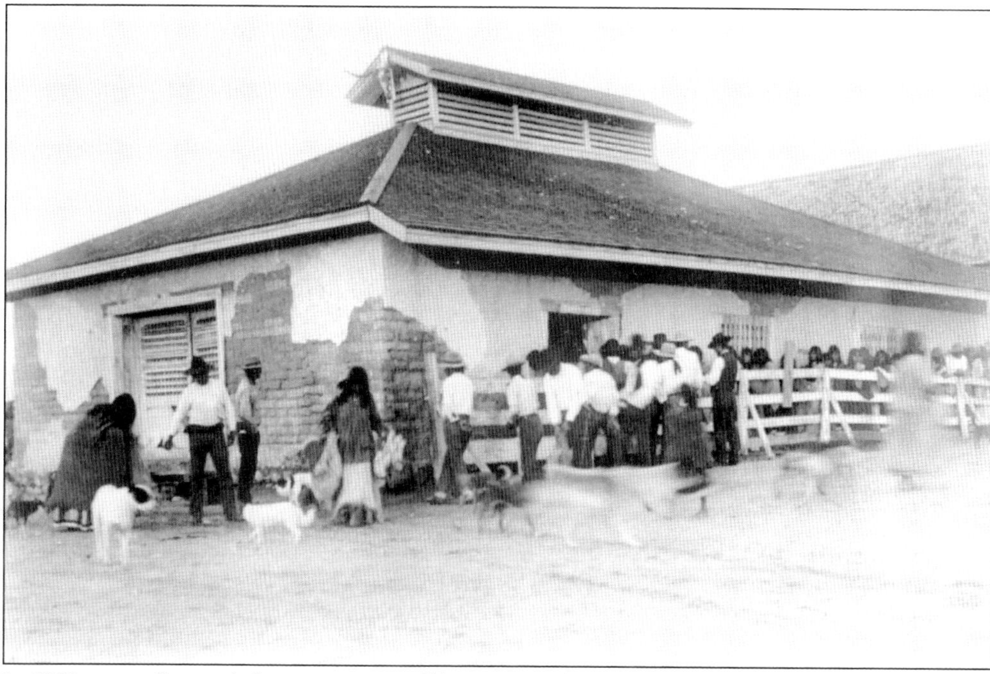

In 1921, critically needed rations were still being issued to 318 of the total reservation population of 2,525 Apaches. The rations included beef, bacon, baking powder, beans, coffee, corn, flour, salt, soap, and sugar—at a total cost of $23.89 per 100 rations. (Courtesy GCHS, GM 27-143.)

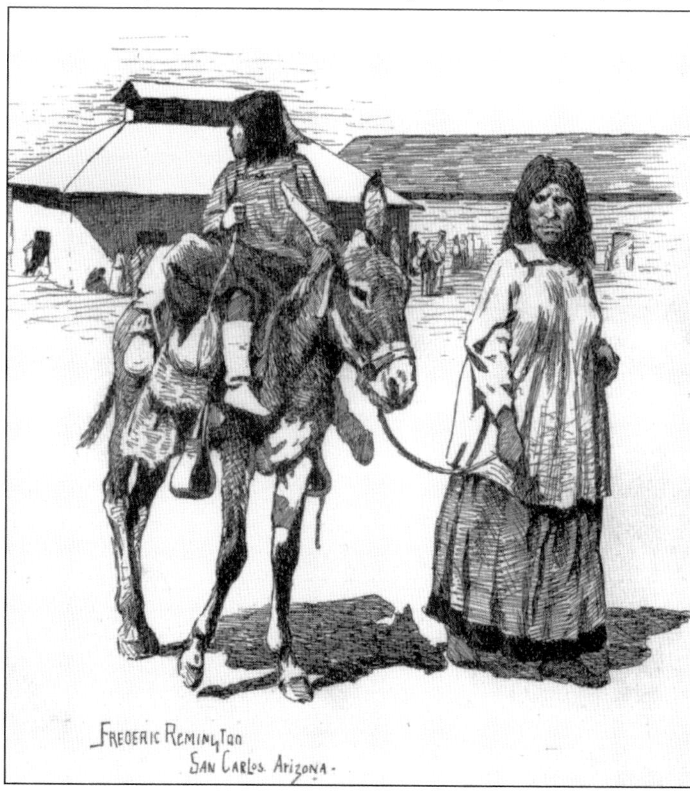

The events associated with ration day attracted the attention of artist Frederick Remington, who visited San Carlos in 1888. This illustration, published in *Century Magazine* in 1889, shows an Apache woman with rations returning to her home. (Courtesy authors' collection.)

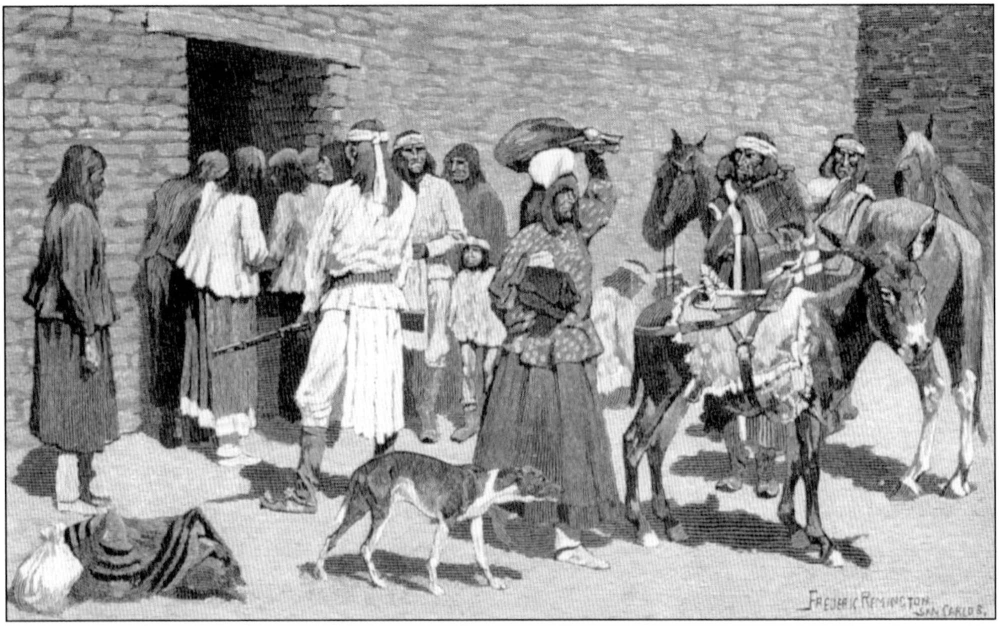

This Frederic Remington illustration, published in 1889 in *Century Magazine*, shows the distribution of beef at the San Carlos Agency. Rations were still being issued in 1925 but only to 164 persons consisting of aged and decrepit men and women, and orphaned children. (Courtesy authors' collection.)

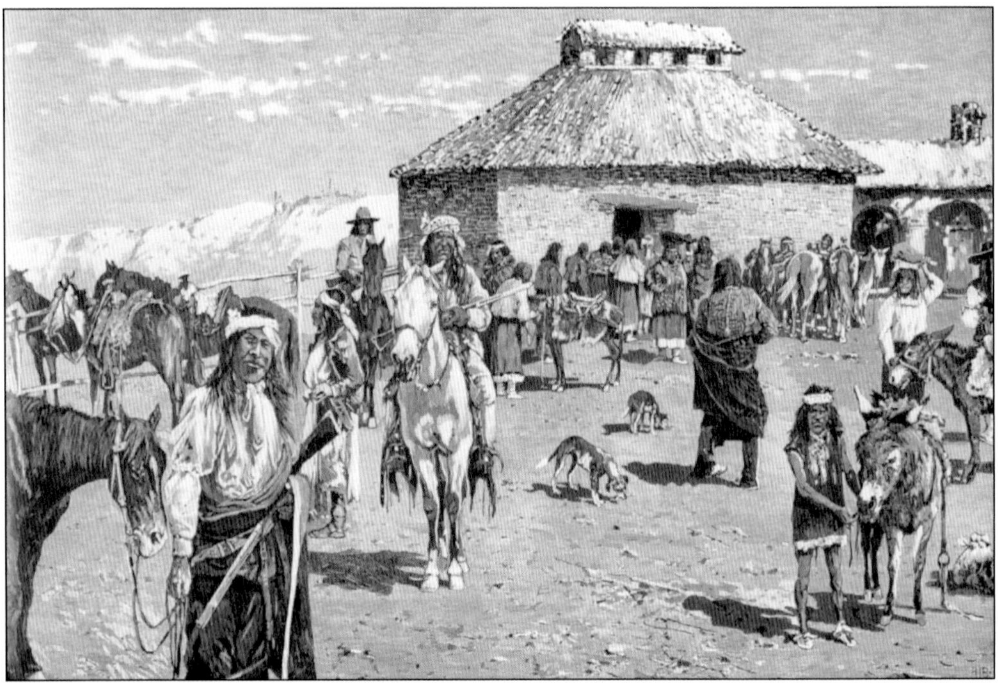

The San Carlos ration day was such an event that it attracted foreign attention. This illustration by an artist named Richter was published in the German publication, *Das Buch fur Elle*, in 1893. The translated caption reads, "Distributing food from Indian agency of Apache in Arizona Territory." (Courtesy authors' collection.)

This photograph, taken in 1875, shows agent John Clum (center) with two Apache leaders of the time—Diablo (Es-kim-law) at left and Eskiminzin at right. Diablo was at first friendly to the agent but turned hostile after being forced to move to the agency. Diablo was killed by White Mountain Apaches near Fort Apache in 1880. (Courtesy NARA, RG 111, Signal Corps Collection, No. 94849.)

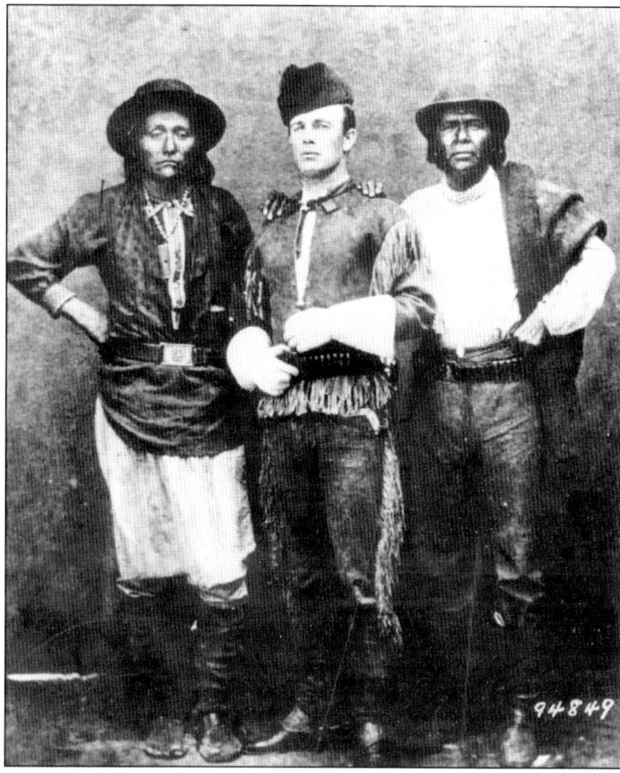

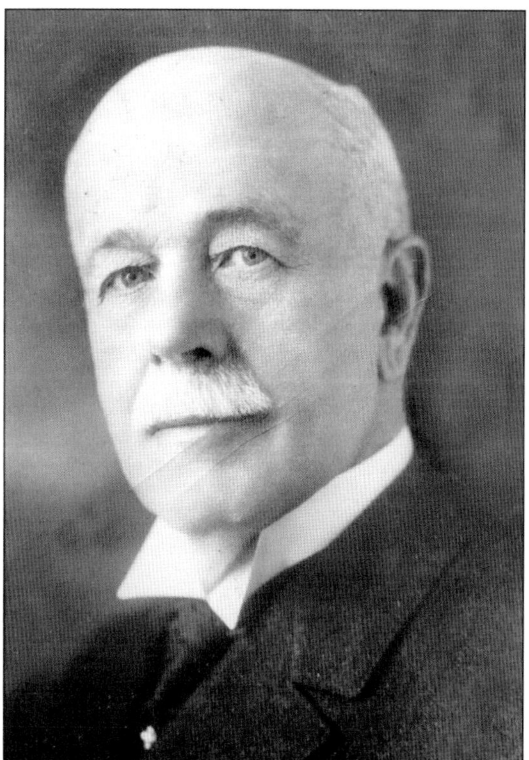

John Clum (1851–1932) was the Indian agent at San Carlos from 1874 to 1877. Later he was the first mayor of Tombstone, founder of the *Tombstone Epitaph*, and a friend of Wyatt Earp. He returned to visit the old agency at San Carlos in 1929, just before the final dynamiting of the remaining buildings. (Courtesy GCHS, GM 29-15.)

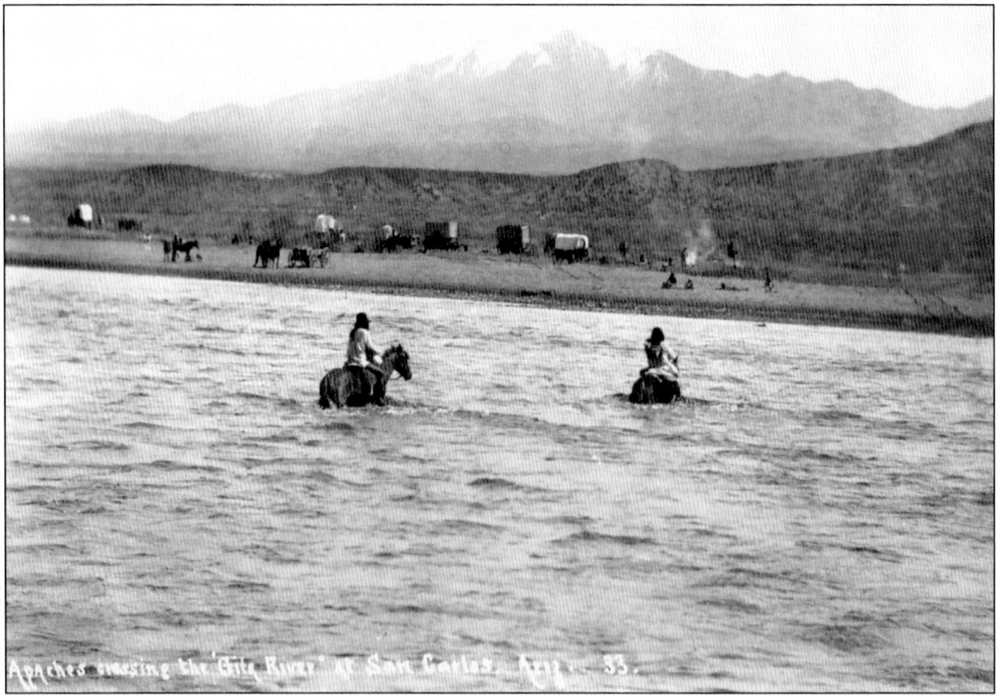

Here San Carlos Apaches or Yavapais cross the Gila River from the agency grounds. A wagon train is camped on the south side of the river, perhaps waiting for the water to subside before crossing to deliver supplies. Mount Turnbull dominates the background. (Courtesy GCHS, GM 27-95.)

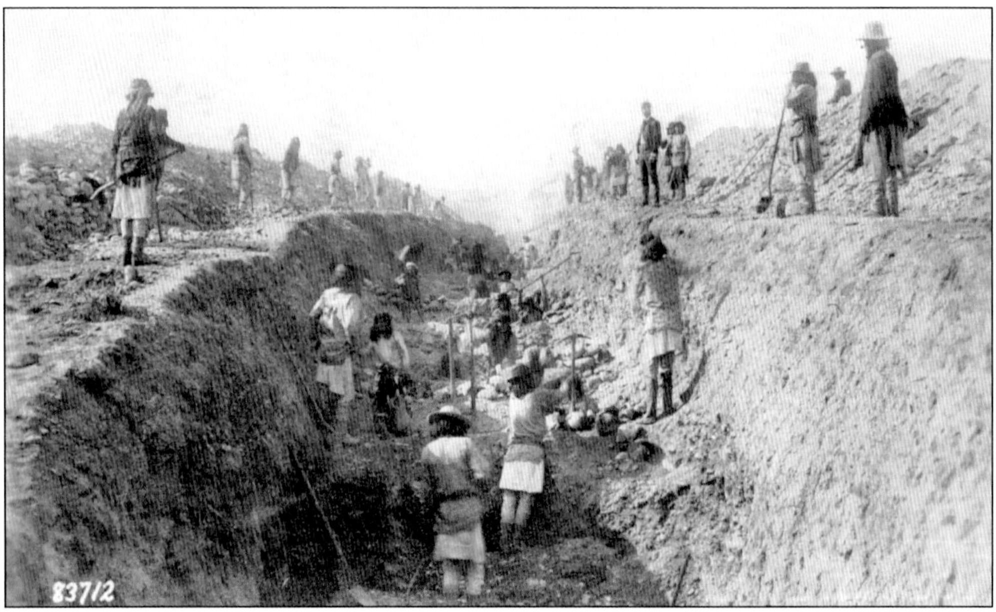

The only way to successfully raise crops at San Carlos was by irrigation. Several large diversion ditches were dug over the years to supply water to the fields; this ditch is under construction in 1886. The photograph was taken by Lt. J. B. McDonald, 10th Cavalry, the officer in charge of the work. (Courtesy NARA, RG 111, Signal Corps Collection, No. 87312.)

Three

POST OF SAN CARLOS

As noted in the last chapter, setting up the new San Carlos Agency caused considerable unrest among the Apaches. To lend support for the civilian agent, C. F. Larabee, the army had a small detachment of troops encamped adjacent to the agency. On May 27, 1873, an altercation with an Apache man during the issuing of rations ended with the man mortally shooting Lt. Jacob Almy during an attempt to arrest him. This led to the stationing of three companies of the 5th Cavalry at San Carlos two days later. The San Carlos army camp became a sub-post of Camp Apache, located about 70 miles to the north. The post remained at San Carlos until October 26, 1875, when the civilian agent, John Clum, won out with an argument that he and his police could effectively maintain law and order on the reservation without a military presence.

An uneasy peace was maintained at San Carlos in the late 1870s. In 1881, an attack took place in the northern part of the reservation that heightened fears of a major outbreak of disgruntled Apaches, mainly Chiricahuas who were quite unhappy being there. In response, Camp San Carlos was reoccupied in 1882 as a regularly garrisoned post. Throughout the 1880s, a span of years that included the Apache wars, the post remained a tent encampment pending a decision on its permanence. In 1894, the post became a sub-post of Fort Grant, and quarters and other support buildings were constructed. Camp San Carlos was officially abandoned as a military post in the fall of 1901, and the buildings were placed under control of the Indian agency.

Because of its resident native population, San Carlos was a preferred recruitment site for Apache scouts during the ensuing Apache conflicts and in the years beyond. Many Yavapais then living at San Carlos also enlisted as scouts. Ethnic diversity increased at San Carlos during the late 1880s and early 1890s as several companies of the 9th and 10th Cavalry and the 24th Infantry units, the celebrated buffalo soldiers, served at the post.

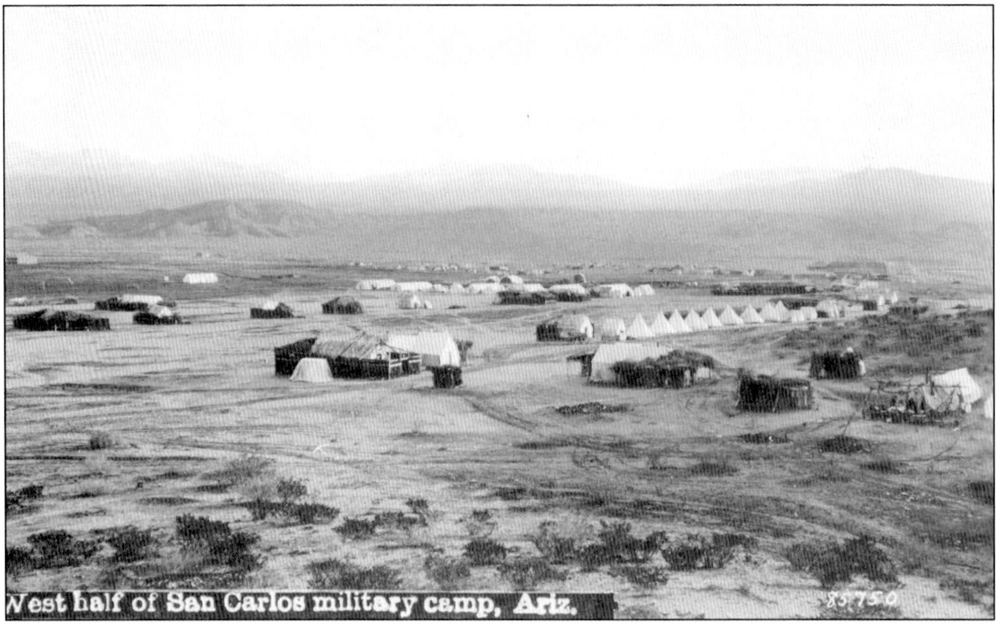

The military post of San Carlos was irregularly occupied from 1873 to 1875. Beginning in 1882, the post was reestablished and regularly garrisoned until 1901. Looking south, this mid-1880s image shows the semipermanent tent encampment; the agency buildings can be seen in the background. Brush enclosures and covers protected the tents from the elements. (Courtesy NARA, RG 111, Signal Corps Collection, No. 85750.)

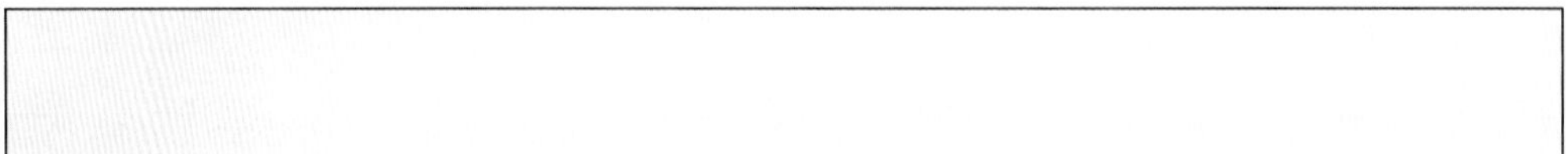
This image from around 1885, looking south toward Mount Turnbull, shows Camp San Carlos with the agency school building complex behind it. The camp was an important source of income for the native population, who provided firewood, wild grass hay, and barley to the military. The army officers and soldiers also bought basketry and beadwork from the Apaches. (Courtesy AHF, Sacks Collection, No. SCS-175.)

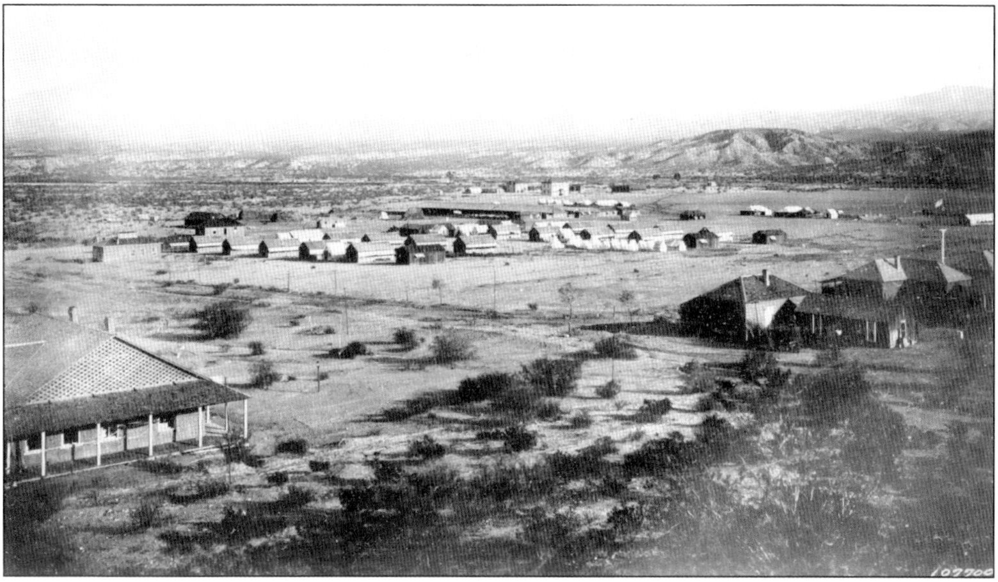

By 1894, more permanent frame and adobe buildings had replaced the tents at Camp San Carlos. The corner of the post hospital can be seen at lower left, the enlisted barracks at center, and the officers' quarters at right. Again, the agency school buildings are in the background. (Courtesy NARA, RG 111, Signal Corps Collection, No. 107700.)

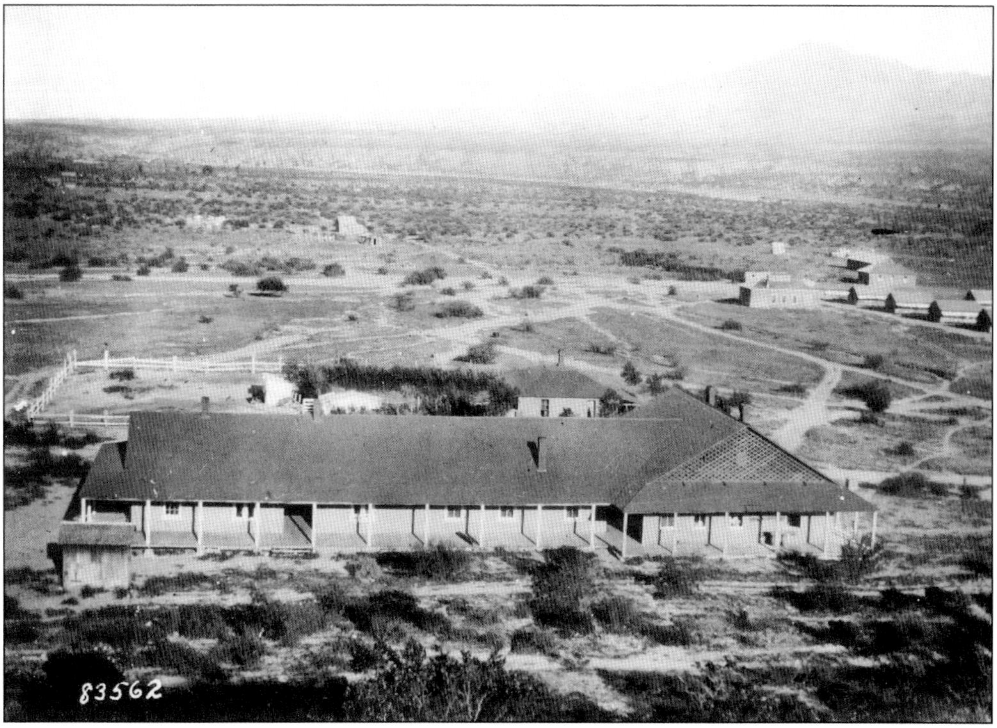

The post hospital is shown in this 1895 photograph, looking east. Following abandonment by the army, the building became a hotel for travelers in 1904. In 1912, a portion of the building was reestablished as a hospital for Apaches with a dispensary, living quarters for the nurse, and four tent houses outside for patients. (Courtesy NARA, RG 111, Signal Corps Collection, No. 83562.)

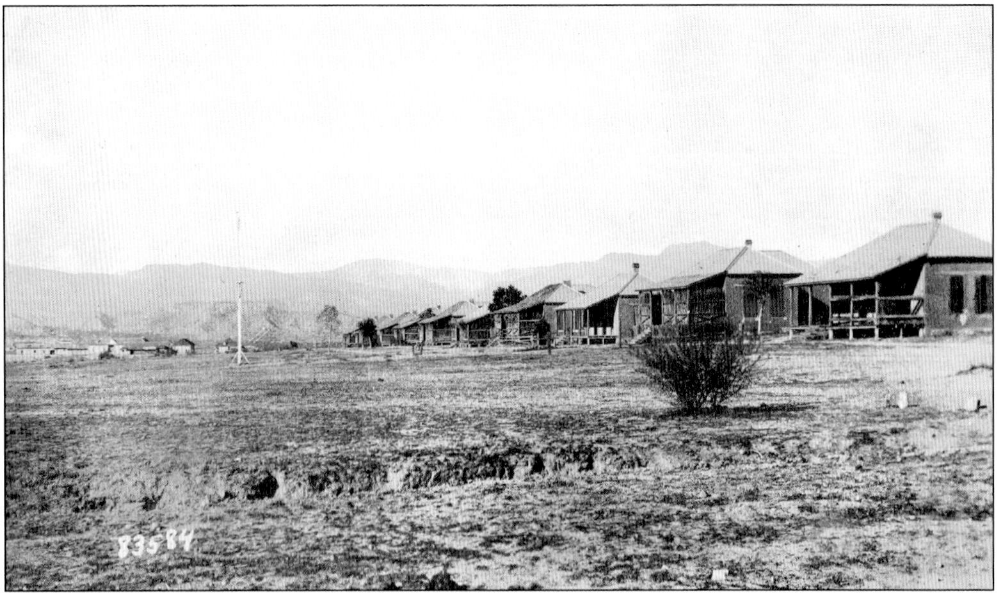

The officers' row at San Carlos is pictured in this image, taken between 1893 and 1897, with the parade ground and flagpole to the left. The agency offices and warehouse can be seen in the distance, left center of the view. (Courtesy NARA, RG 111, Signal Corps Collection, No. 83584.)

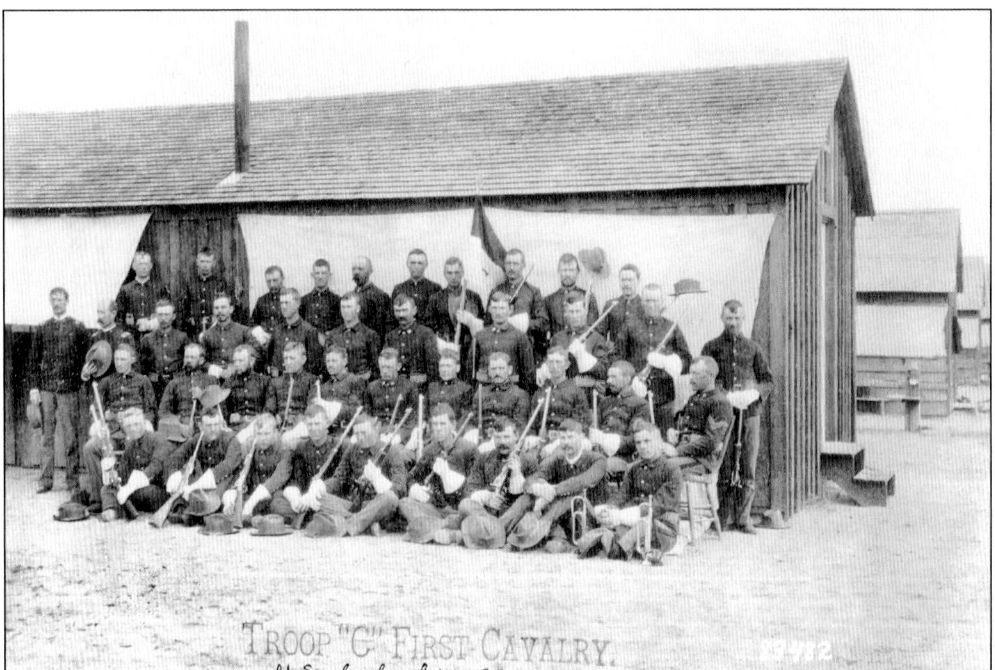

The frame enlisted barracks can be seen behind this company photograph of Troop C, 1st Cavalry, taken at San Carlos in 1892. Note the canvas added to the sides of the buildings to provide extra protection from the elements, particularly the persistent dusty winds. (Courtesy NARA, RG 111, Signal Corps Collection, No. 83482.)

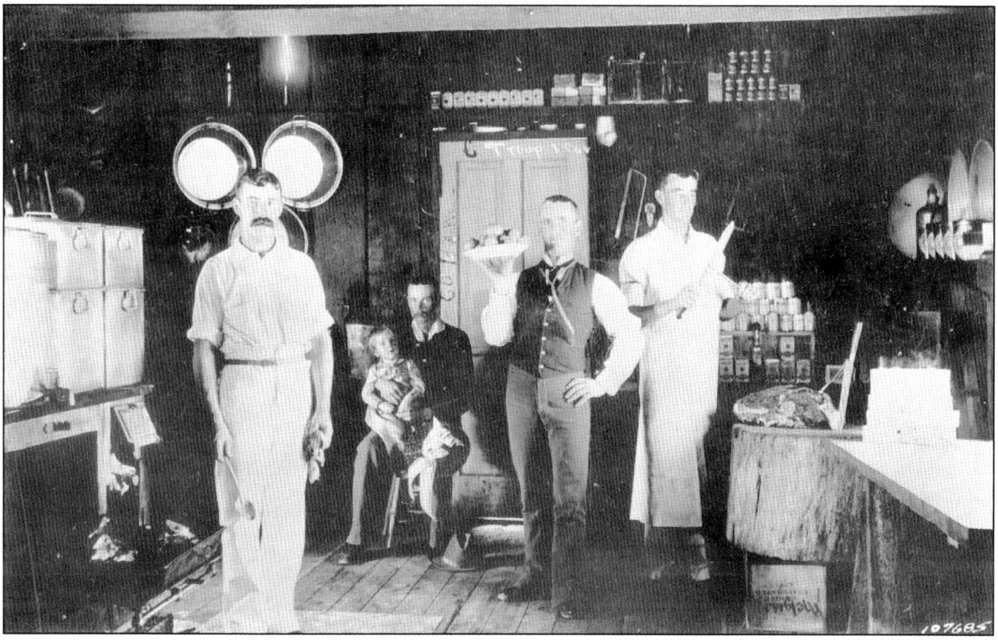

This 1894 photograph shows the kitchen of Company C, 1st Cavalry at San Carlos. The presence of the child in the soldier's lap reflects a change in earlier policy. During the more turbulent times of the 1880s, military dependents were not permitted at the post. (Courtesy NARA, RG 111, Signal Corps Collection, No. 107685.)

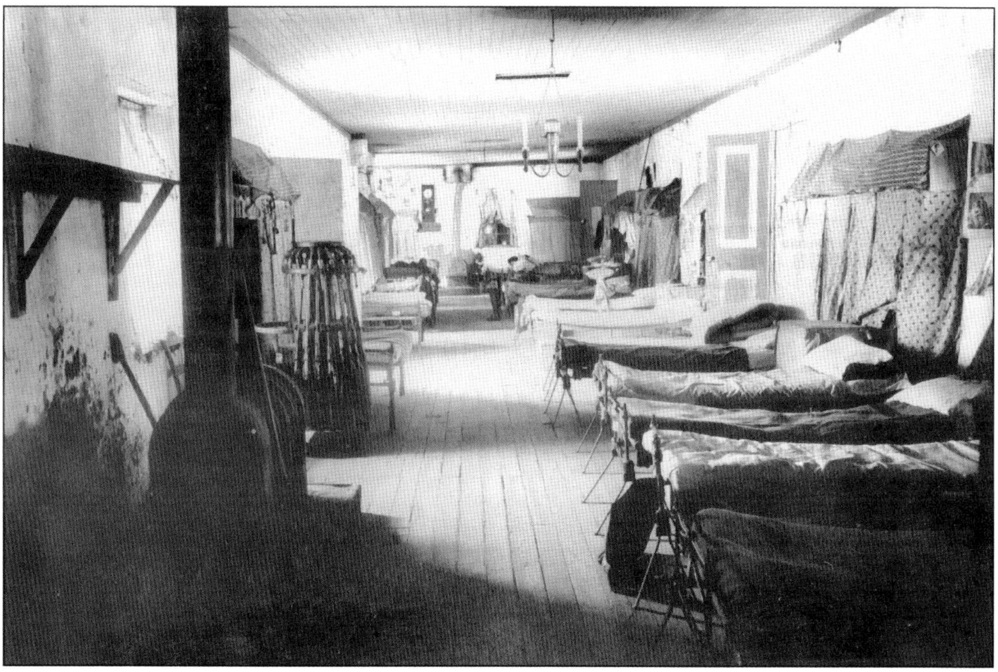

This picture of the interior of an enlisted barracks building is said to be from San Carlos; however, because of the type of building, it is more likely from another post in the region. Nonetheless, the image represents a good example of what the barracks at San Carlos would have looked like at the time. (Courtesy GCHS, GM-121.)

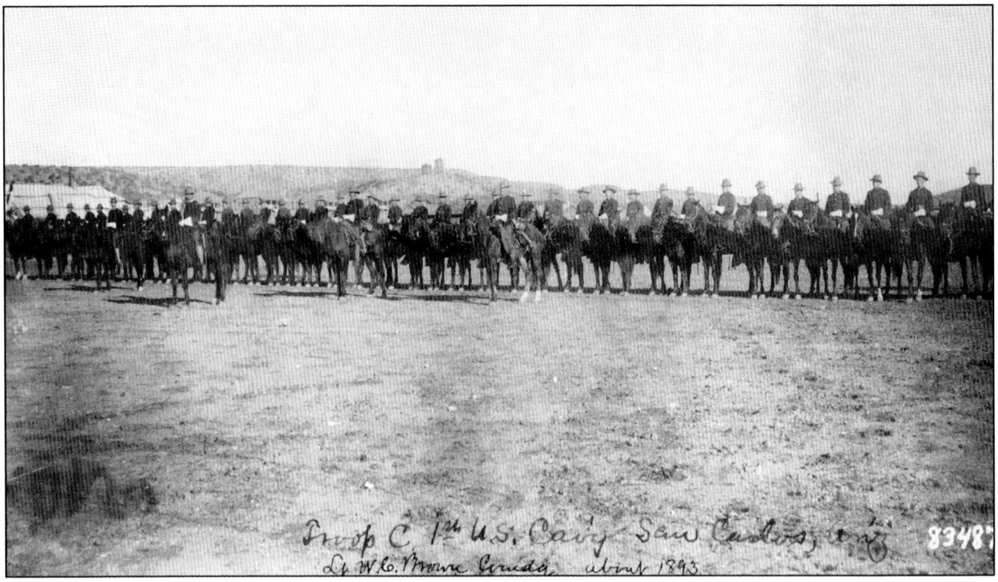

A cavalry formation is on the parade ground at Camp San Carlos in this photograph, taken around 1893. The unit in the image is Troop C, 1st Cavalry, under the command of Lt. W. C. Brown. (Courtesy NARA, RG 111, Signal Corps Collection, No. 83487.)

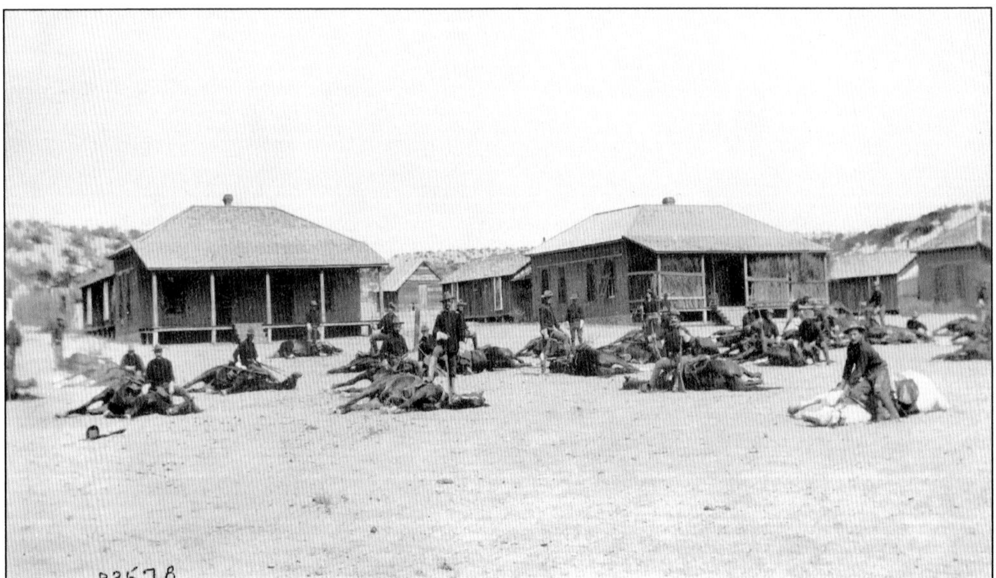

Here Capt. William J. Nicholson's troop of the 7th Cavalry practices horse maneuvers at San Carlos in 1894. The training activity is taking place in front of the officers' housing. (Courtesy NARA, RG 111, Signal Corps Collection, No. 83578.)

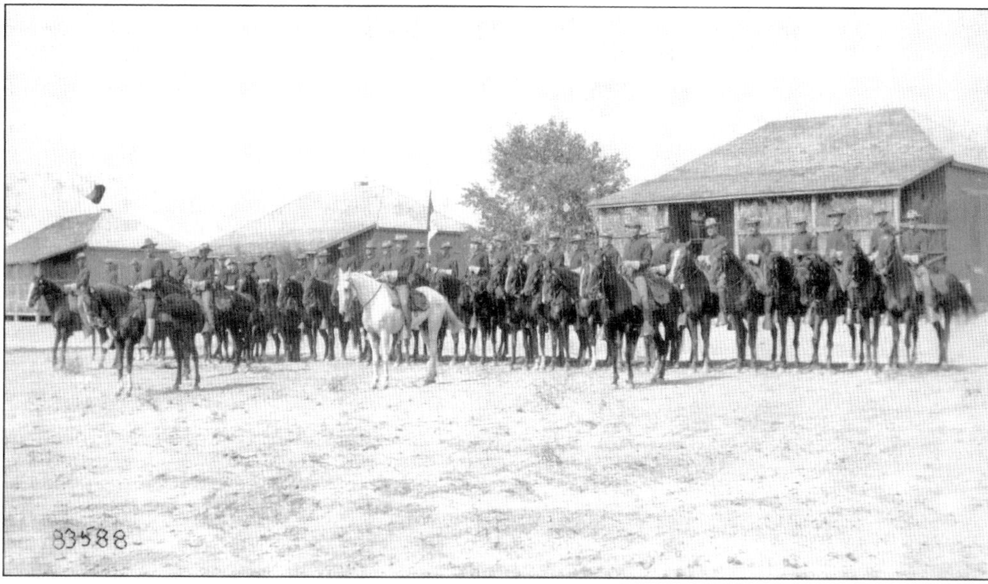

Another view of Capt. William J. Nicholson's 7th Cavalry troop is shown in this image, also from 1894. Nicholson later became a brigadier general in the army. He and another 20 officers that served at San Carlos rose to the rank of brigadier general or higher later in their careers. (Courtesy NARA, RG 111, Signal Corps Collection, No. 83588.)

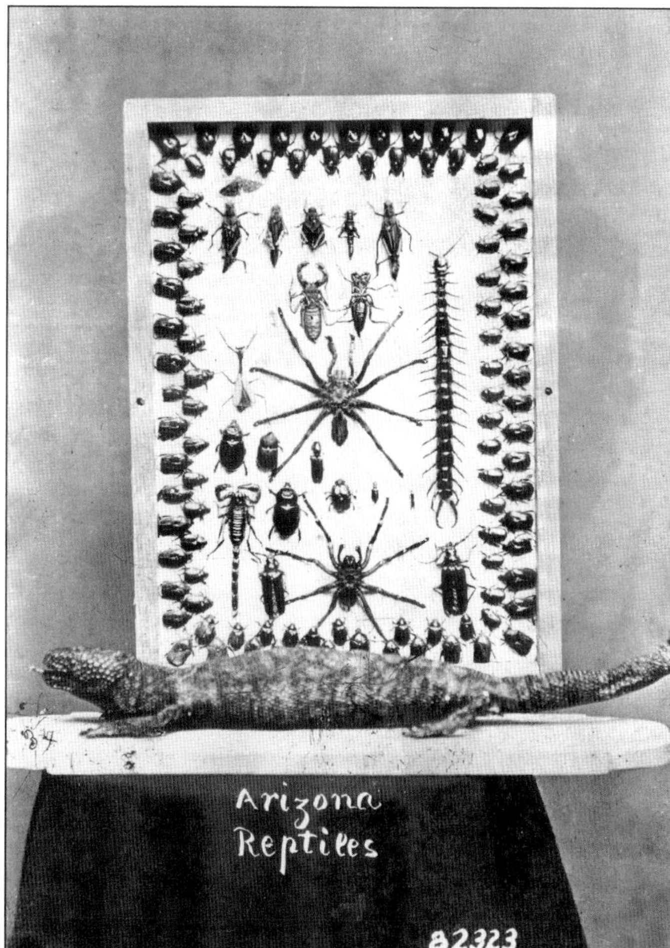

This image is captioned as follows: "Some of Britton Davis' occasional bedfellows." Lt. Britton Davis commanded the Apache scout companies at San Carlos in the early 1880s and made this collection of insects and other animals during his stay. (Courtesy NARA, RG 111, Signal Corps Collection, No. 82323.)

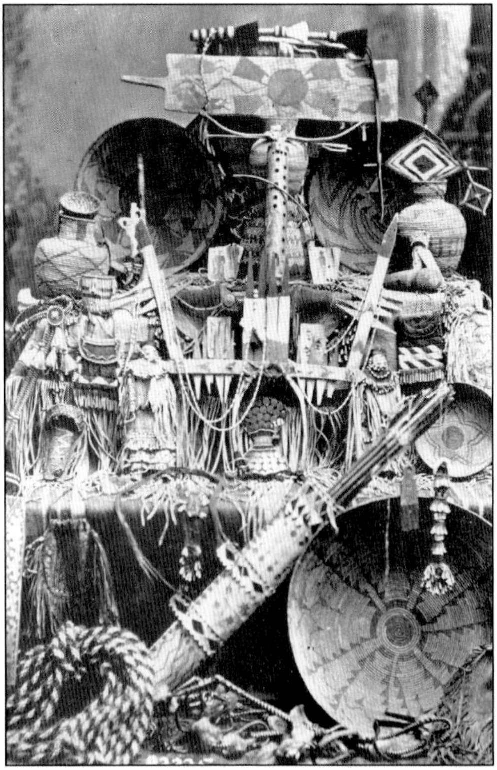

Several army officers were attracted to collecting ethnographic items during their tours in Arizona. During his tour at San Carlos, Lt. Britton Davis assembled this diverse collection of Apache beadwork, ornaments, basketry, weapons, religious paraphernalia, and other artifacts. (Courtesy NARA, RG 111, Signal Corps Collection, No. 82325.)

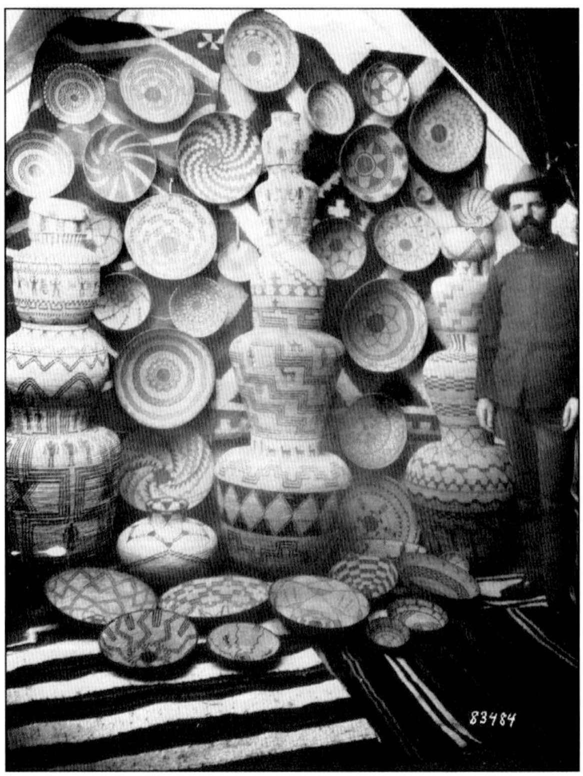

While stationed at San Carlos during 1891–1893, Lt. L. P. Davidson of the 11th Infantry, shown at right in the photograph, amassed an impressive collection of Apache basket specimens. (Courtesy NARA, RG 111, Signal Corps Collection, No. 83484.)

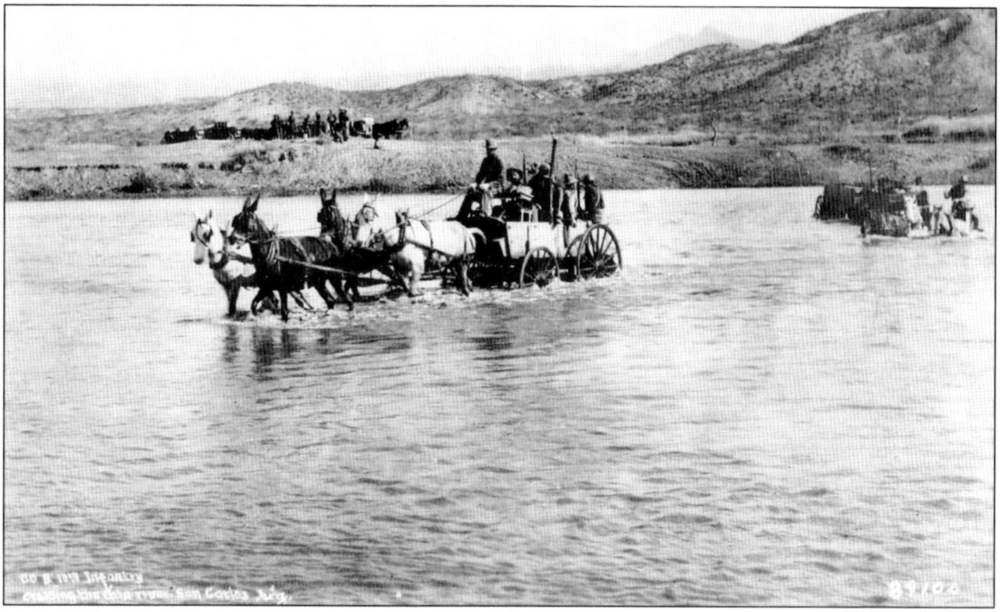

Company B, 10th Infantry crosses the Gila River toward the agency and military camp. Because of the conditions at San Carlos, troops were only stationed there for periods between one and six months. This company is likely arriving from Fort Thomas for their San Carlos tour of duty. (Courtesy NARA, RG 111, Signal Corps Collection, No. 89105.)

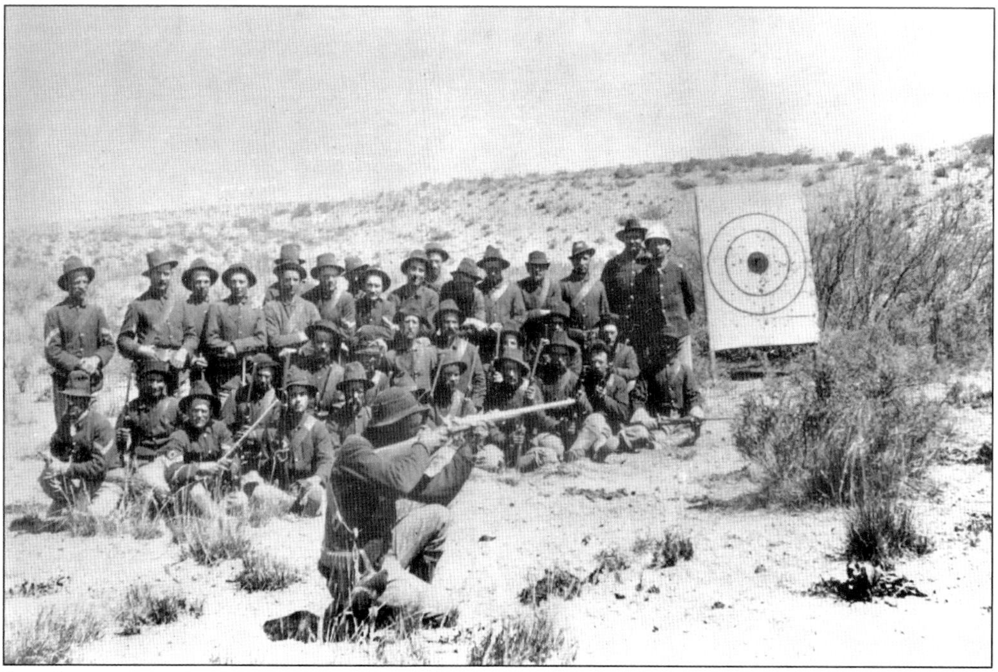

Regular target practice was a requirement for troops serving in the Arizona Territory. This image, possibly not at San Carlos, shows troopers on the range with their Springfield Trapdoor carbines. At San Carlos, the range was on the mesa west of the camp. An officer there noted that after target practice, the Apaches collected animals that had been unintentionally killed on the range for food. (Courtesy NARA, RG 111, Signal Corps Collection, No. 89498.)

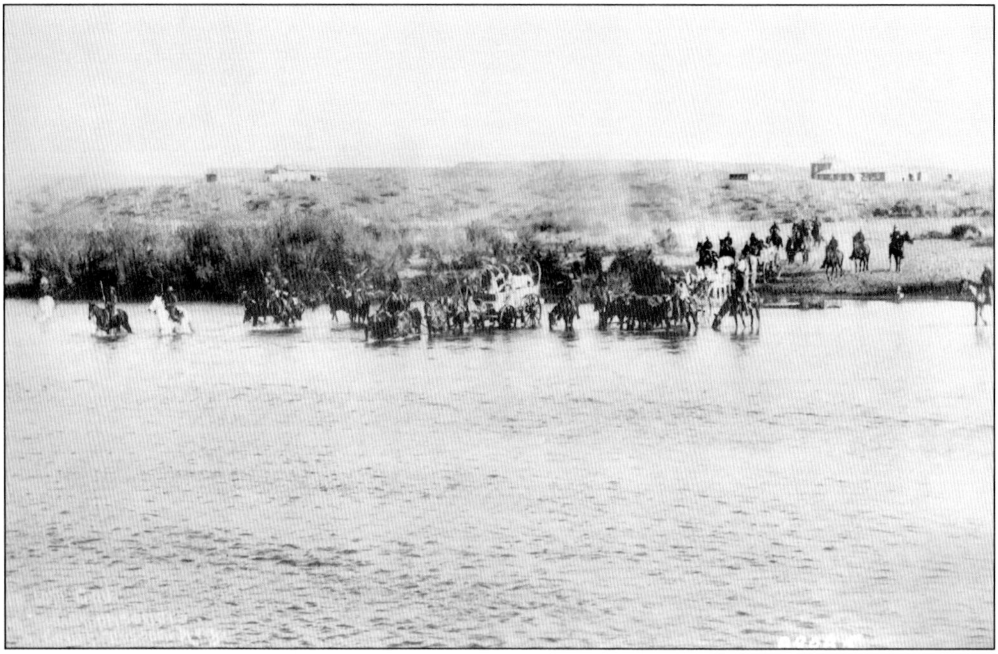

In 1885, a congressional act gave jurisdiction to U.S. courts for serious crimes committed on reservations. Here an 1886 image shows Troop G, 10th Cavalry taking prisoners to the District Court in Tucson. The San Carlos Agency offices and school buildings can be seen in the background, at the left and right, respectively. (Courtesy NARA, RG 111, Signal Corps Collection, No. 89085.)

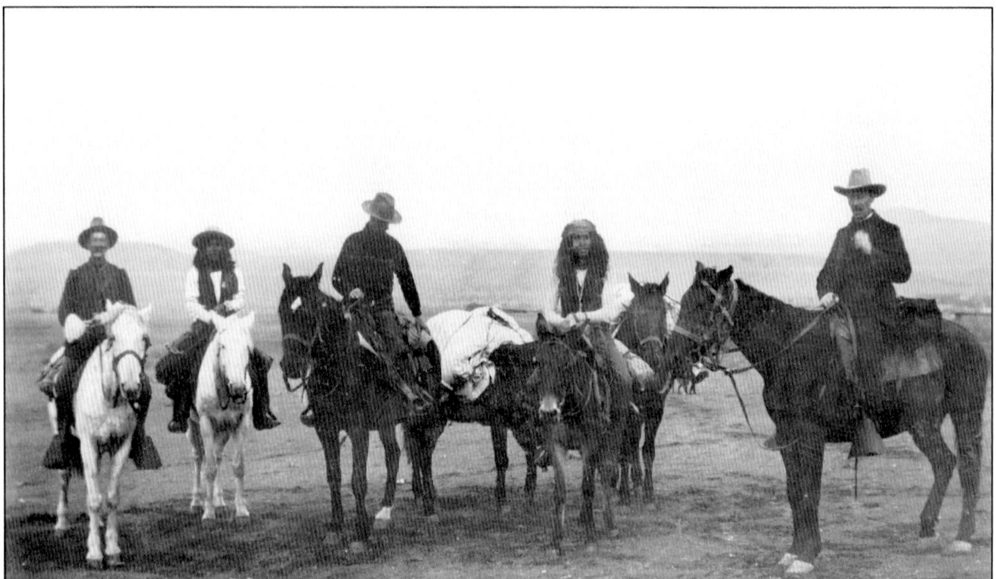

Troops and scouts were regularly sent off the San Carlos Reservation after hostiles. In this 1895 photograph, Capt. James E. Macklin is seen with his Apache scouts, starting on a reconnoiter for the notorious Apache Kid. (Courtesy NARA, RG 111, Signal Corps Collection, No. 83579.)

Noted artist Frederic Remington visited San Carlos in 1888, in the company of a troop of black soldiers of the 10th Cavalry. Along the way, he photographed both scenes and people that he later converted to sketches. In this sketch, published in 1889, Remington shows the interaction between an Apache scout and a buffalo soldier at San Carlos. (Courtesy authors' collection.)

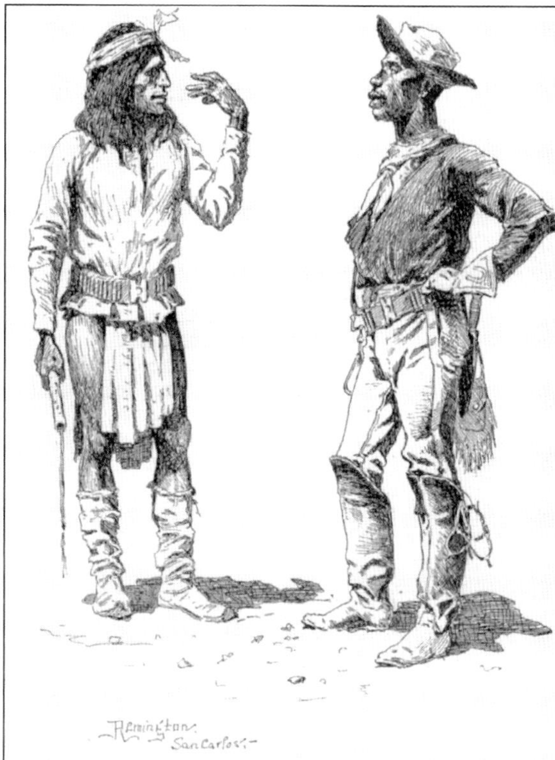

THE SIGN LANGUAGE.

Frederic Remington accompanied the 10th Cavalry on a two-week scout from Fort Grant to San Carlos and vicinity in 1888, led by his friend Lt. Powhattan Clarke, a later Medal of Honor winner for his actions in the Apache wars. During the course of the expedition, Remington relied on his sketch pad and Scovill Detective box camera to record activities of the troops. (Courtesy authors' collection.)

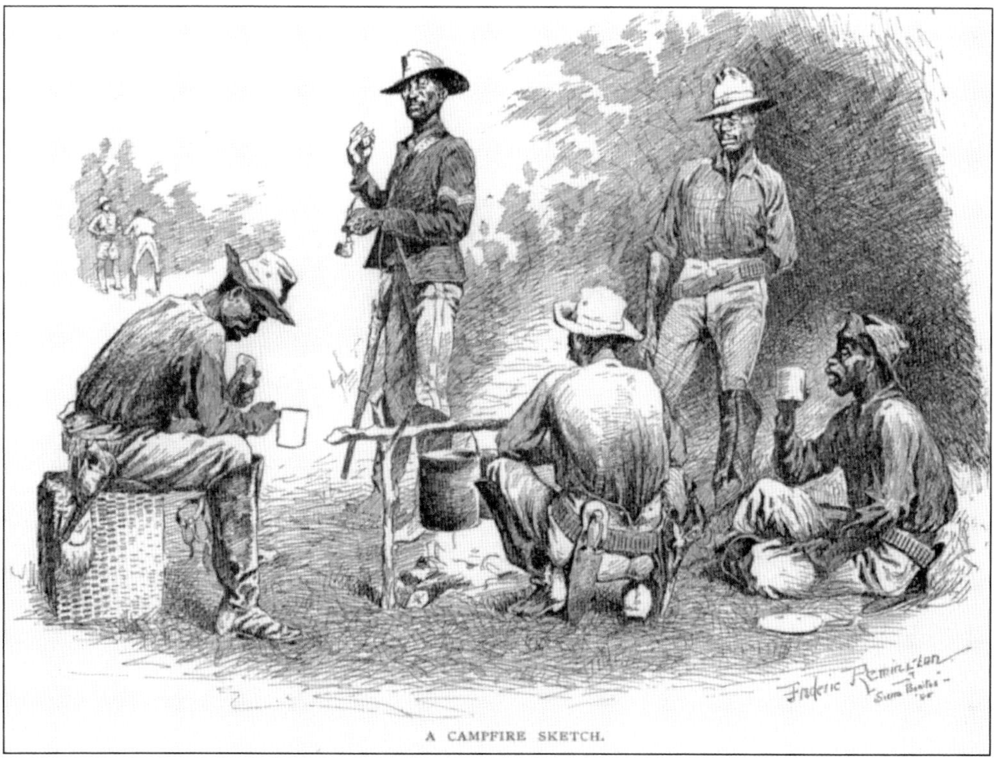

A CAMPFIRE SKETCH.

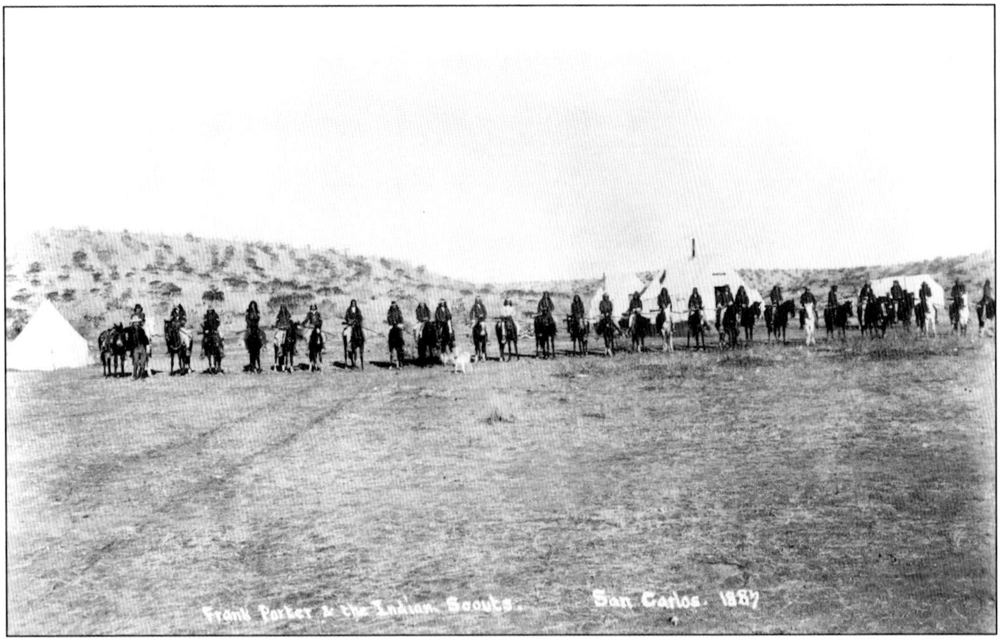

Companies of 25 Indian scouts were often recruited and stationed at Camp San Carlos after 1882, as shown in this 1887 photograph of Frank Porter, civilian chief of scouts (dismounted at left of line), with his mounted company of scouts. (Courtesy NARA, RG 111, Signal Corps Collection, No. 107513.)

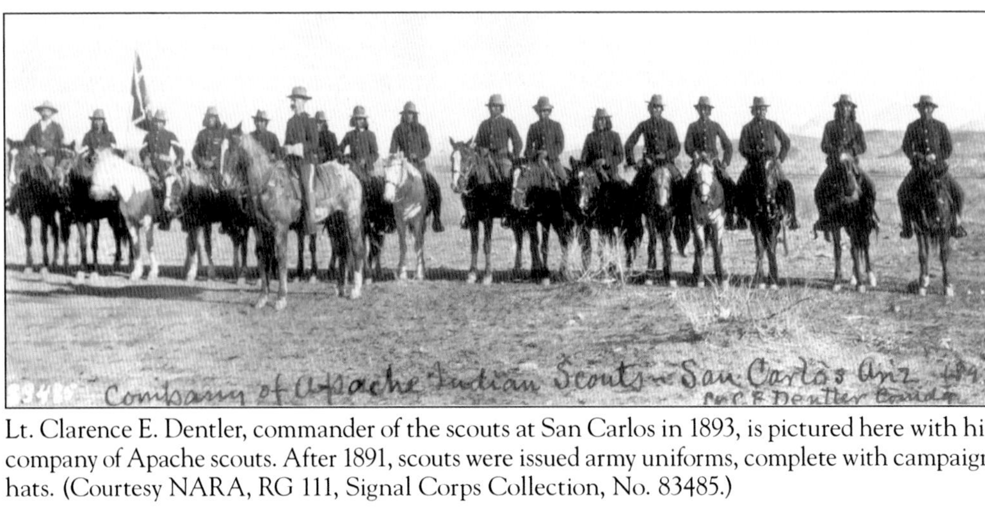

Lt. Clarence E. Dentler, commander of the scouts at San Carlos in 1893, is pictured here with his company of Apache scouts. After 1891, scouts were issued army uniforms, complete with campaign hats. (Courtesy NARA, RG 111, Signal Corps Collection, No. 83485.)

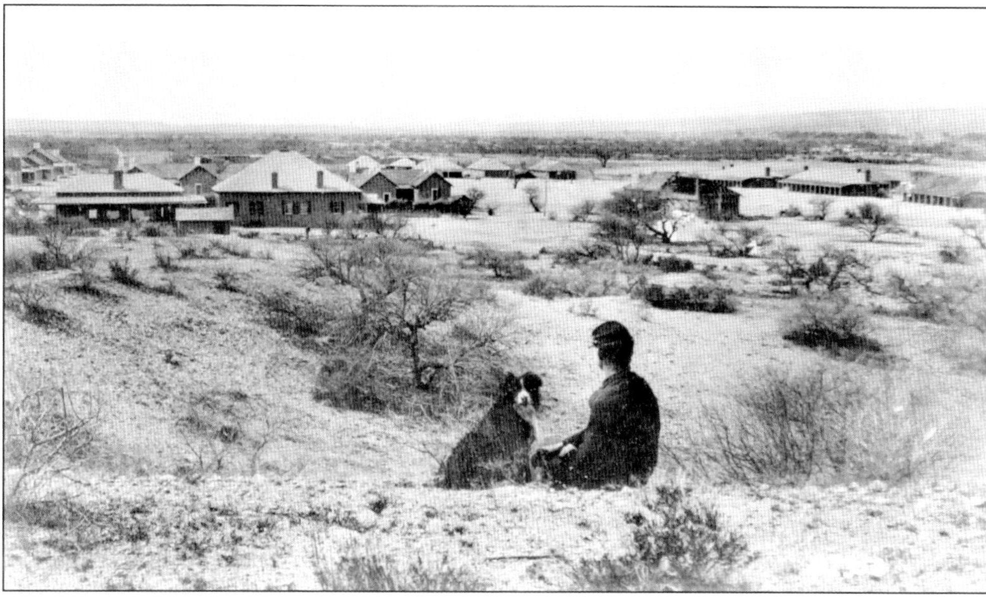

Camp Thomas, later known as Fort Thomas, was established about 28 miles upriver from San Carlos in 1876 to control Apaches on the San Carlos Reservation. The name honored Gen. Lorenzo Thomas, adjutant general of the army, who had died the previous year. During the 1880s, troops from Fort Thomas were sent on temporary assignments to San Carlos; after Fort Thomas was abandoned in April 1891, troops for San Carlos were provided from Fort Grant, located about 30 miles south of the Fort Thomas site. The above photograph shows the buildings at the fort in the mid-1880s. Large-scale improvements to the post had been made in 1883–1884. In the image below, a cavalry encampment is pictured on the Gila River near the fort in 1885, with Mount Turnbull in the background. (Above, courtesy NARA, RG 111, Signal Corps Collection, No. 82358; below, courtesy NARA, RG 111, Signal Corps Collection, No. 89095.)

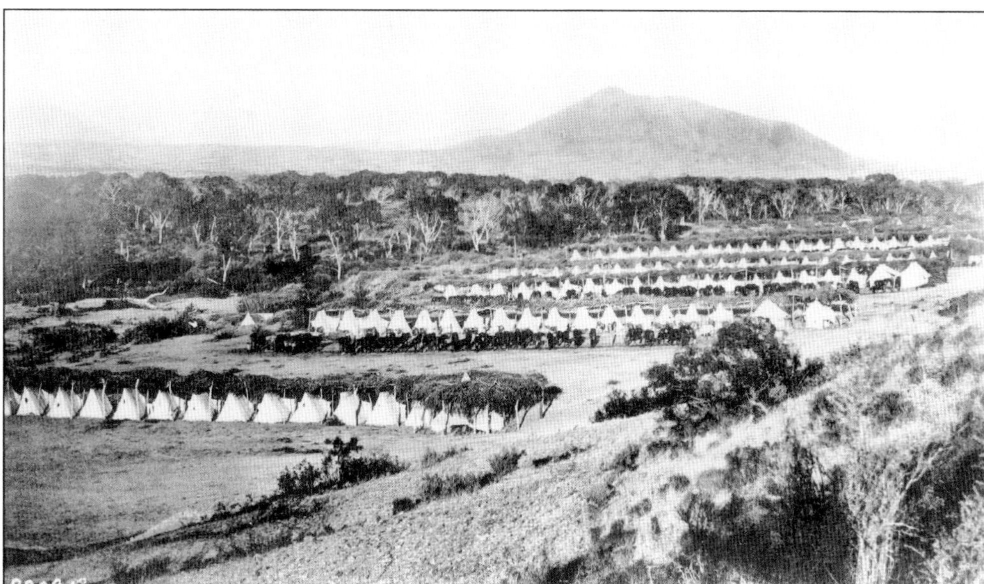

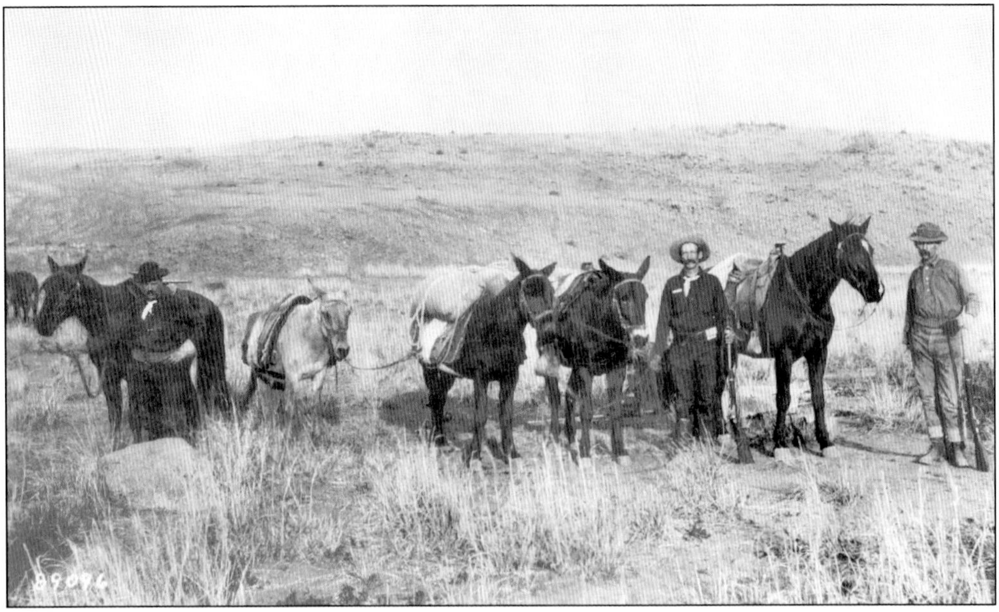

Mule pack trains were crucial to the army's ability to leave established wagon roads and follow hostile Apaches through the terrain of southern Arizona, New Mexico, and northern Mexico. This 1883 image shows government pack mules, along with civilian packers, near the San Carlos subagency (Geronimo). (Courtesy NARA, RG 111, Signal Corps Collection, No. 89096.)

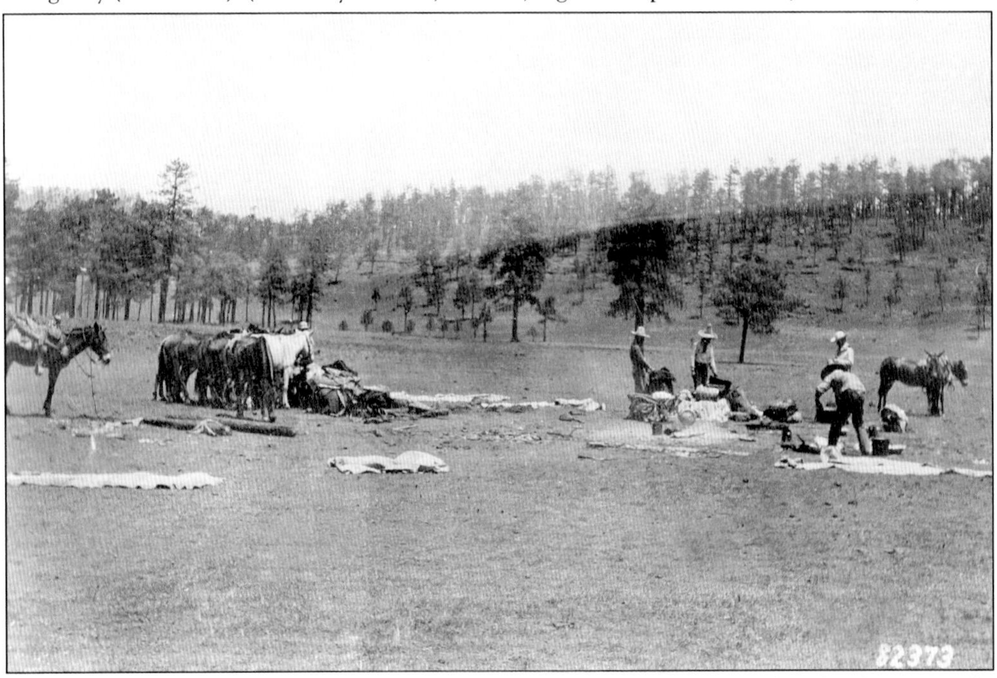

Government pack trains consisted of a bell horse and about 50 mules under the direction of a civilian pack master or chief packer and a dozen or so packers. Each mule carried loads averaging 250 pounds. An average day's march was 30 miles; 15 miles per day in mountainous terrain. The animals were able to subsist entirely on wild grasses. (Courtesy NARA, RG 111, Signal Corps Collection, No. 82373.)

George Crook (1828–1890), who rose to a permanent rank of major general, was closely associated with the Apache wars, having served two terms as commander of the Department of Arizona, from 1871 to 1875 and from 1882 to 1886. During these periods, General Crook made several visits to San Carlos to direct military operations and to consult with the Apaches and Yavapais. (Courtesy NARA, RG 111, Signal Corps Collection, No. 89516.)

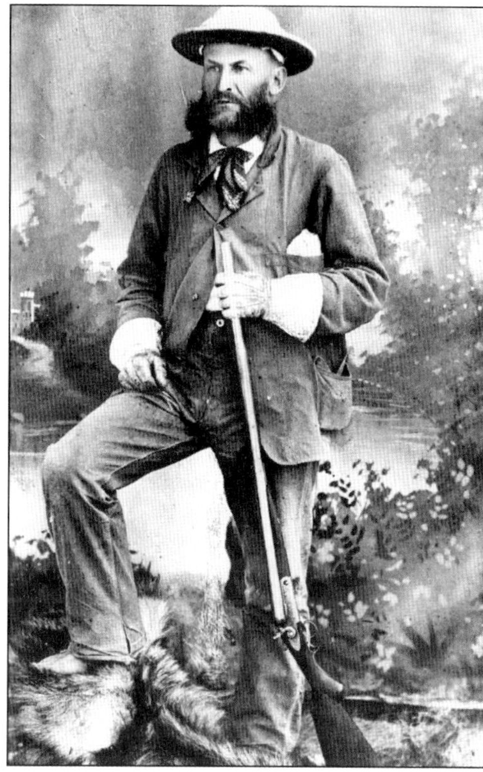

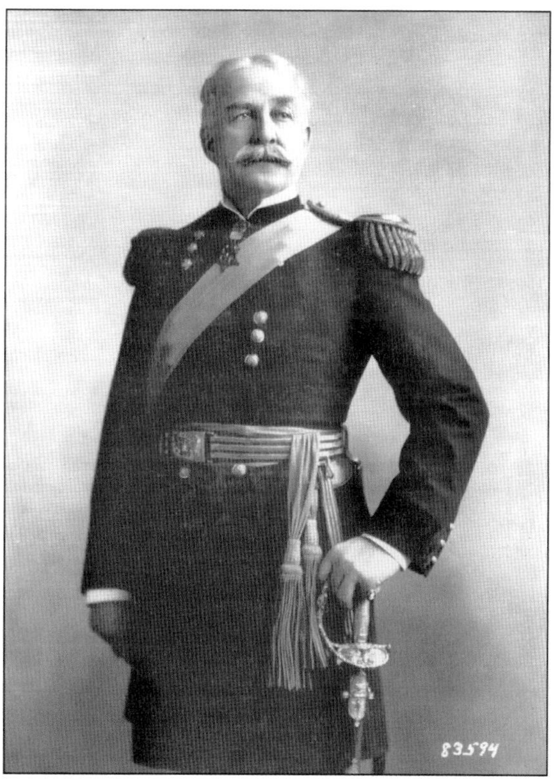

Gen. Nelson A. Miles (1839–1925) replaced Crook as commander against Geronimo's forces in 1886–1887. Geronimo, along with 19 men and 28 women and children, surrendered on September 3, 1886, ending the Apache wars. Miles had the Chiricahua people exiled to Florida five days later. (Courtesy NARA, RG 111, Signal Corps Collection, No. 83594.)

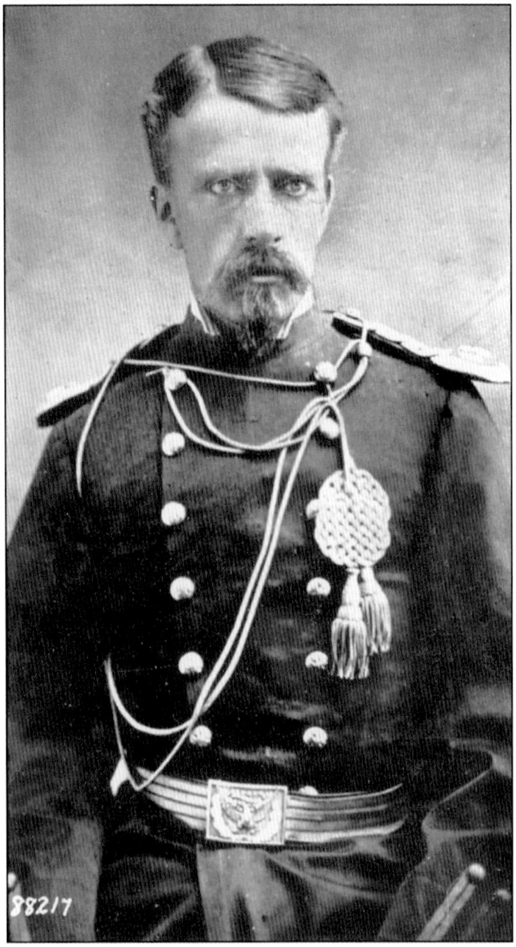

Capt. Emmet Crawford (1844–1886), 3rd Cavalry, was assigned to Fort Thomas in 1882. Later that same year, he was assigned to command Camp San Carlos by General Crook. He participated in Crook's 1883 Mexico campaign and continued to enlist and train scouts at San Carlos. He was accidentally shot and killed by Mexican irregular troops in January 1886 during the Geronimo campaign. (Courtesy NARA, RG 111, Signal Corps Collection, No. 88217.)

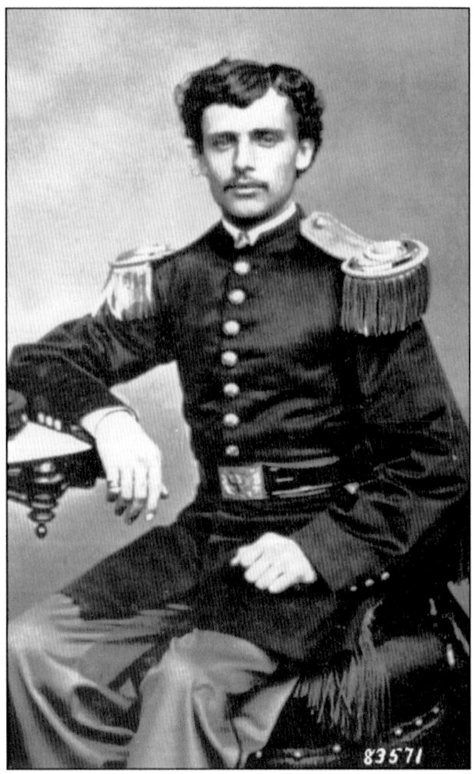

Capt. Albert L. Myer, 11th Infantry, served as acting Indian agent at San Carlos from August 25, 1893, to November 11, 1897. This was during the period that the U.S. Army was not only stationed at Camp San Carlos, but also had sole authority over the San Carlos Indian Agency, normally a role filled by a civilian. (Courtesy NARA, RG 111, Signal Corps Collection, No. 83571.)

James H. Cook was one of two James Cooks who served as civilian pack-train masters for General Crook's supply trains. Cook also served as a scout and guide for the 5th Cavalry during the Apache wars. He later moved to western Nebraska where he ran a ranch until his death in the 1930s. (Courtesy NARA, RG 111, Signal Corps Collection, No. 89497.)

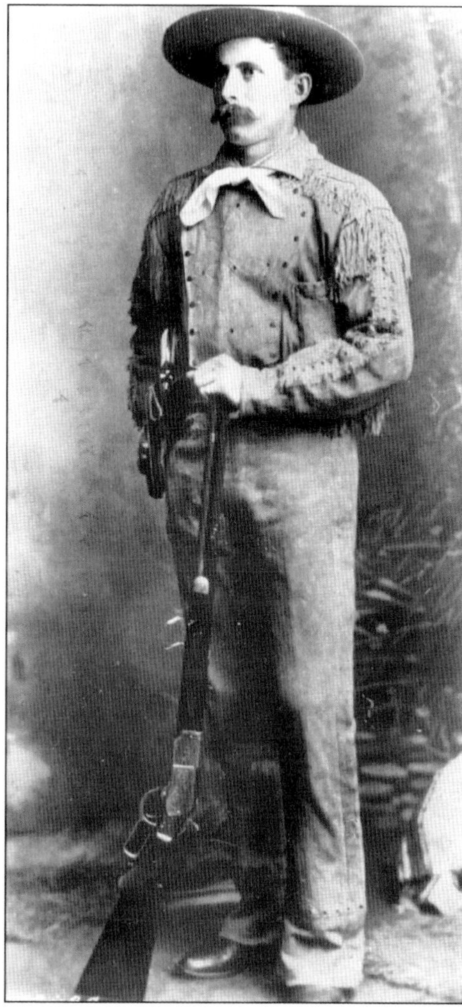

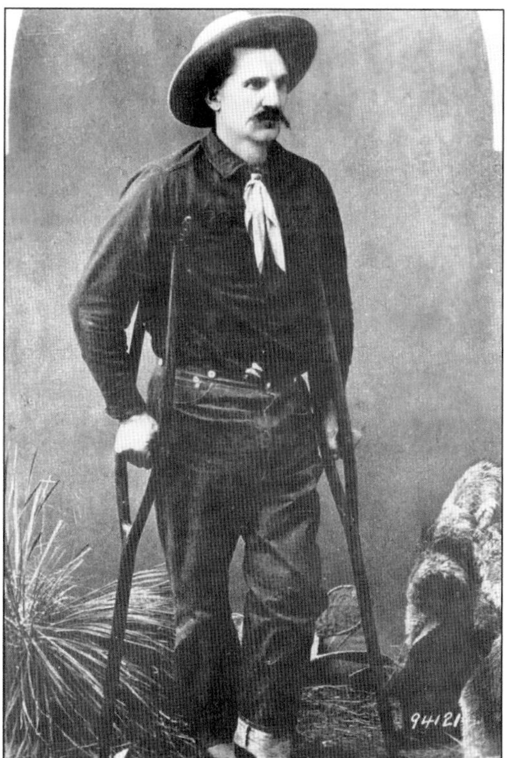

Albert Siebler (1843–1907), born in Germany, came to the United States in 1849. By 1871, he was chief of scouts for General Crook in Arizona and, in 1875, oversaw the removal of the Yavapais and Tonto Apaches to San Carlos. He continued both civilian and military employment at San Carlos until 1891. (Courtesy NARA, RG 111, Signal Corps Collection, No. 94121.)

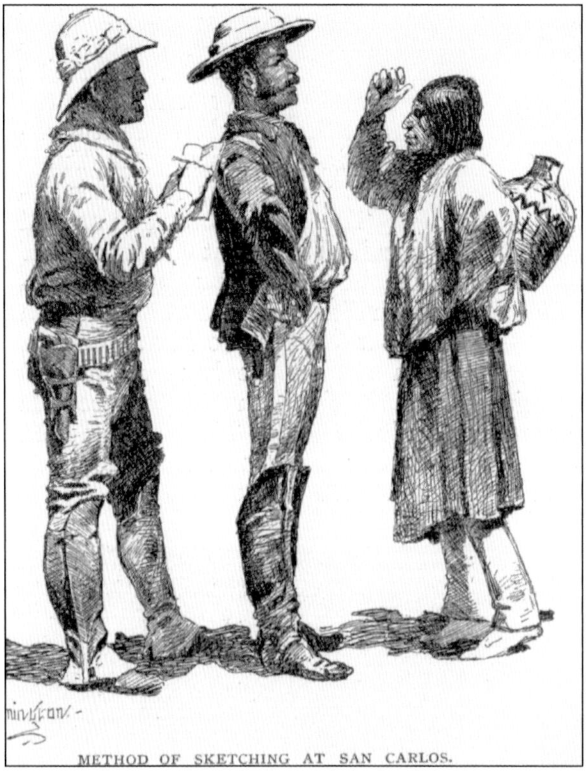

In this self-portrait, Frederick Remington is shown using Lt. Powhattan Clarke as a prop and shield while sketching at San Carlos. The Apache people did not appreciate Remington's efforts to portray them. Remington remarked: "San Carlos is a hotter place than I ever intend to visit again." (Courtesy authors' collection.)

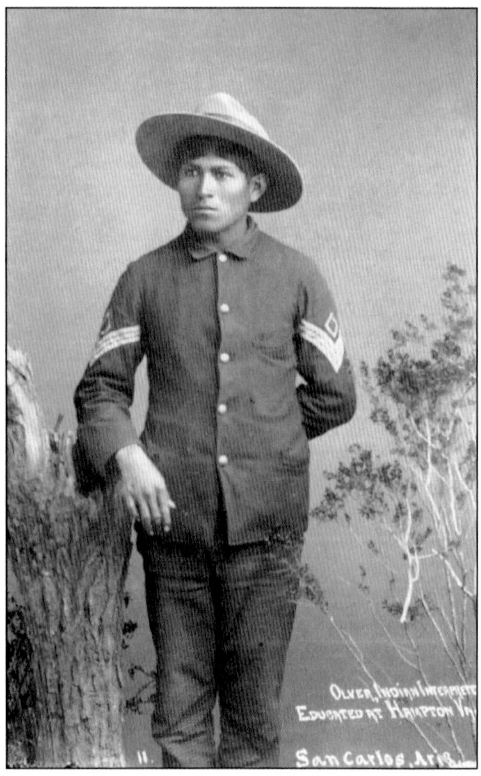

Oliver Eaton (A-mo-ha-ma), a full-blooded Yavapai, was sent from San Carlos to Hampton Institute, Virginia, during the years 1881–1885. Upon returning, he served as an interpreter at San Carlos and as a scout for General Miles during the 1886 Geronimo campaign. He died in 1895. (Courtesy ASUL, Sammy Jones Collection, SJ-165.)

Merejildo Grijalva (1840–1912) was born to Opata Indian parents in Mexico. He was captured by the Chiricahua in 1849 but escaped 10 years later. He served on and off as a scout and interpreter at San Carlos and elsewhere in the region from the 1860s to the 1890s. In 1893, he became chief of scouts at San Carlos. (Courtesy NARA, RG 111, Signal Corps Collection, No. 94115.)

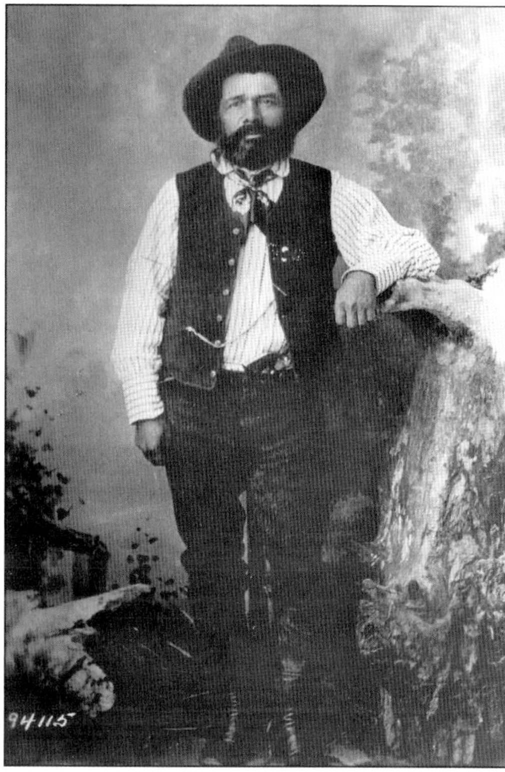

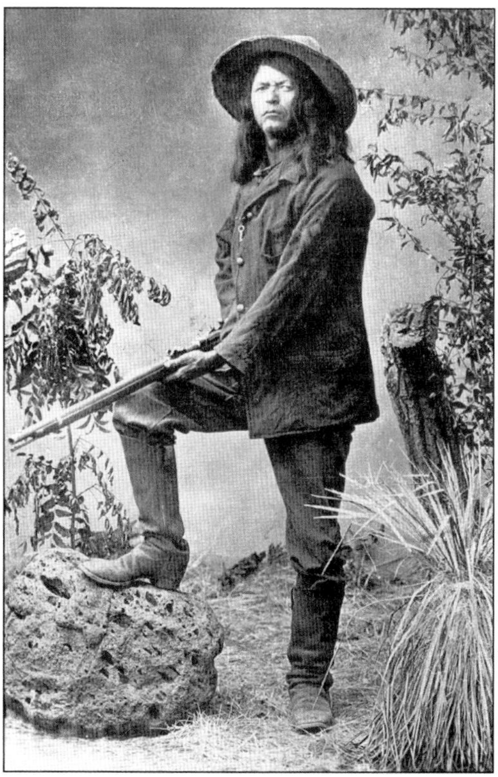

Born Felix Telles to Mexican parents, Mickey Free (1847–1914) was captured by Apaches from his Irish stepfather's southern Arizona ranch in 1861. Raised by Apaches, Free became a scout for General Crook in 1871 and served as an interpreter, scout, and policeman at San Carlos and elsewhere for the next 25 years. This photograph was taken at Willcox in 1884. (Courtesy NARA, RG 111, Signal Corps Collection, No. 89506.)

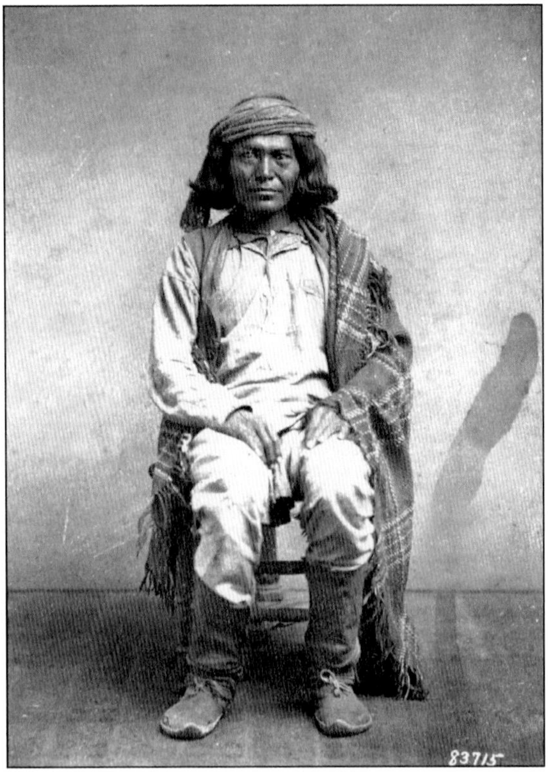

Nah-diz-az, a Tonto Apache, gained infamy when he shot and killed Lt. Seward Mott, 10th Cavalry and commander of the scouts, at San Carlos on March 10, 1887. He was also known as the "Carlisle Kid," having attended the Carlisle Indian School. He was tried in Globe and subsequently hanged in 1889, the first legal hanging in Gila County. (Courtesy NARA, RG 111, Signal Corps Collection, No. 83715.)

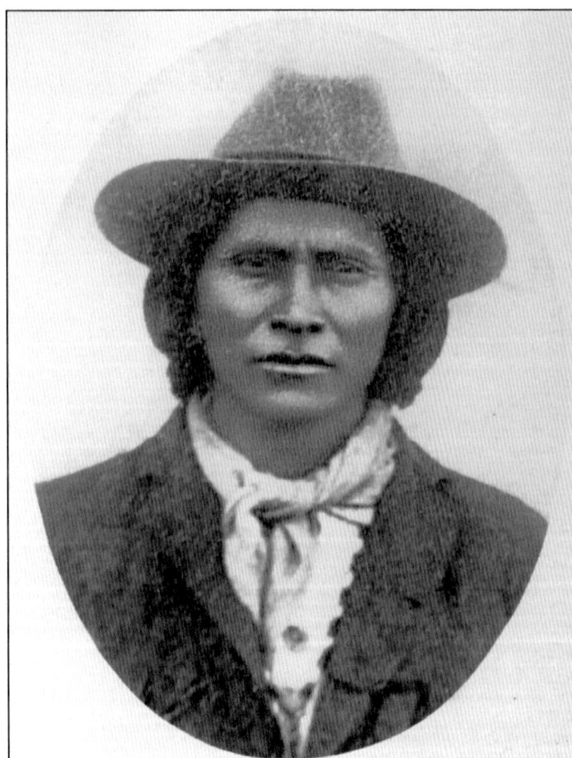

The "Apache Kid" (Es-ki-bi-nadel) was born in 1860. He served as scout at San Carlos with several enlistments between 1881 and 1887. Kid got into trouble in 1887 and was charged with mutiny and desertion. Following other transgressions, he was sentenced to prison in 1889. He escaped on the way to prison and was sought for several years, but he was never captured. (Courtesy AHF, Biography Collection; photograph by F. A. Hartwell.)

Four

Apache and Yavapai Police and Scouts

When agent John Clum arrived at San Carlos in 1874, he immediately created a police force made up of men from each of the Apache groups that had initially been brought to the agency. As more Apache and Yavapai groups came under his supervision, he added policemen from those bands as well. Additionally, Clum appointed Apache judges to adjudicate crimes committed at the agency and on the larger reservation. The Apache policing system worked so well at San Carlos that it became a model for other reservations across the country and was continued for decades at the reservation.

The concept of using Apache against Apache as scouts preceded the creation of the San Carlos Agency, first occurring when Gen. George Crook came to Arizona in 1871 to enforce control over the various Apache groups. He immediately recruited a company of Apaches to lead his troops in terrain that was unfamiliar to the U.S. Army. The enlistment of Apache scouts during the Apache wars of the 1880s was a primary tool in subjugating hostile Apache groups in both Arizona and farther south in Mexico. The primary recruiting points for Apache scouts were San Carlos and Fort Apache in the northern part of the reservation. Many Yavapais were also recruited at San Carlos.

At times, considerable overlap existed between Apache police and scouts in terms of both personnel and duties at San Carlos. Since scouts were only enlisted for six months at a time and only when needed, many scouts served multiple enlistments over time. When not needed by the army, many scouts became policemen. During the years that the military actually assumed authority over the agency, scouts served a dual policing role while stationed at Camp San Carlos.

After 1890, the number of Apache scouts needed by the army was greatly reduced. Scout companies remained in service at Fort Apache. When Fort Apache was abandoned in 1922, all remaining Apache scouts were sent to Fort Huachuca, where they served until the unit was disbanded in 1943. Three Apache scouts, the last of their number, retired from active service in 1948.

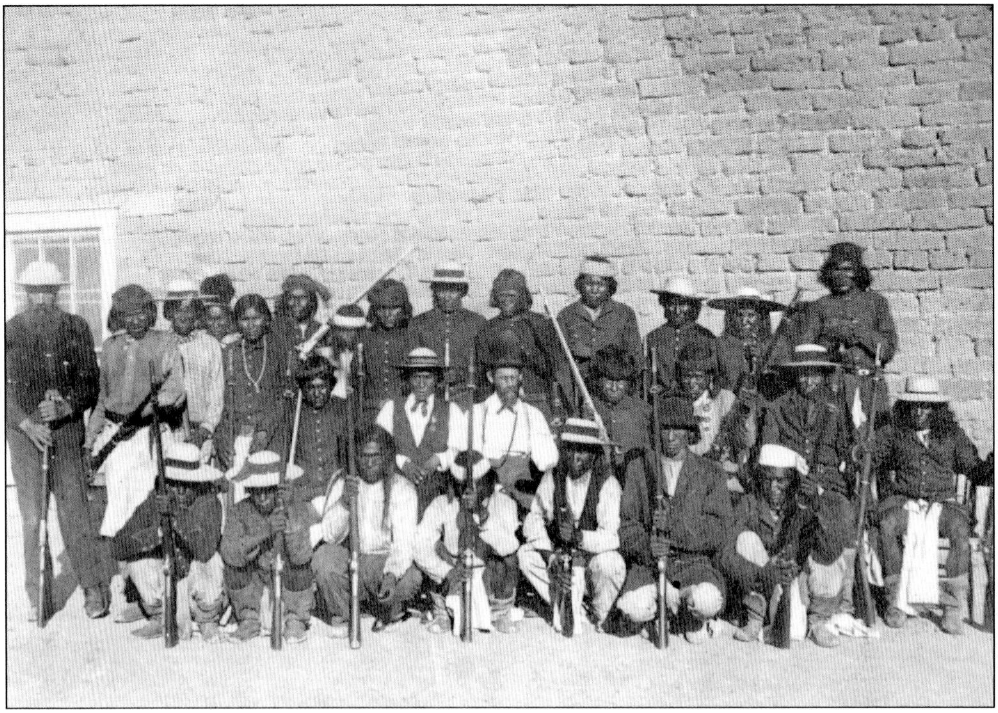

Initiation of a Native American police force in 1874 at the new San Carlos Agency is seen as one of John Clum's major achievements. The first men were paid at a rate of $15 per month, and their functions included arresting insubordinates, guarding of prisoners, and general police duty on the reservation. The San Carlos policemen are pictured here in the late 1870s. (Courtesy AHF, Rothrock Collection, No. 52; stereograph by George H. Rothrock.)

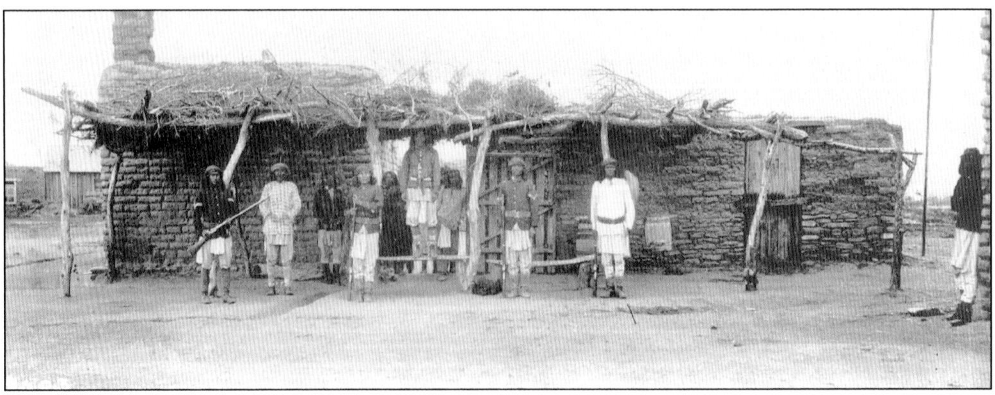

The guards at the first San Carlos Agency guardhouse are at the ready in this 1880 photograph. In this instance, the guards appear to be Apache scouts rather than agency policemen. It was in this rather fragile-looking structure that John Clum first jailed Geronimo in 1876. (Courtesy NARA, RG 111, Signal Corps Collection, No. 89503.)

John Clum and his agency police force are in Tucson in 1876 on their way to Warm Springs, New Mexico, to remove Geronimo and other Chiricahua Apaches to San Carlos. Interpreter Merejildo Grijalva is standing at left. The matching uniforms were apparently supplied by the citizens of the city. (Courtesy NARA, RG 111, Signal Corps Collection, No. 89536.)

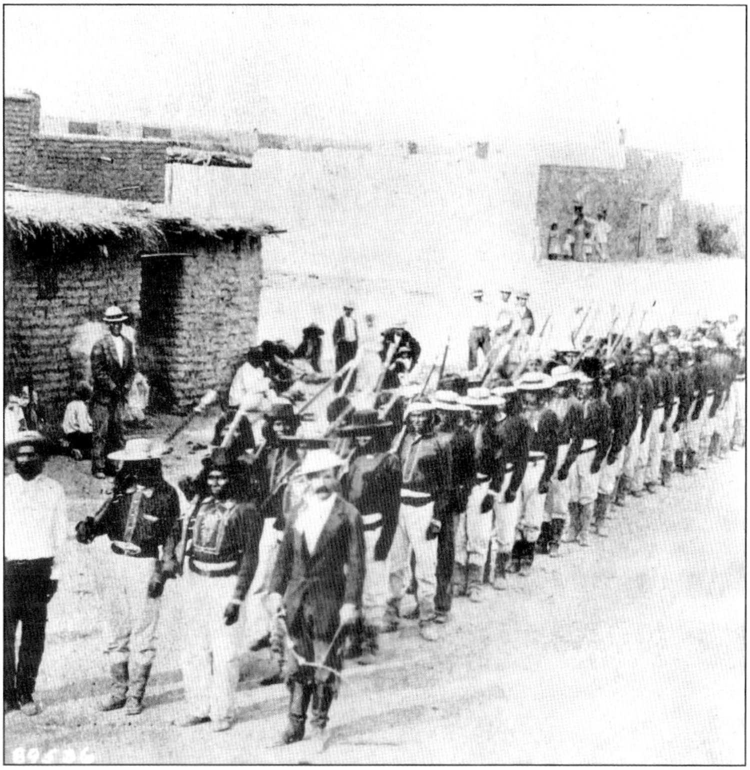

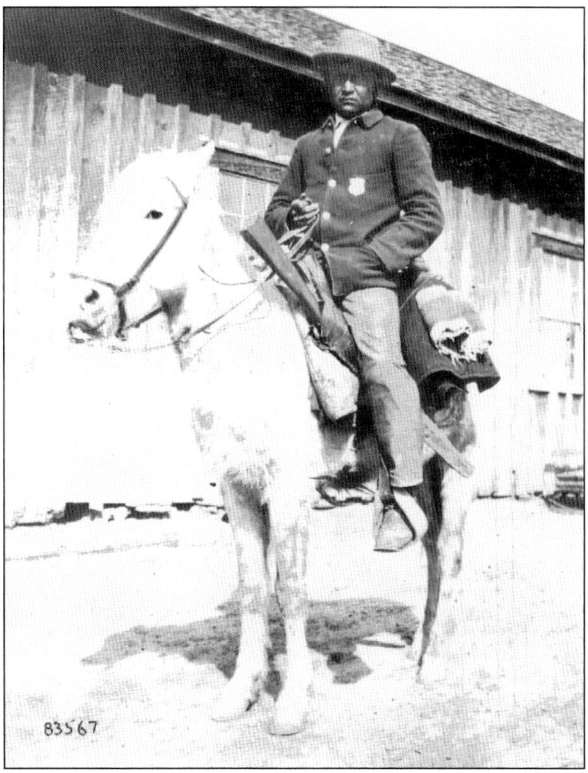

A mounted San Carlos Apache policeman was photographed at the agency in 1895. With bedroll in tow, he appears ready to hit the trail for points elsewhere on the reservation. (Courtesy NARA, RG 111, Signal Corps Collection, No. 83567.)

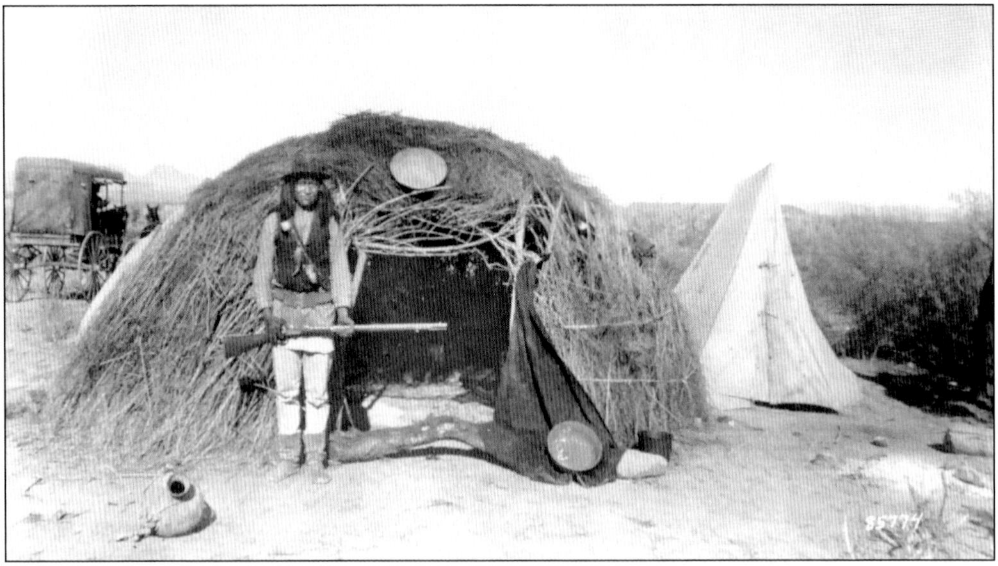

Policemen were enlisted from each of the groups that had been placed on the San Carlos Reservation. In this case, a Tolkepaya Yavapai policeman, or perhaps scout, is shown at his camp. He wears the traditional war-charm necklace over the right shoulder and under the left arm. (Courtesy NARA, RG 111, Signal Corps Collection, No. 85774.)

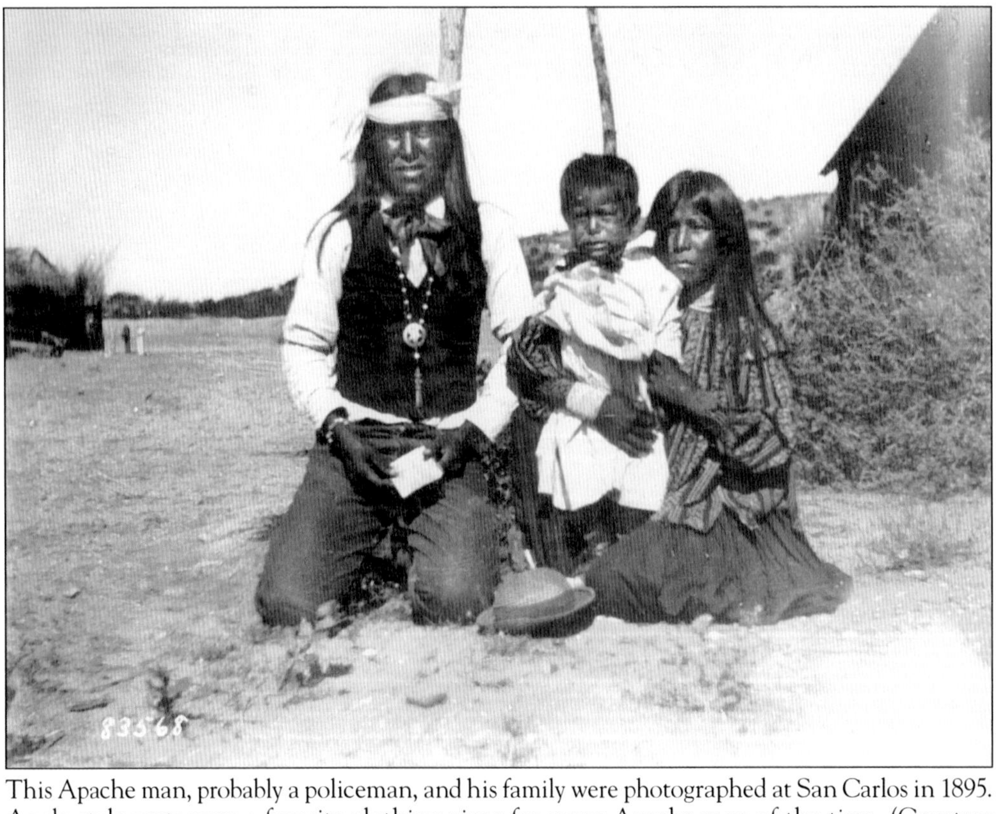

This Apache man, probably a policeman, and his family were photographed at San Carlos in 1895. Anglo-style vests were a favorite clothing piece for many Apache men of the time. (Courtesy NARA, RG 111, Signal Corps Collection, No. 83568.)

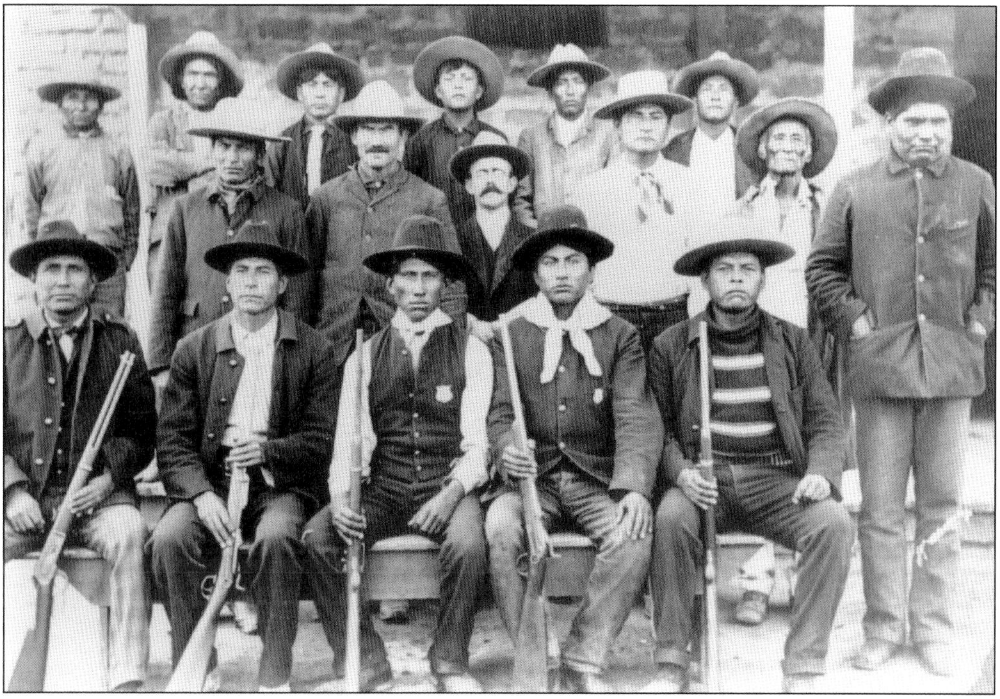

Two troops of San Carlos Apache policemen, along with their sergeants, are seen in these photographs taken in front of the agency guardhouse around 1900. The Anglo man in the center of the photograph above is unidentified but may be the agency superintendent at the time. Weaponry in nearly every case is the Springfield Trapdoor carbine, probably originally of military issue. (Above, courtesy GCHS, GM 27-137; below, courtesy GCHS, GM 27-138.)

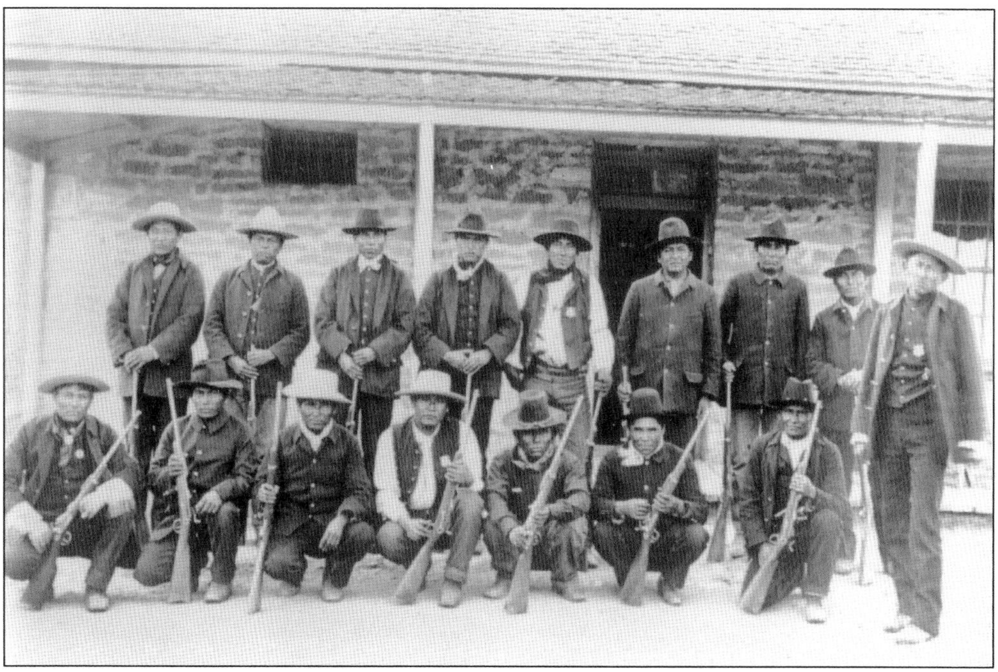

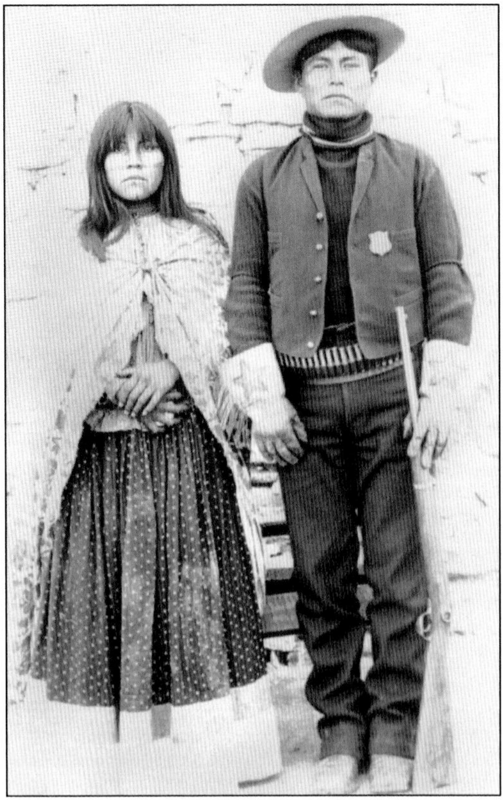

A young San Carlos policeman and (presumably) his wife are shown in this image from around 1900. According to Capt. W. J. Nicholson, a member of the 7th Cavalry and the acting Indian agent, one of the most serious types of trouble faced by the reservation police in 1900 was associated with the ease that Apaches could procure whisky and other intoxicating liquor in the towns adjacent to the reservation—Globe and Geronimo. (Courtesy GCHS, GM 27-131.)

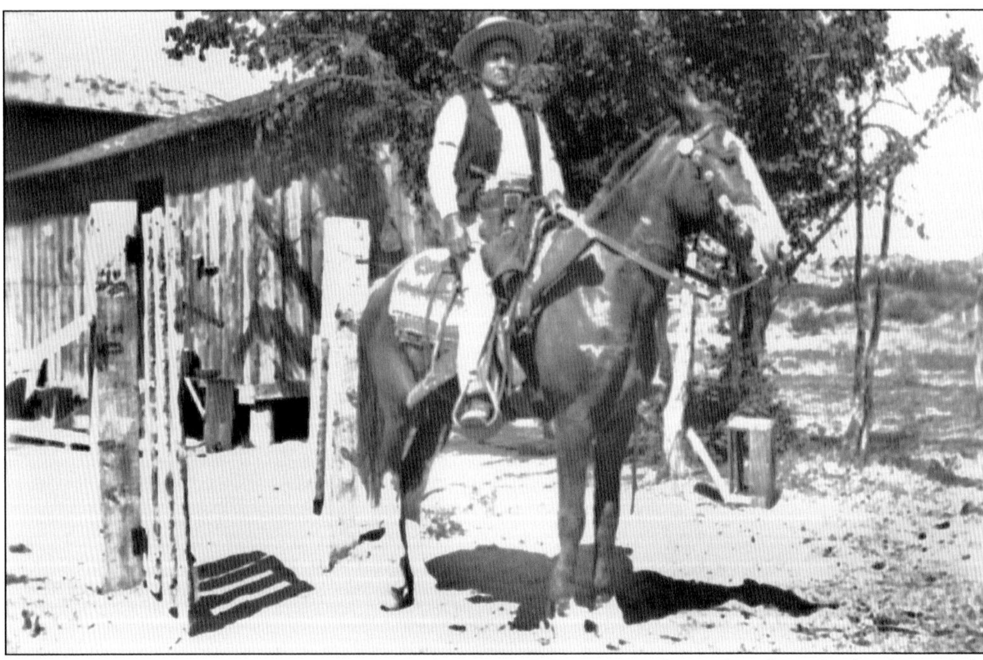

Owing to the vastness of the reservation, elements of the San Carlos police force had to be mobile. This mounted policeman, probably photographed in the 1920s, appears ready to make his patrol. (Courtesy ASUL, Francis J. Uplegger Collection, SPC 187:4.134.)

Two San Carlos Apache guards, either policemen or scouts, along with another youth at the left rear, are shown with their prisoners in this 1880s cabinet card image. Since the photograph was made in a studio, it is impossible to tell if the scene is real or staged. (Courtesy ASUL, Sammy Jones Collection, SJ-166.)

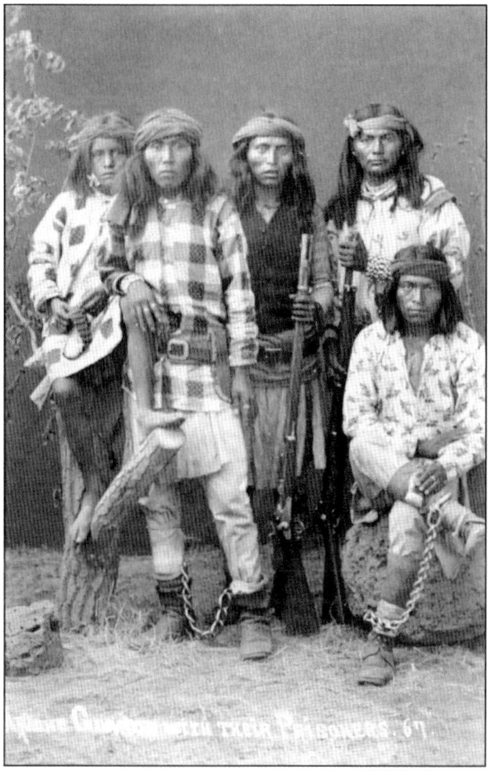

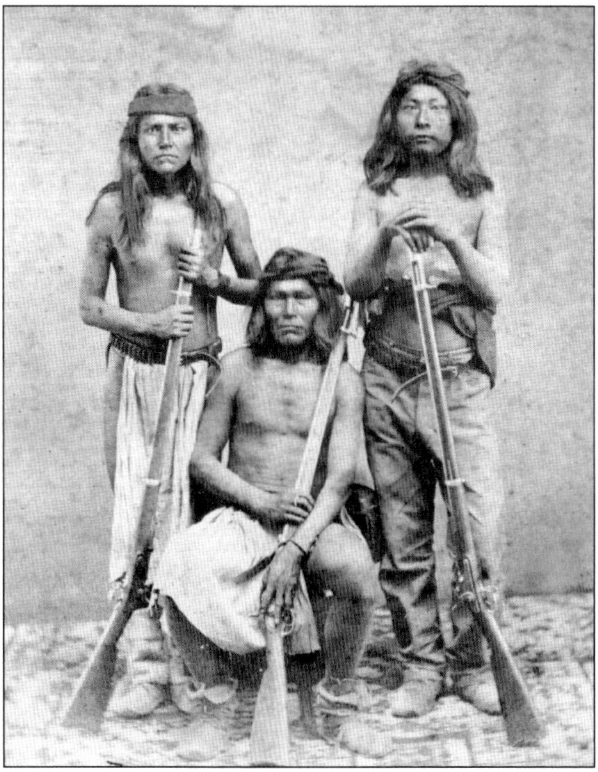

Three Apache scouts, with their military issue Springfield carbines and ammunition belts, are posed in this *c.* 1880 image. As can be seen in this picture, as well as others in this chapter, General Crook came up with a system whereby scouts wore red cloth headbands to distinguish them from other Apaches, particularly hostiles, during action. (Courtesy AHF, Apache Collection, IA-44; stereograph by Henry Buehman.)

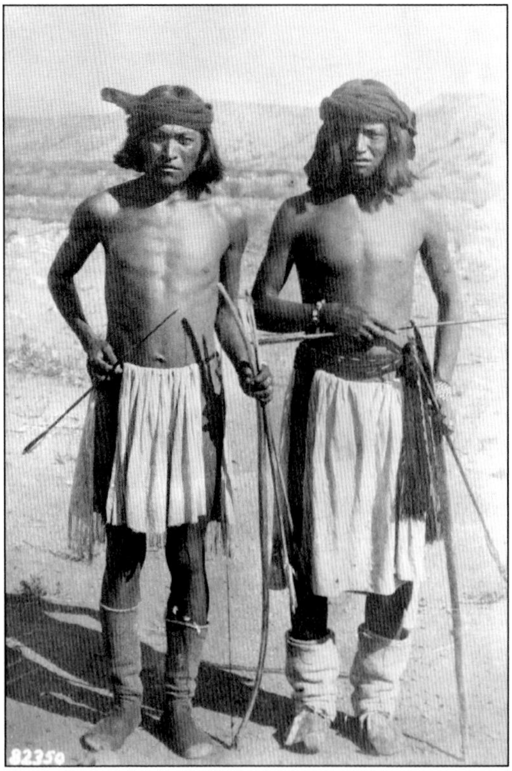

These two Apache scouts, photographed at San Carlos in 1888, are pictured in "war costume." As a battle neared, Apache scouts preferred to strip to their loincloths and footgear. Interestingly, the scout on the left appears to be wearing a pair of military issue woolen socks. (Courtesy NARA, RG 111, Signal Corps Collection, No. 82350.)

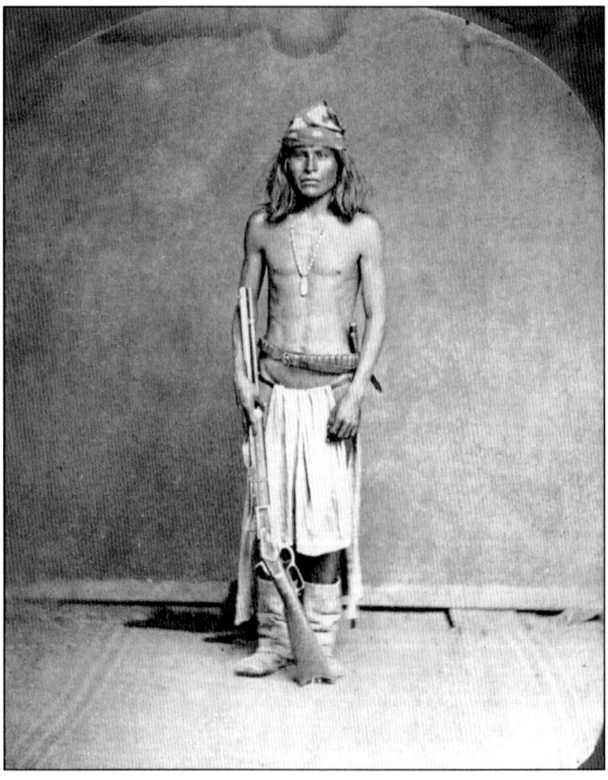

This image from the late 1870s shows an Apache scout in the classic "ready for action" appearance. Stripped down to headband, loincloth, and buckskin moccasins, the only other articles are his rifle and 40-round ammunition belt with a butcher knife stuck in it. Around his neck, he wears tweezers for removing facial hair. (Courtesy AHF, Rothrock Collection No. 34; stereograph by George Rothrock.)

The two mounted San Carlos scouts in these images are virtually identical in appearance, except for the headgear. The image at right is a drawing by Frederic Remington, published in *Century Magazine* in 1889. Remington identifies this person as being Tolkepaya Yavapai. Both men are wearing loose-fitting calico shirts and loose cotton drawers reaching to buckskin moccasins. Scouts were required to provide their own horse and horse equipment but were reimbursed by the army at a rate of 40¢ per day, or about $12 a month, in addition to their regular monthly pay. Each scout was issued a Springfield rifle and, on an as needed basis, 40 rounds of ammunition. (Right, courtesy authors' collection; below, courtesy ASUL, Sammy Jones Collection, SJ No. 163.)

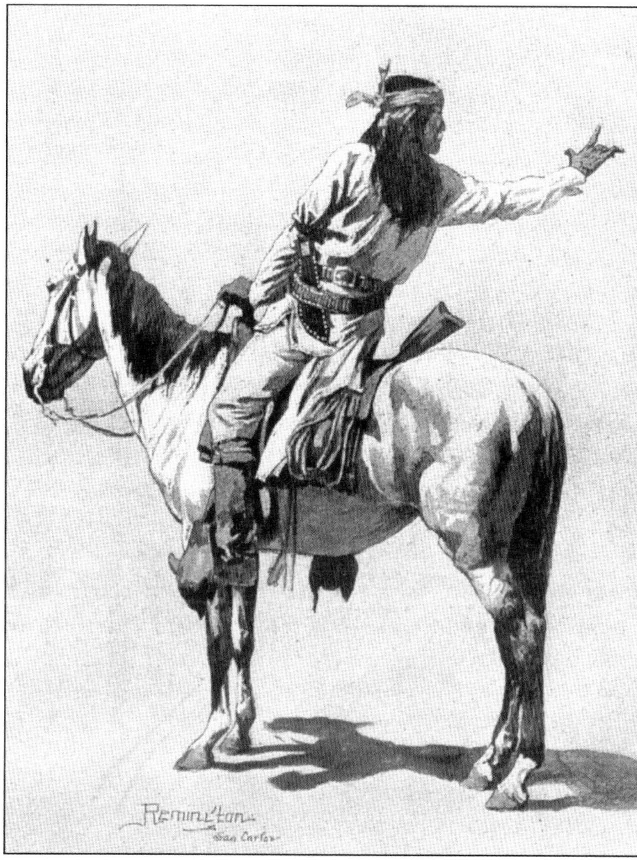

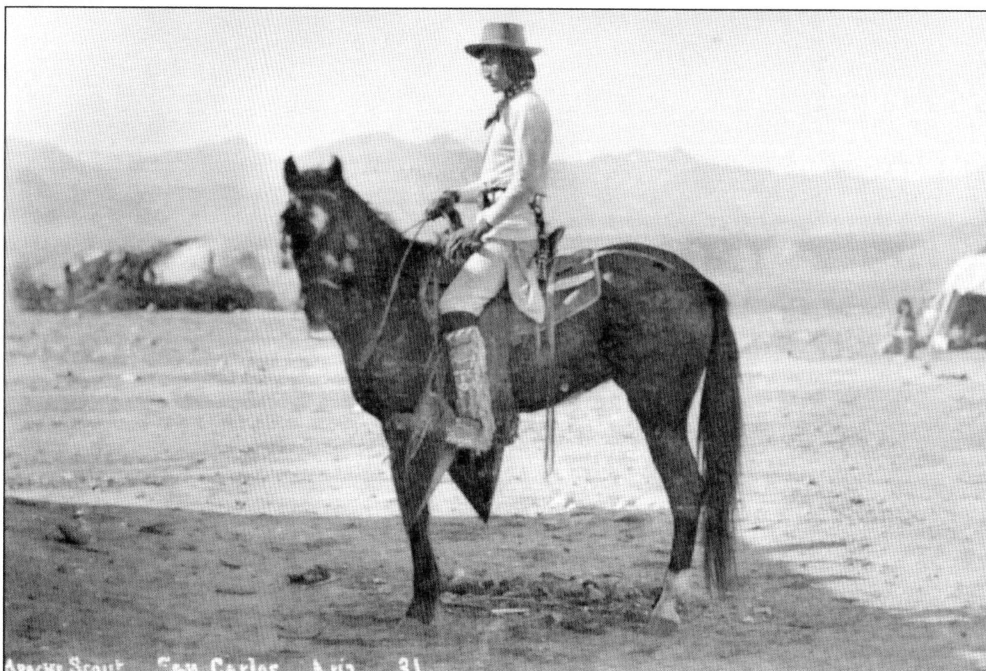

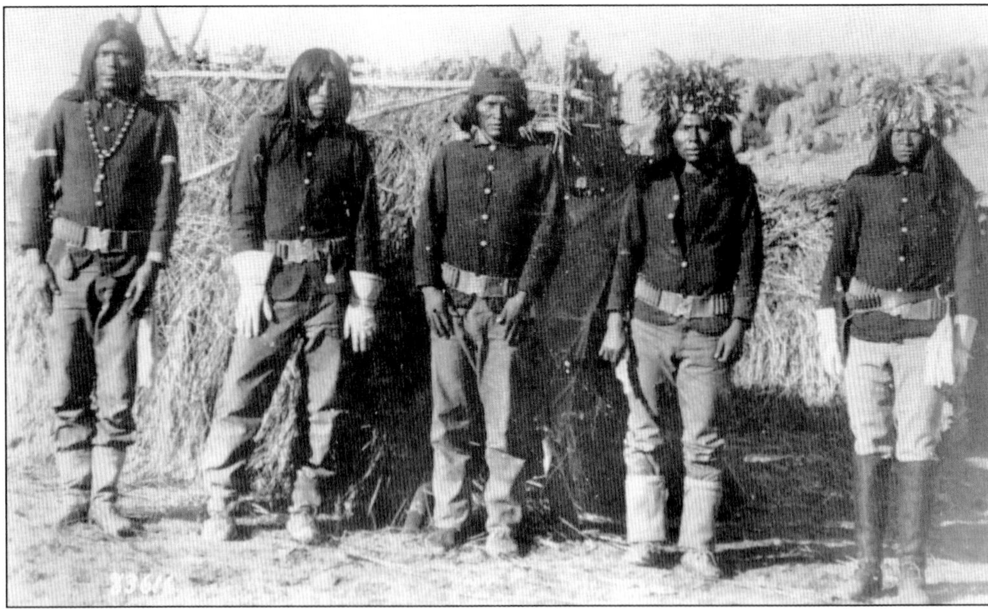

This image from the early 1890s shows a group of Apache scouts in more formal military-issue clothing, complete with 1887 Mills ammunition belts and, in two cases, army-issue gauntlets. The two at right wear turkey and quail feather caps. The corporal at left carries a small buckskin bag at his belt containing sacred pollen. (Courtesy NARA, RG 111, Signal Corps Collection, No. 83616.)

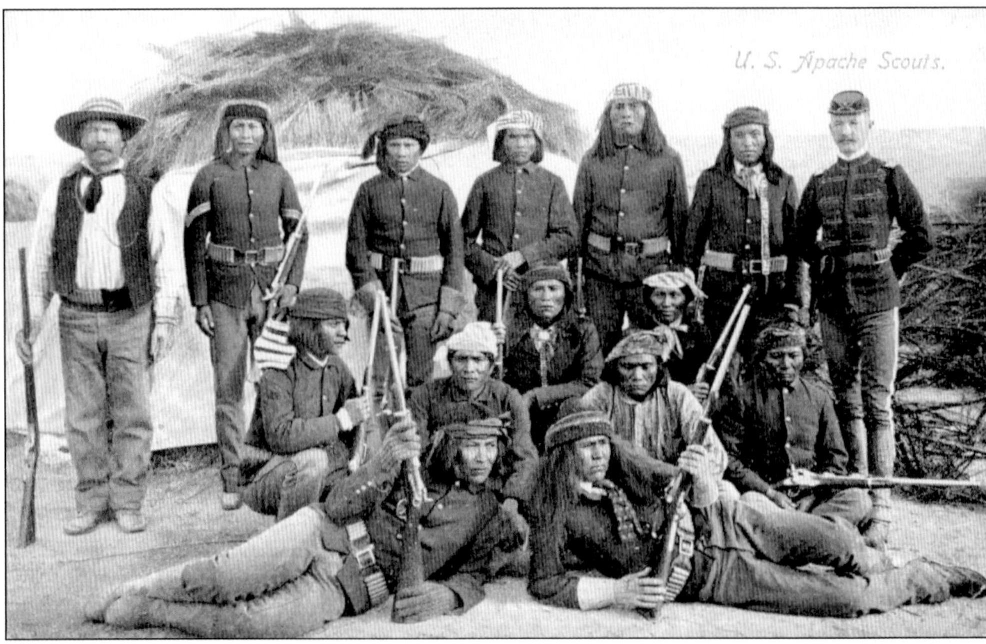

This image shows an Apache scout company at San Carlos around 1890. From left to right are (first row) Kilchyun and Eskinnutkada; (second row) Belgodo, Tom Smith, Nansetinne, Haddo, Dastane, and Mezetaha; (third row) Merejildo Grijalva, interpreter; Sgt. Billy Thompson; Jack Thompson; Jack Many Hats; Big John; Dude; and Maj. C. E. Tayman, 24th Infantry. (Courtesy authors' collection; identifications courtesy AHF.)

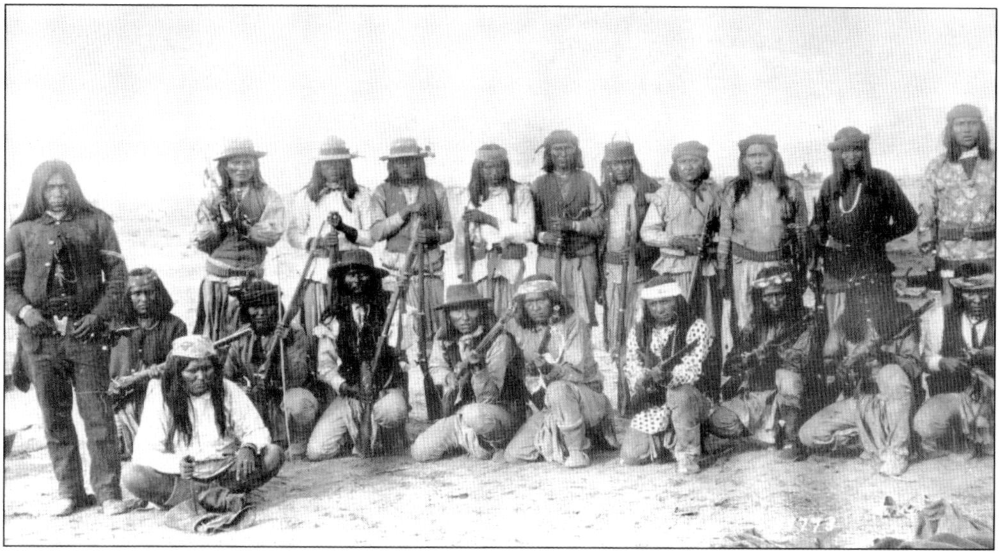

This group of scouts was photographed about 1882. Scouts were enlisted for a six-month period, with many serving multiple enlistments over the years. A 1917 act provided small pensions for scouts in the Indian wars who served during limited years. In 1927, the act was amended to include all scouts or their spouses who were still living and could prove service. (Courtesy NARA, RG 111, Signal Corps Collection, No. 85773.)

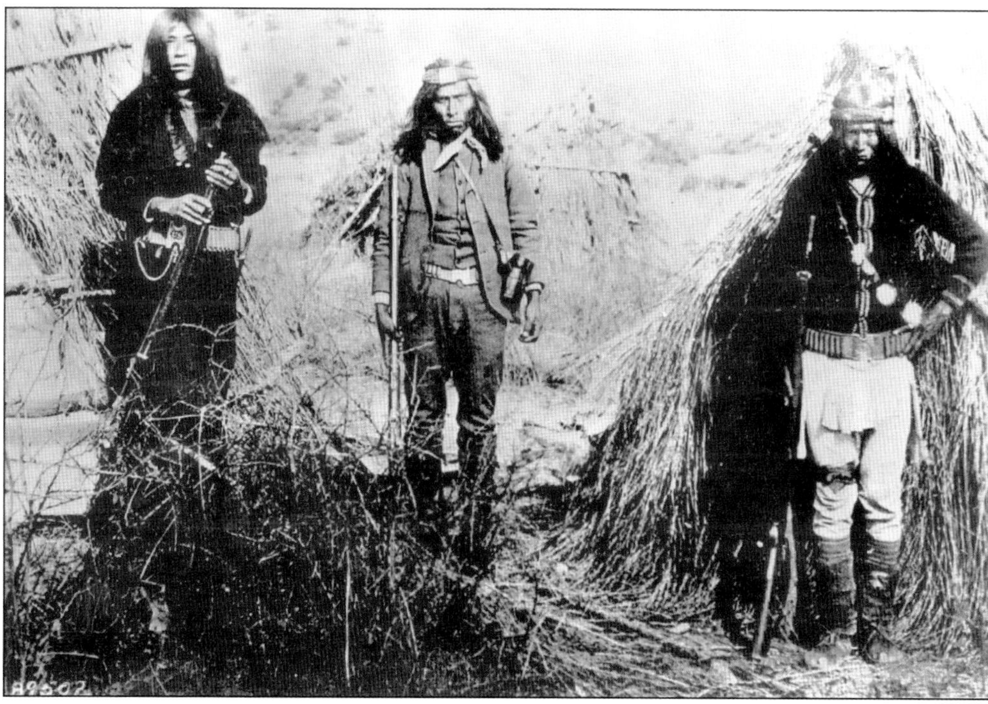

From left to right, this 1886 photograph shows Ma-si, a Chiricahua scout who was soon thereafter sent to Florida but escaped the train and returned to Arizona; the Apache Kid, then sergeant of scouts before turning outlaw, and Rowdy, who was awarded the Medal of Honor in 1890 for heroic action. (Courtesy NARA, RG 111, Signal Corps Collection, No. 89502; photograph by C. S. Fly.)

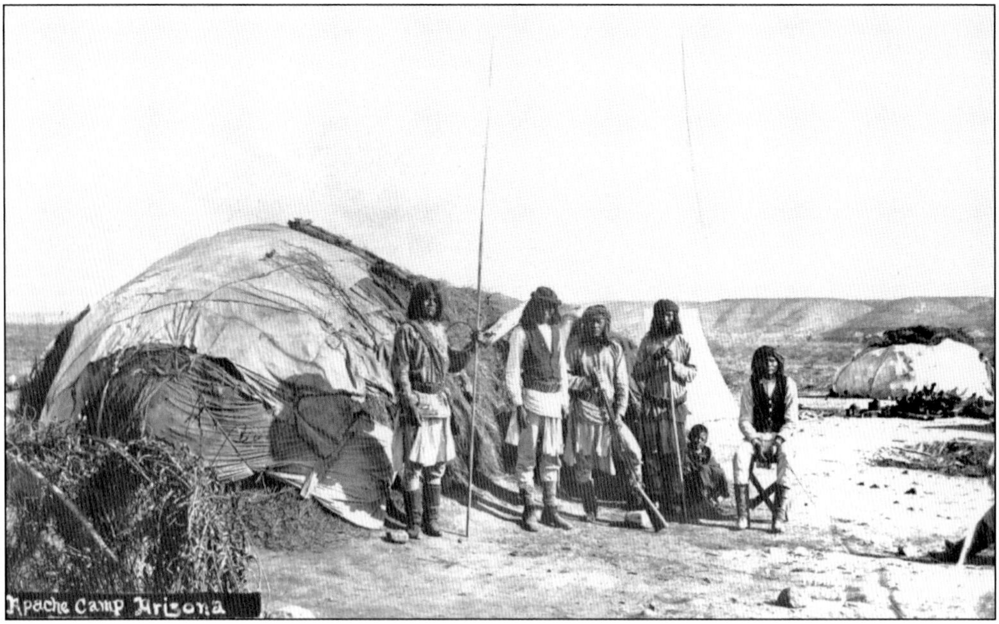

New Mexico photographer Ben Wittick (1845–1903) visited Arizona in the 1880s and made many fine posed photographs in the Fort Apache and San Carlos areas. The two on this page were taken at the Chiricahua scout camp at San Carlos. The man at left in the photograph above holds hoop-and-pole game paraphernalia. This game was a favorite recreational game of Apache men and was played to pass downtime in the scout camps. The game was played by two men who rolled the hoop ahead and then threw the poles alongside it so that when the hoop fell over to one side, points were scored depending on where the hoop fell in relation to the poles. The game required a great deal of skill. (Above, courtesy AHF, Zonta Collection, ZO-64; below, courtesy NARA, RG 111, Signal Corps Collection, No. 85775.)

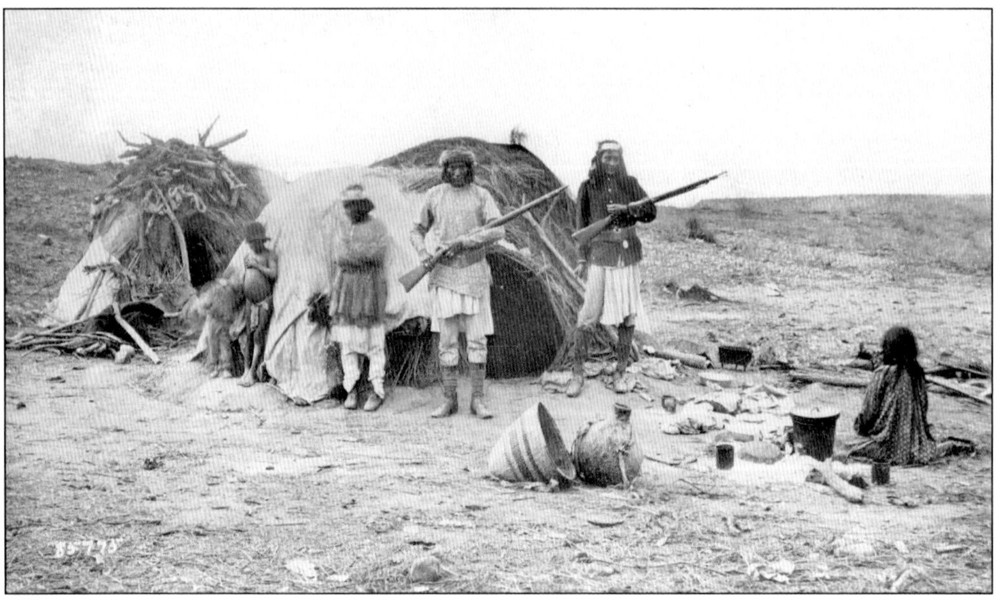

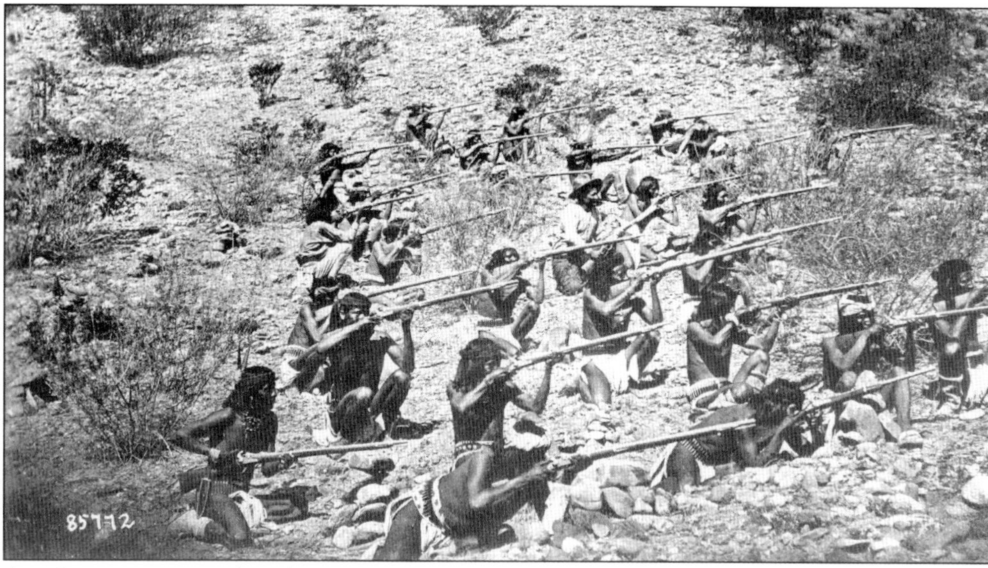

Apache scouts were enlisted in companies of 25 men. Later, during the Geronimo campaigns, the size of the companies was increased. The scout companies were commanded by an Anglo army officer, who relied on a civilian chief of scouts for hands-on supervision. Actual military training for the scout companies was limited. In these two views from San Carlos, however, some training in attacking a target in the field is evident. In the above photograph, the scouts are stripped for action. (Above, courtesy NARA, RG 111, Signal Corps Collection, No. 85772; below, courtesy GCHS, GM 27-28.)

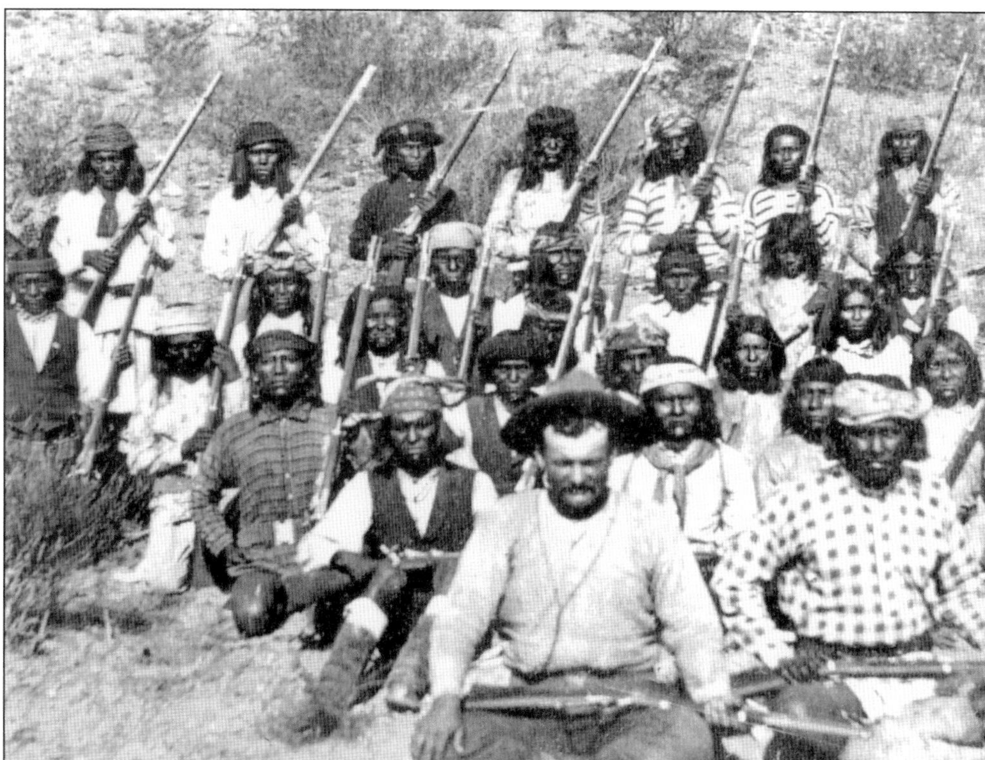

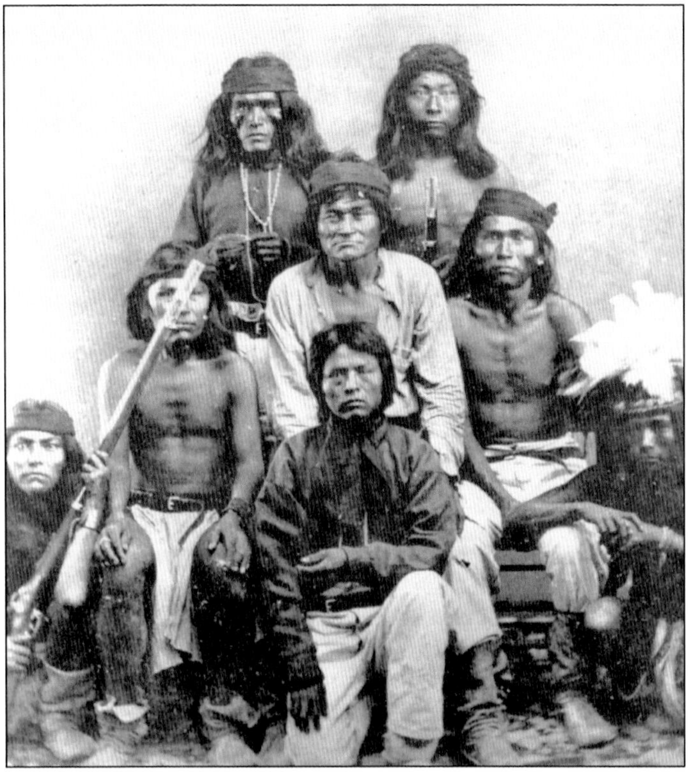

General Crook strongly believed in the usefulness and dependability of his Apache scouts. When he personally led the 1883 expedition to Mexico's Sierra Madre Mountains in pursuit of Geronimo and his band, Crook's entire force consisted of 42 Anglo soldiers, including the San Carlos scout commander Capt. Emmet Crawford and chief of scouts Al Sieber, and 193 Apache scouts. (Courtesy AHF, Sacks Collection, SCS-168.)

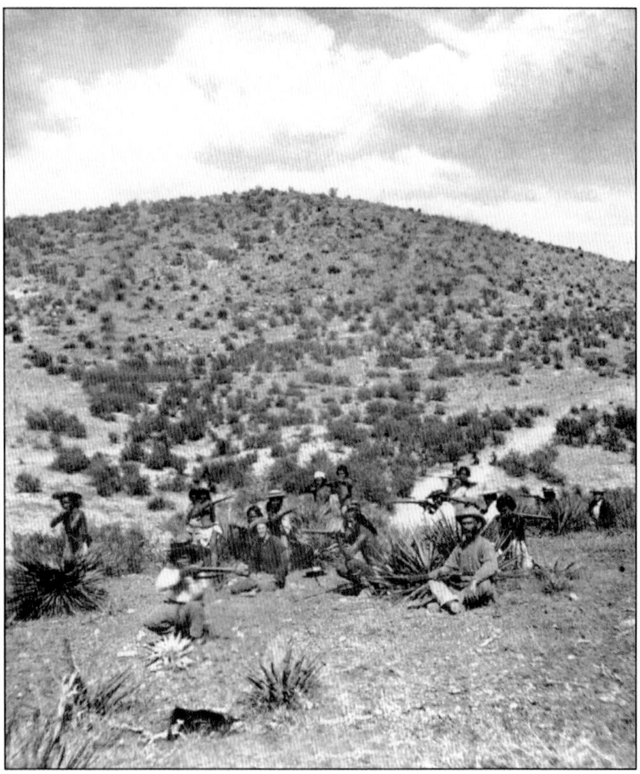

A civilian chief of scouts drills his Apache scouts in the desert environment around the San Carlos Agency. Because of their cultural background, the scouts were exceedingly self-sufficient when on a scout. They often collected their own plant and animal foodstuffs during the day's march for preparation during the evening camp. (Courtesy AHF, Rothrock Collection, I-9; stereograph by George Rothrock.)

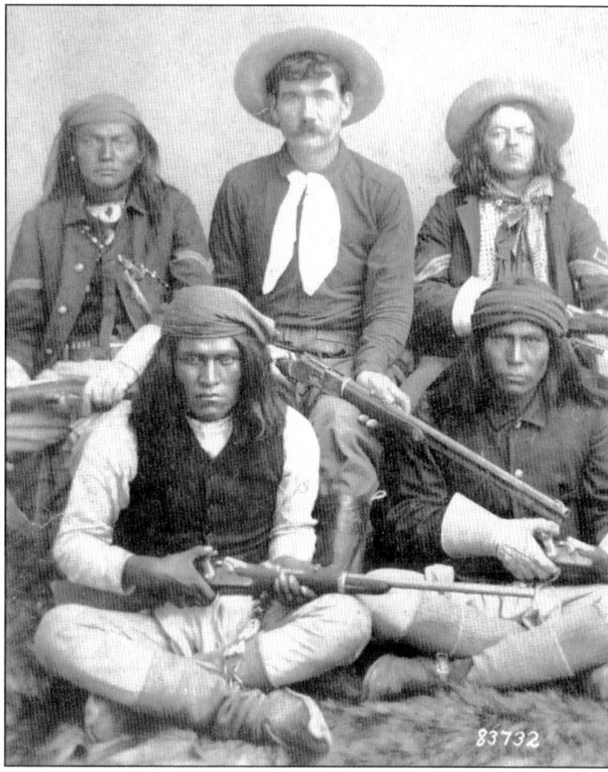

This contingent of scouts includes the civilian chief of scouts along with 1st Sgt. Mickey Free at upper right. (Courtesy NARA, RG 111, Signal Corps Collection, No. 83732.)

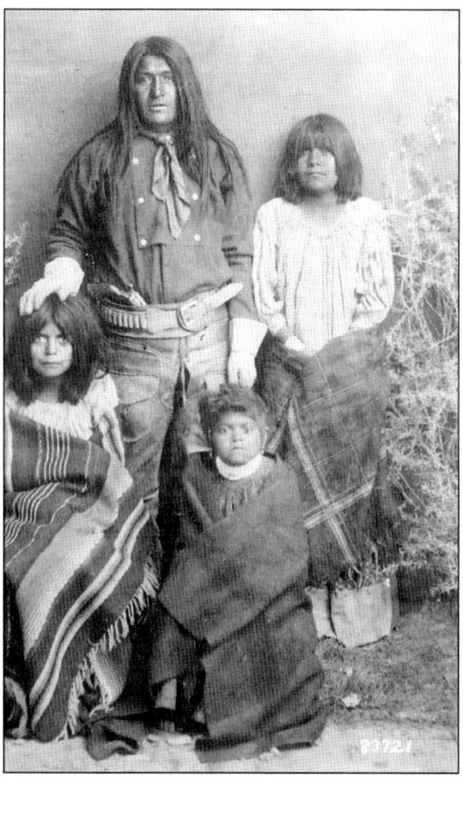

Captain Jack, a Tolkepaya Yavapai scout, and his family are pictured here around 1885–1887. (Courtesy NARA, RG 111, Signal Corps Collection, No. 83721.)

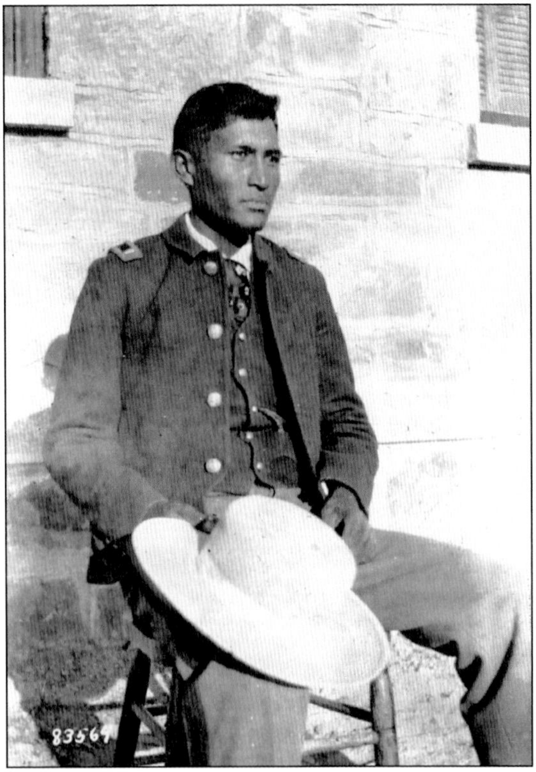

The caption for this 1895 photograph says it is of a full-blooded Apache scout at the San Carlos Indian Agency, but this individual could be a regular Apache soldier, an experiment tried by the U.S. Army from 1891 to 1897, where each cavalry and infantry regiment could have one all-Native American company unit. (Courtesy NARA, RG 111, Signal Corps Collection, No. 83564.)

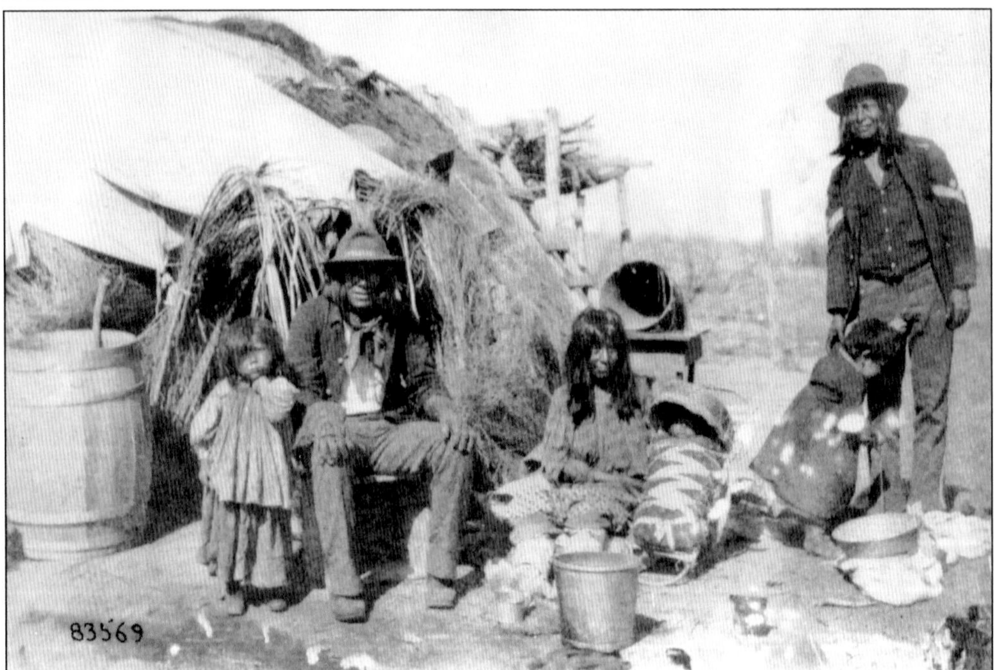

The caption for this photograph reads, "Indian scout and family at home—Billie and Merihilda's boy." It would seem that the man at right in the first sergeant's uniform may be a son of interpreter and scout Merejildo Grijalva. (Courtesy NARA, RG 111, Signal Corps Collection, No. 83569.)

Jim, a White Mountain Apache scout, posed for this photograph in 1883. Enlisted at San Carlos, he served as a sergeant in Capt. Emmet Crawford's 1885–1886 campaign in Mexico. (Courtesy NARA, RG 111, Signal Corps Collection, No. 88213.)

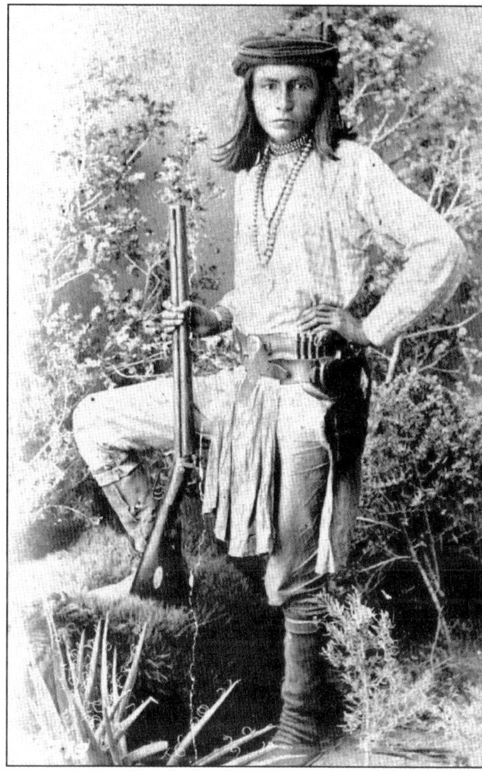

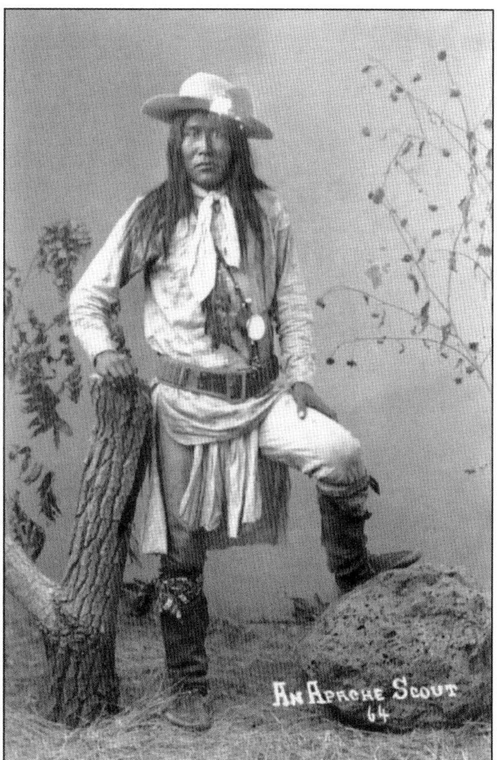

This cabinet-card image of an Apache scout shows the typical style of dress for scouts in the 1880s, including an elaborate war-charm necklace for warding off blows and missiles, particularly bullets, during battle. (Courtesy ASUL, Sammy Jones Collection, SJ-164.)

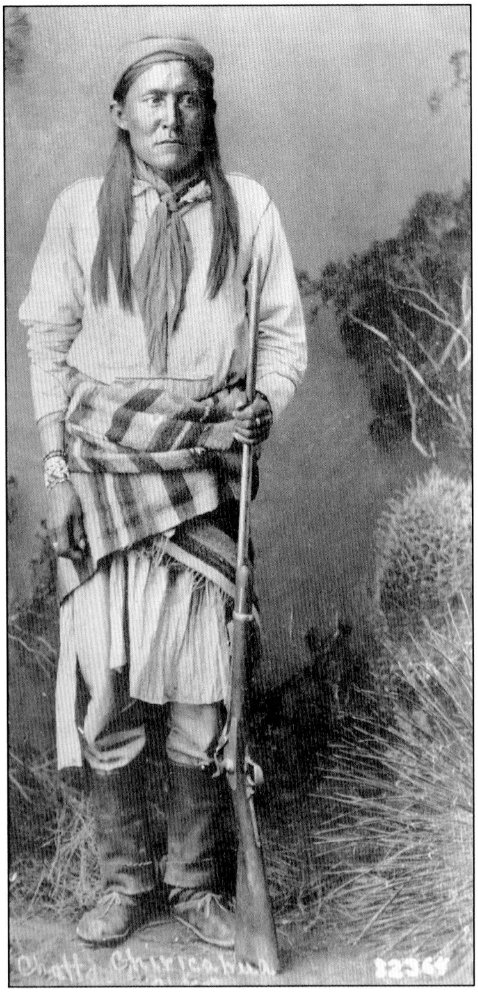

Chatto (1854–1934) led Chiricahua warriors on raids in Arizona in 1882–1883. Captured in Mexico in 1884, he returned to San Carlos and became a sergeant in Gen. George Crook's scouts against Geronimo. He was sent to Florida to be with the other Chiricahua Apaches. (Courtesy NARA, RG 111, Signal Corps Collection, No. 82364; photograph by A. Frank Randall.)

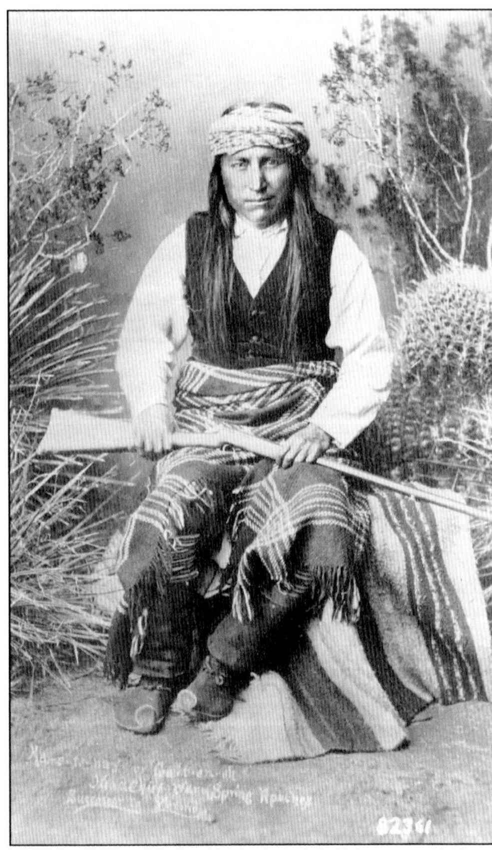

Kay-e-ten-ae was a Warm Springs Apache leader. He was arrested in 1884 for threatening Lt. Britton Davis, tried at San Carlos, and sent to Alcatraz prison. Gen. George Crook had him released early in 1885, and Kay-e-ten-ae scouted for Crook during the Geronimo campaign. Despite still being in the service, he was sent to Florida with the rest of the Chiricahua. (Courtesy NARA, RG 111, Signal Corps Collection, No. 82361.)

Tzoe, a member of the Canyon Creek band of the Cibeque Apaches, was called "Peaches" by the Anglos because of his fair complexion. Peaches became a scout for Gen. George Crook in 1881 and then left the reservation with Geronimo's hostiles. Surrendering in 1883, he again enlisted and became one of the army's most trusted scouts during the remainder of the Apache wars. He is seen in the image at right and in the center of the photograph below. Frank Randall took both photographs in 1884 at Willcox. (Right, courtesy NARA, RG 111, Signal Corps Collection, No. 82346; below, courtesy No. 87294, photograph by A. Frank Randall.)

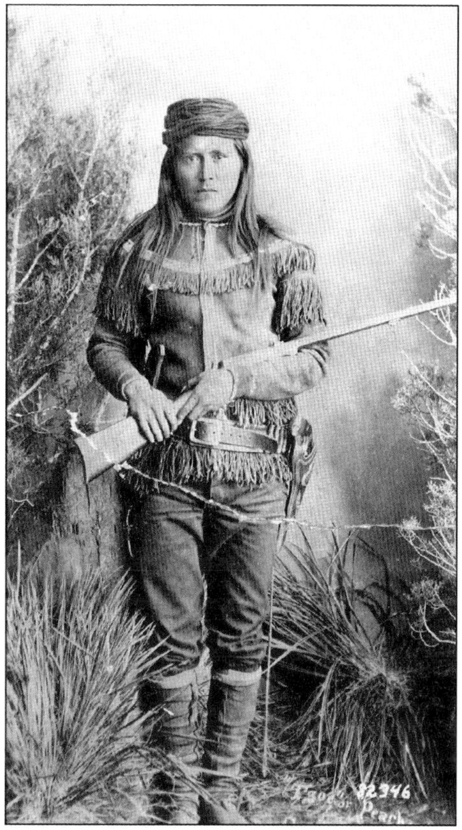

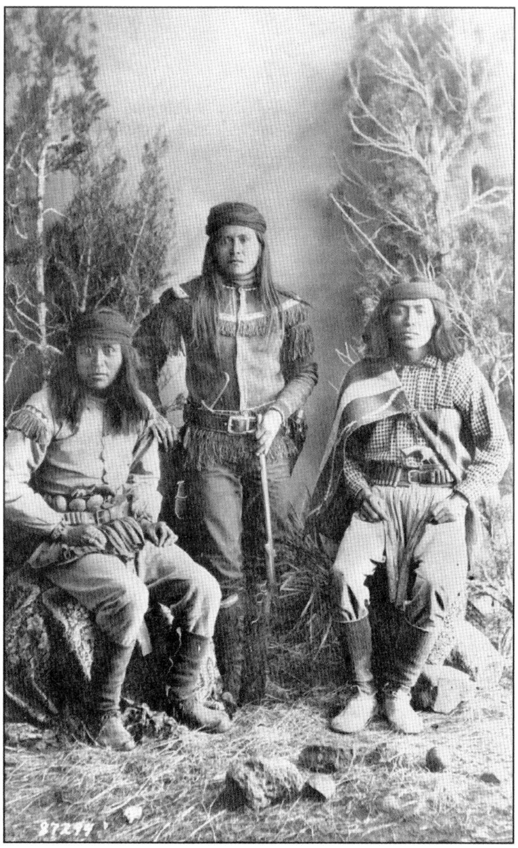

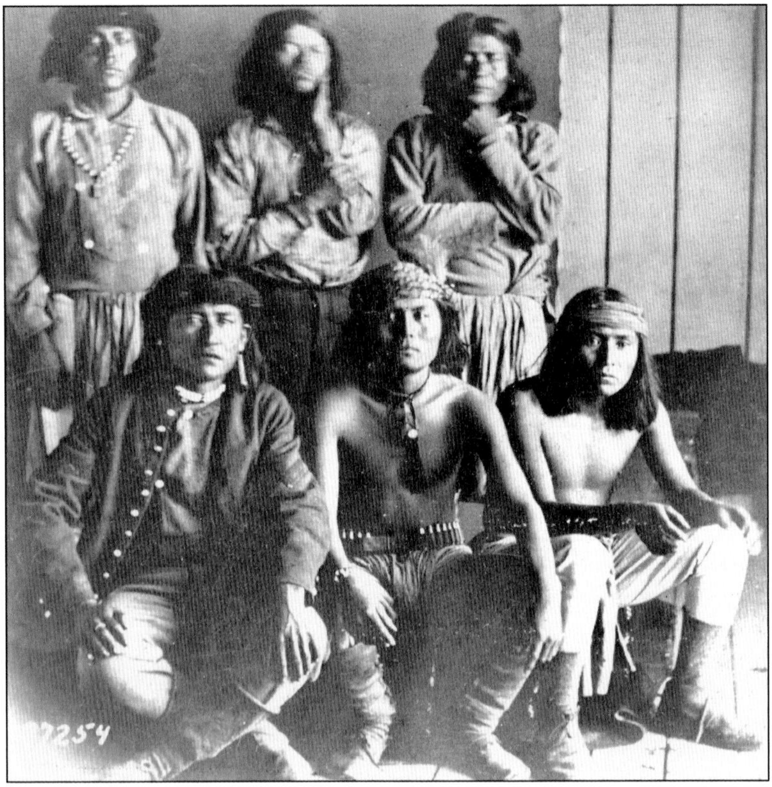

Six Apache scouts of B Company are seen in this photograph from around 1880. Longtime scout Mickey Free is standing in the center of the second row. (Courtesy NARA, RG 111, Signal Corps Collection, No. 87254.)

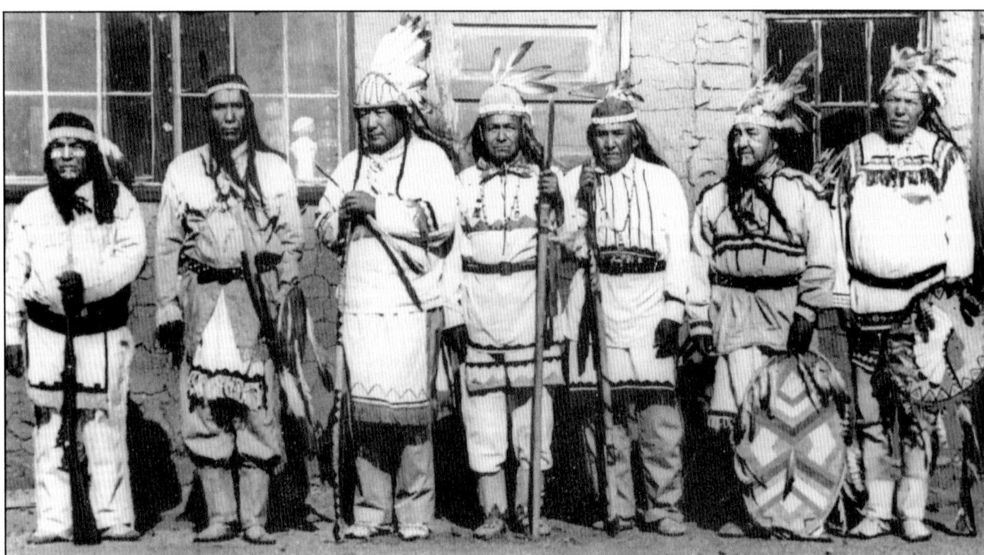

The last of the Apache scouts are shown here in 1930. Pictured are Sgt. Sinew Riley, Joe Keesay, Ivan Antonio, Jessie Billie, Alejo Quintero, William Major, and Jim Lane. (Courtesy GCHS, GM 27-146.)

Five

San Carlos Agency after 1900

On April 1, 1901, a new era began at the San Carlos Agency when civilian George D. Corson relieved Capt. W. J. Nicholson, 7th Cavalry, as Indian agent. A few months later, the U.S. Army, down to a detachment of 10 men at that time, left San Carlos for good. Back in the hands of the U.S. Indian Service, the San Carlos Agency spent the next 25 years or so attempting to improve the economic and social well being of the Apache people. The reservation's infrastructure was upgraded as roads and bridges were constructed using Apache laborers. In 1898, the railroad reached the reservation as the line from Safford to the east was extended to Globe, just west of the reservation boundary.

Importance was placed on improving the health, education level, and housing conditions at the agency and elsewhere on the Apache lands. Aside from the agency proper, small communities were developed at Bylas, Peridot, and a place called Rice Station, located about 12 miles north of the agency. A school had been in place at the agency for several years. Around 1900, a boarding school was established at Rice, and day schools were later started at Bylas and at Peridot, the latter sponsored by the Lutheran Church. An agency doctor and nurse were employed, and health specialists, known as field matrons, were placed in the various communities to visit individual homes. Even in the first decades of the 20th century, the Apaches strongly preferred to inhabit the traditional wickiup homes, despite the fact that the agents had for years advocated moving into frame houses. It would not be until the late 1920s that the housing shift would take hold.

While farming had been seen by federal authorities as the economic future of the Apaches since the opening of the agency, the restricted availability of arable lands and the limitations of water supply repeatedly held back such aspirations. Thus there was an emphasis placed on labor employment on the reservation, such as in road construction and at sawmill, the establishment of a cattle industry, and finding seasonal off-reservation labor for Apache men and women.

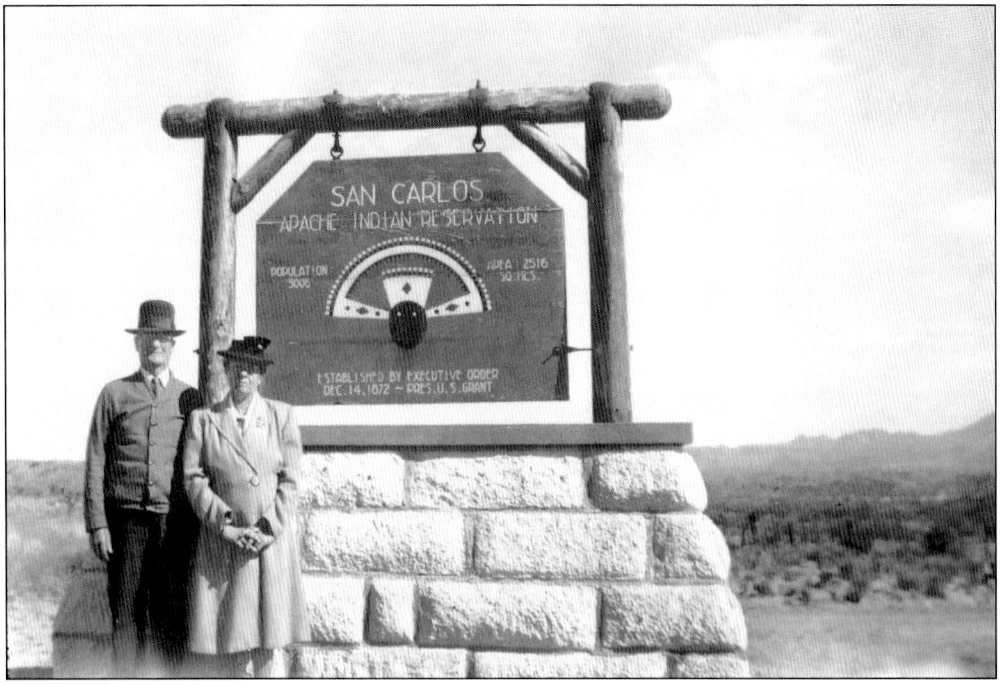

When established in 1872, the original White Mountain Reservation, with the agency at San Carlos, included nearly 4,000 square miles. After 1900, following some executive order land reductions and the splitting off of the Fort Apache Reservation in 1897, the San Carlos Reservation consisted of just over 2,500 square miles. (Courtesy GCHS, GM 27-78.)

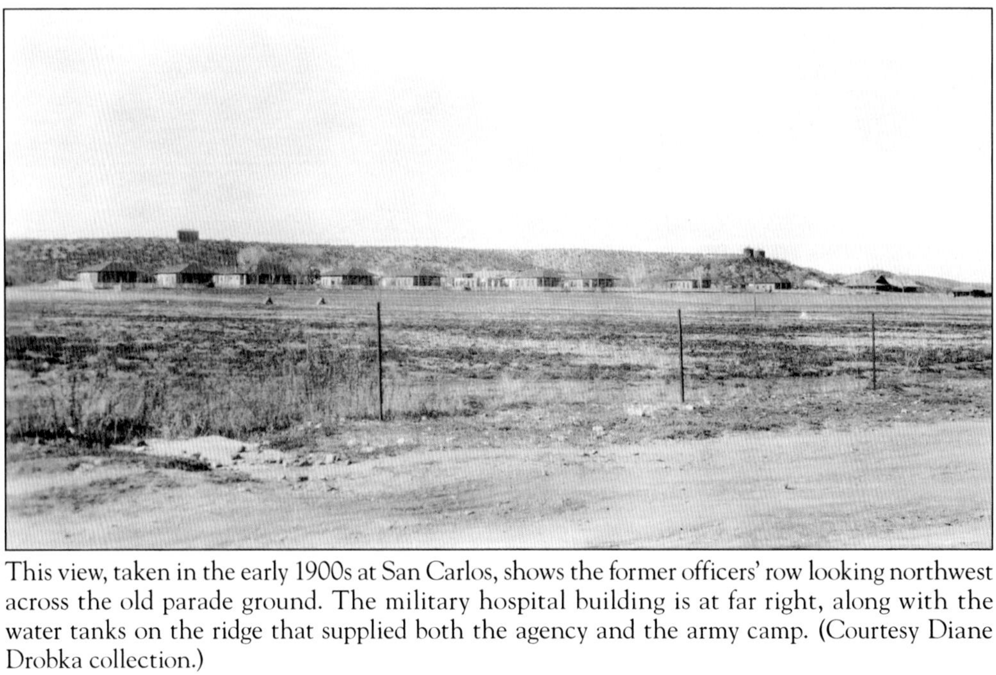

This view, taken in the early 1900s at San Carlos, shows the former officers' row looking northwest across the old parade ground. The military hospital building is at far right, along with the water tanks on the ridge that supplied both the agency and the army camp. (Courtesy Diane Drobka collection.)

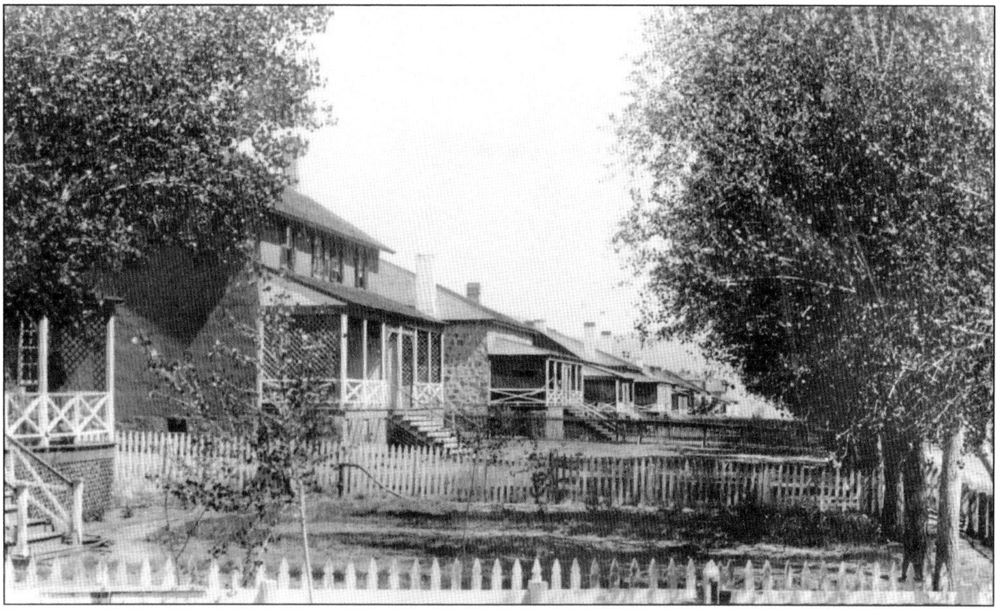

Porches and 60 shade trees were added to the employee cottages in 1904, followed by extensive remodeling of the agent's house and others in 1912–1914. During the remodeling phase, two of the former officers' quarters were torn down, and the materials were reused to remodel the remaining cottages. (Courtesy GCHS, 27-119.)

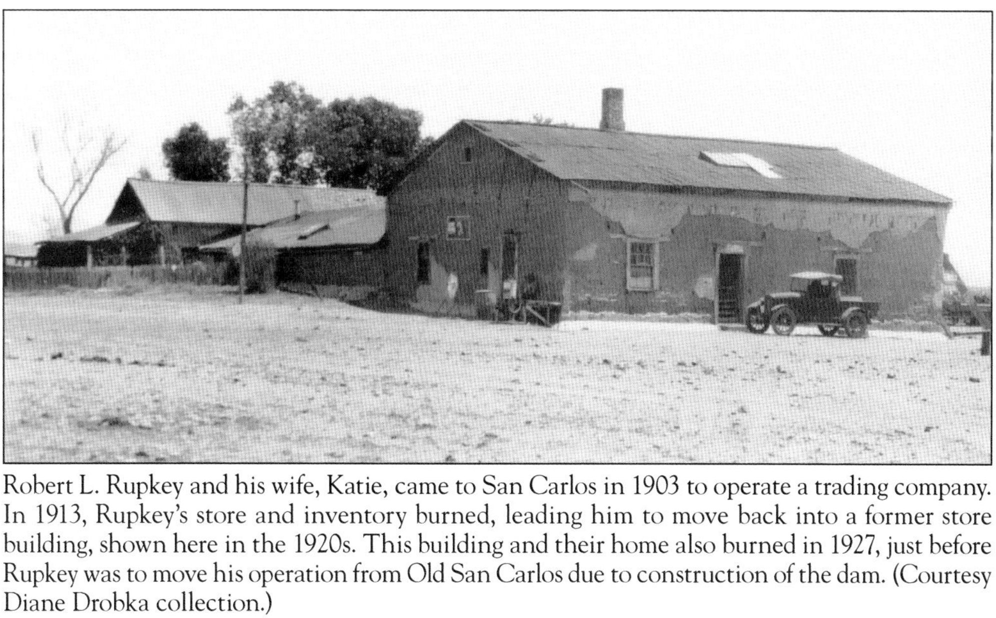

Robert L. Rupkey and his wife, Katie, came to San Carlos in 1903 to operate a trading company. In 1913, Rupkey's store and inventory burned, leading him to move back into a former store building, shown here in the 1920s. This building and their home also burned in 1927, just before Rupkey was to move his operation from Old San Carlos due to construction of the dam. (Courtesy Diane Drobka collection.)

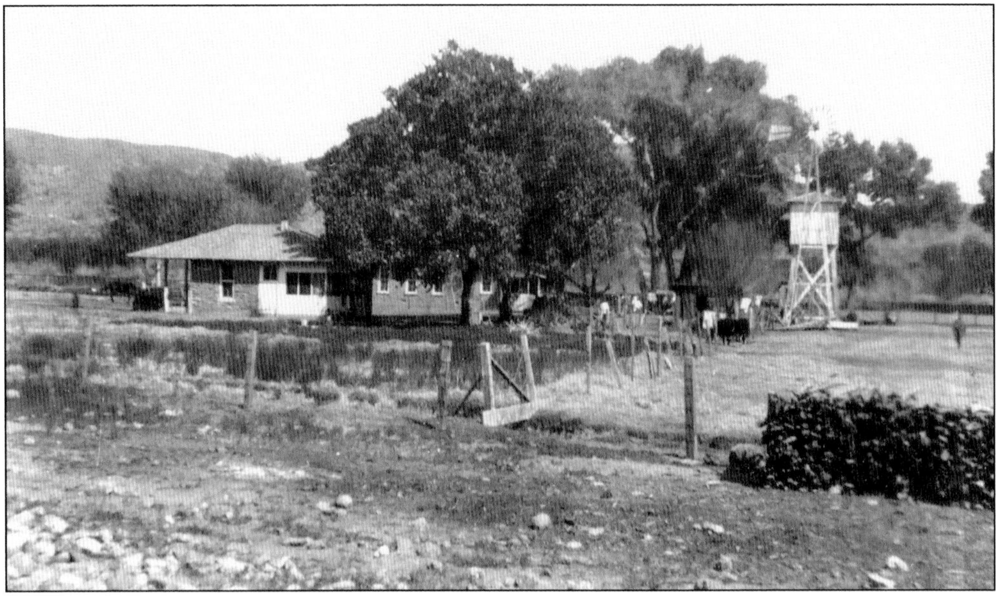

This 1924 image shows the homes of a Mr. Surface, the agency farmer at Peridot Farm Station, and the field matron, Mary A. Seward. The field matron's cottage was constructed in 1912. The role of the agency farmer was to assist the Apache farmers in improving irrigation and cultivation of their fields. (Courtesy NARA, RG 75.)

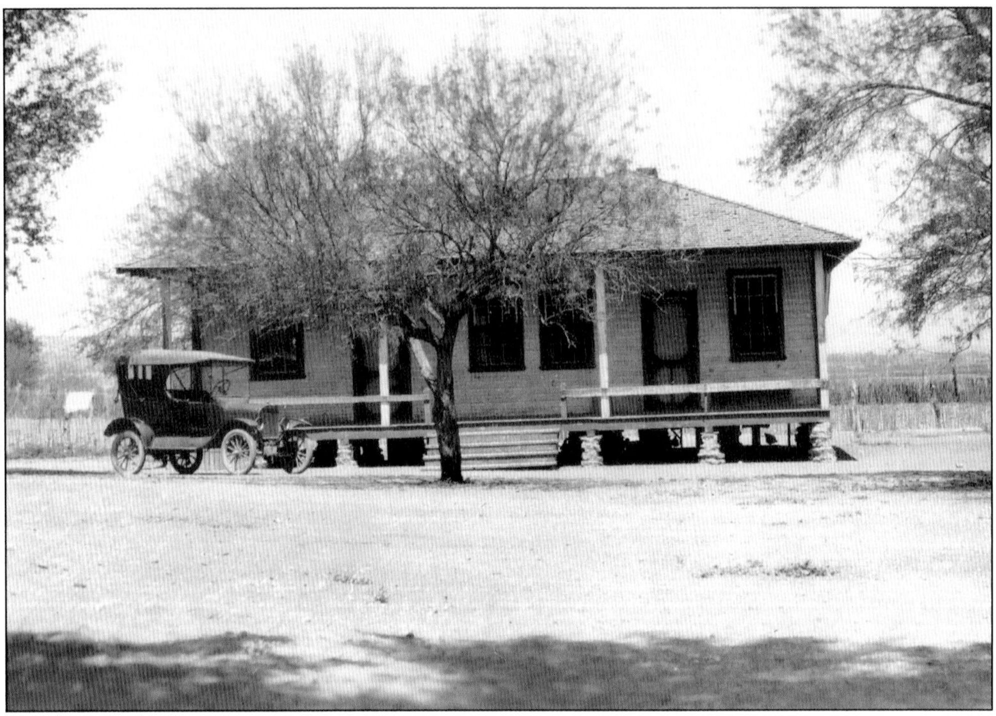

This photograph shows what is probably the field matron's and farmer's housing in Bylas in the 1920s. Gracie S. Taylor was the field matron there from 1918 to about 1929. Her husband, Aaron, was the agency's Bylas farmer in the early 1920s. (Courtesy Diane Drobka collection; photograph probably by Gracie Taylor.)

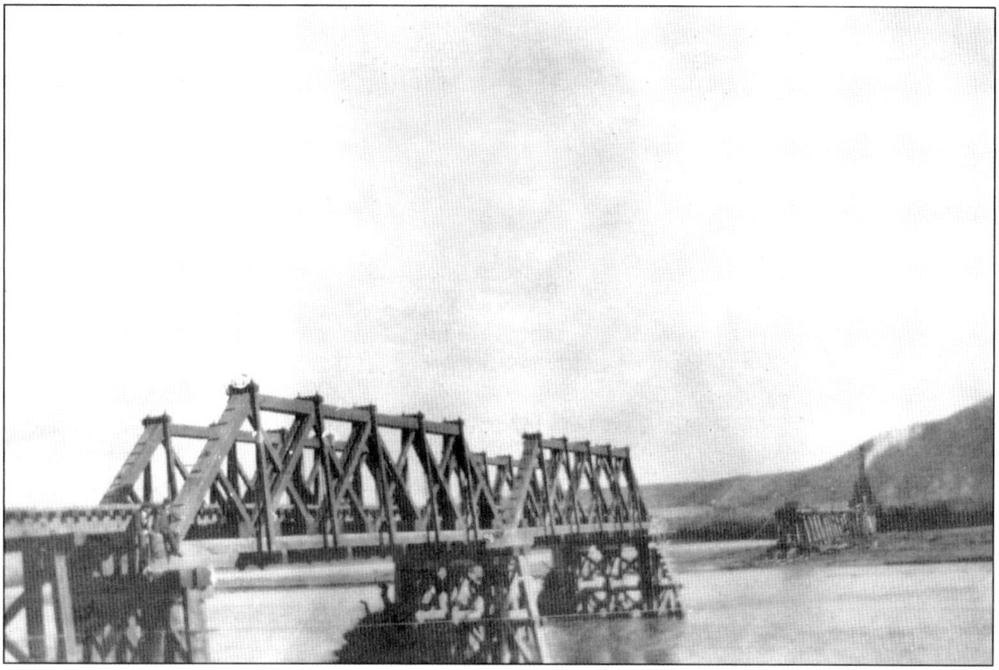

The original wooden railroad bridge over the Gila River, about 1.5 miles east of the agency, was completed by the Gila Valley, Globe, and Northern Railroad in August 1898. It was replaced by a more substantial metal bridge after the first one was damaged by flooding in 1907. This photograph shows the removal of the wooden bridge after the flood. (Courtesy GCHS, GM 28-3.)

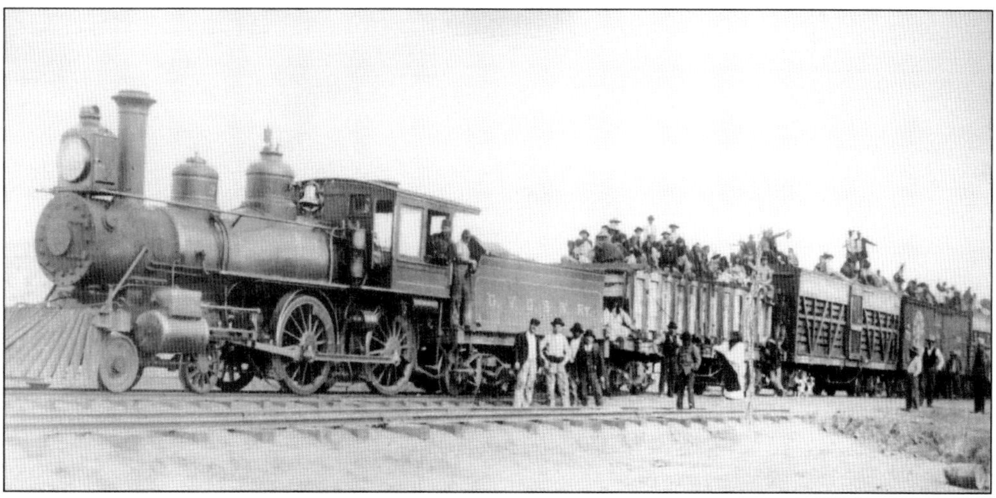

This train is reportedly the first to arrive in Globe on November 11, 1898, after crossing over the newly laid track in the San Carlos Reservation. Passenger service in the early 1900s was called "the Geronimo Route." In February 1910, the Gila Valley, Globe, and Northern Railroad became the Arizona Eastern Railroad, Globe Division. (Courtesy GCHS, GM 28-4.)

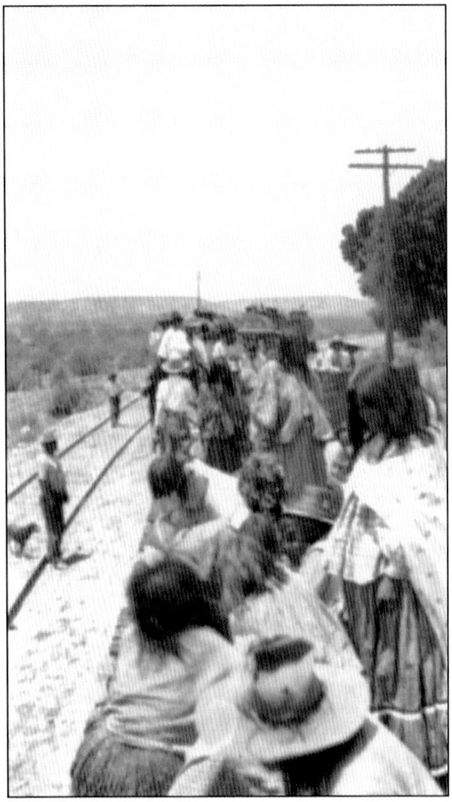

Construction of the railroad from Bowie to Globe was stalled at Geronimo between 1895 and 1898 as the San Carlos tribe balked at construction on reservation lands. In 1895, an agreement between the tribe and the railroad company provided for an $8,000 indemnity payment and compensation for damages to tribal members whose homes and/or land were damaged by construction, as well as free passage on the steps and platforms of baggage and express cars and on empty boxcars for Apaches for a period of 30 years. In 1898, San Carlos agent Sedgwick Rice estimated that one-half of the railroad construction on the reservation had been done by Apache men. These two 1920s snapshots show Apaches from Bylas catching rides to the agency on the train and along the track by handcar. This mode of travel also offered the first opportunity for many Apache people to access off-reservation shopping in the town of Globe. (Left, courtesy ASUL, Francis J. Uplegger Collection, CPSPC 187.4.51; below, courtesy CPSPC 187.4.48.)

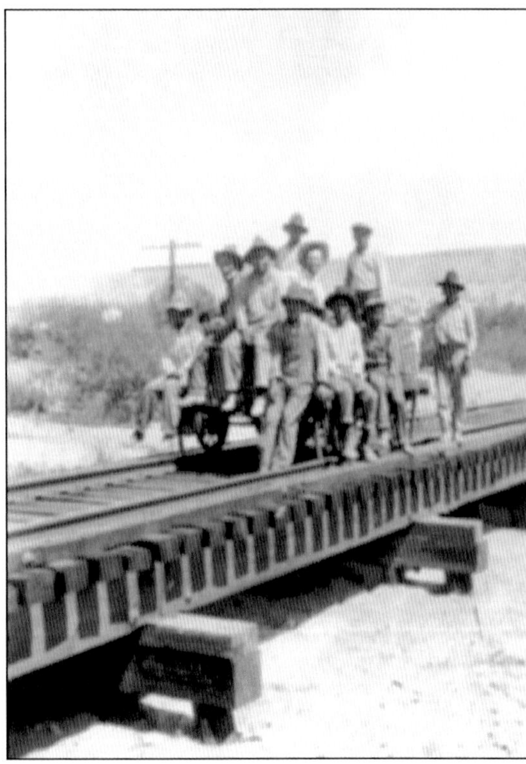

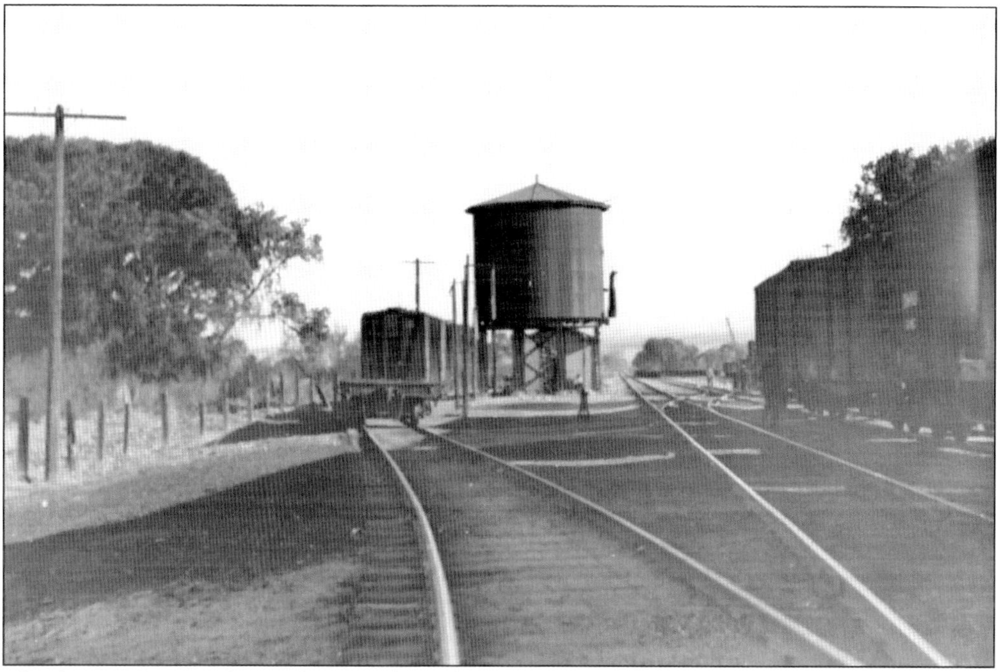

The depot at San Carlos was located about three-quarters of a mile east of the agency. In addition to the depot, there was a water tank, section house, stock pen, and bunkhouse. This photograph was taken in 1928 as part of a railroad study to identify features that would have to be moved because of the construction of the dam. (Courtesy ASUL, Arizona Eastern Railroad Collection, AEPC No. 228; photograph by W. H. Moulthrop.)

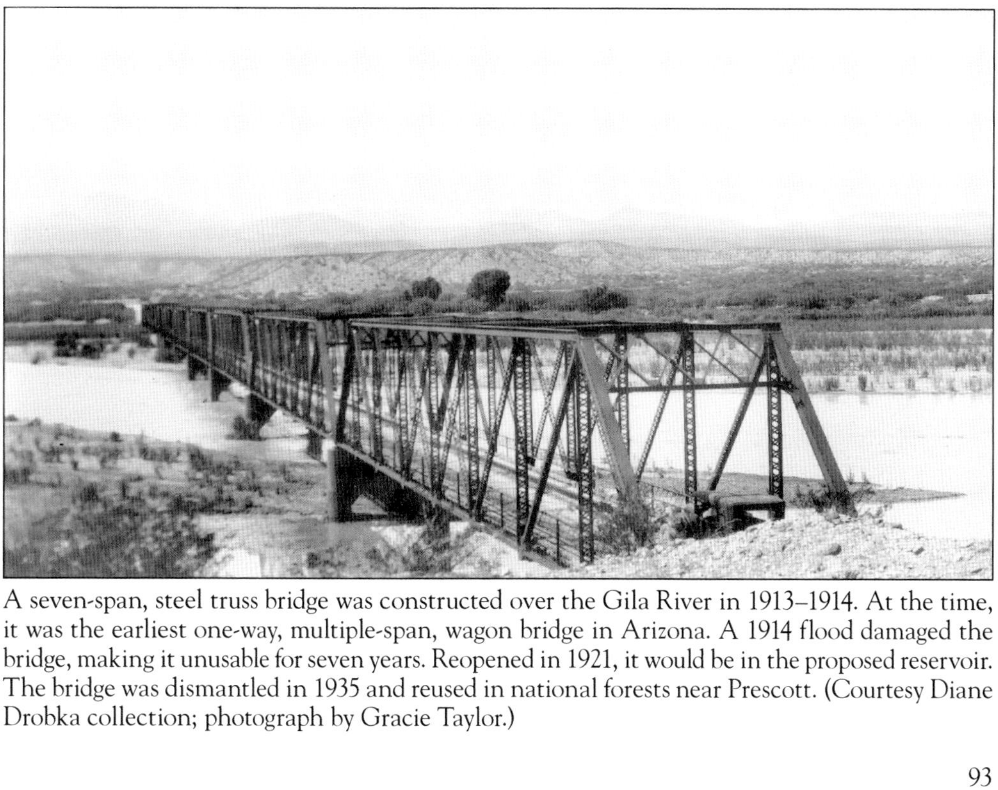

A seven-span, steel truss bridge was constructed over the Gila River in 1913–1914. At the time, it was the earliest one-way, multiple-span, wagon bridge in Arizona. A 1914 flood damaged the bridge, making it unusable for seven years. Reopened in 1921, it would be in the proposed reservoir. The bridge was dismantled in 1935 and reused in national forests near Prescott. (Courtesy Diane Drobka collection; photograph by Gracie Taylor.)

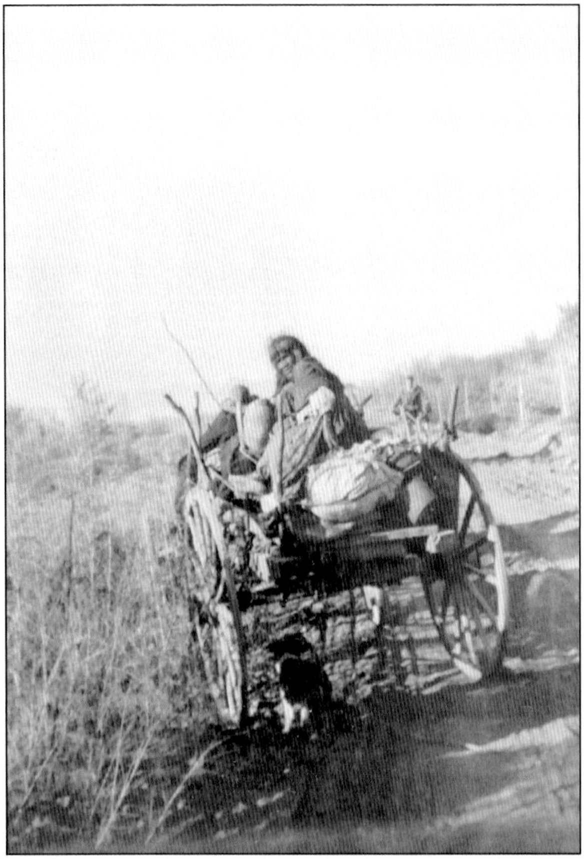

Wagons were the most common means of transportation on the San Carlos Reservation in the early 1900s. Use of automobiles by Apaches did not become common until the late 1920s. This photograph, from about 1900, shows an Apache woman on the road near the agency. (Courtesy GCHS, GM 27-36.)

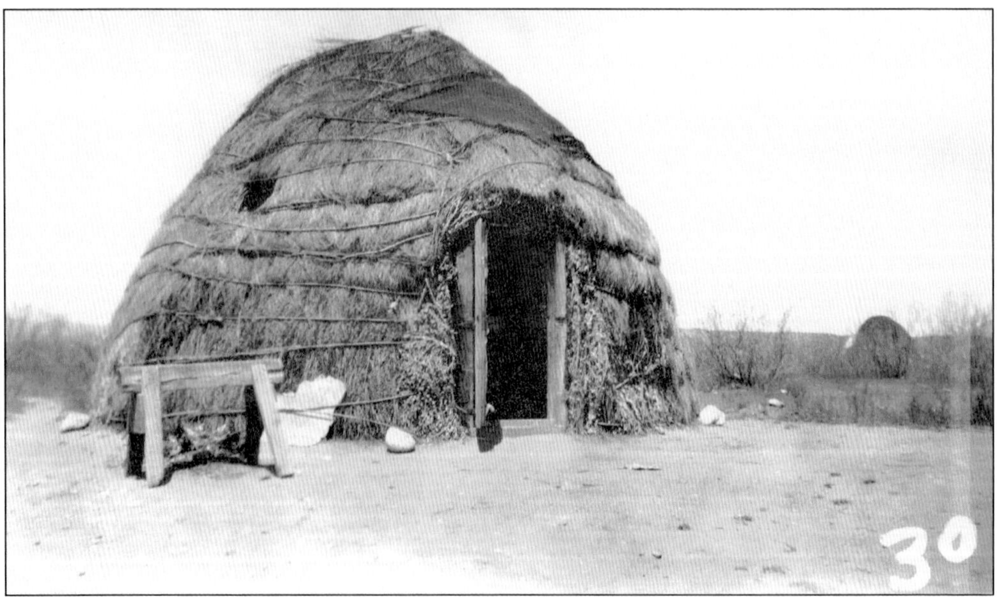

The traditional brush-covered wickiup home was greatly preferred by the San Carlos Apaches well into the 20th century. This 1924 photograph shows the well-maintained home of an elderly Apache by the name of Cyrus Delman. (Courtesy NARA, RG 75.)

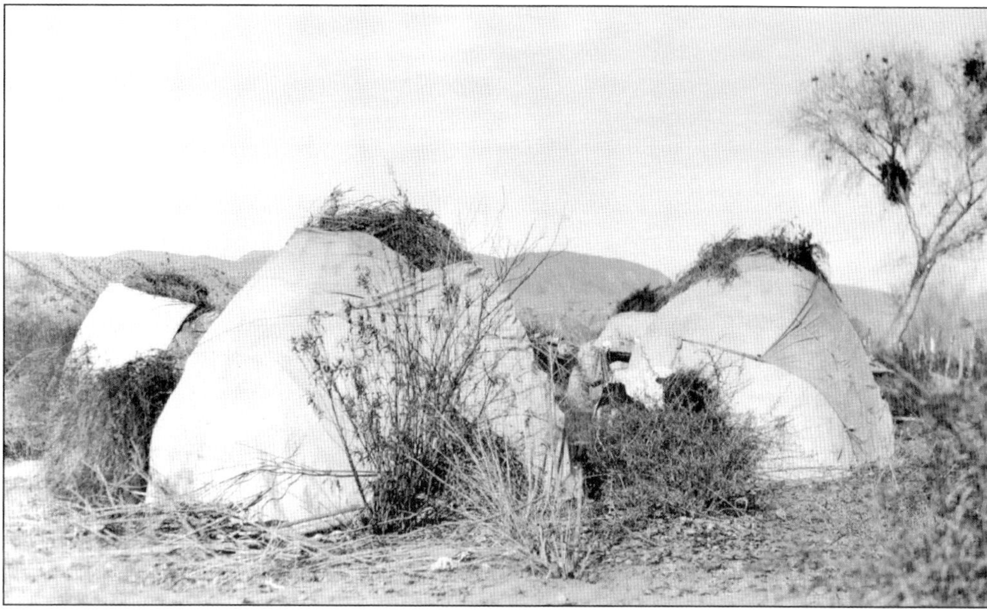

In 1916, the San Carlos Agency superintendent estimated that out of a total population of 2,670 on the reservation, there were some 660 families. Of these, 88 lived in frame houses (79 with wooden floors), and 572 lived in the traditional wickiup homes. (Courtesy Diane Drobka collection; photograph by Gracie Taylor.)

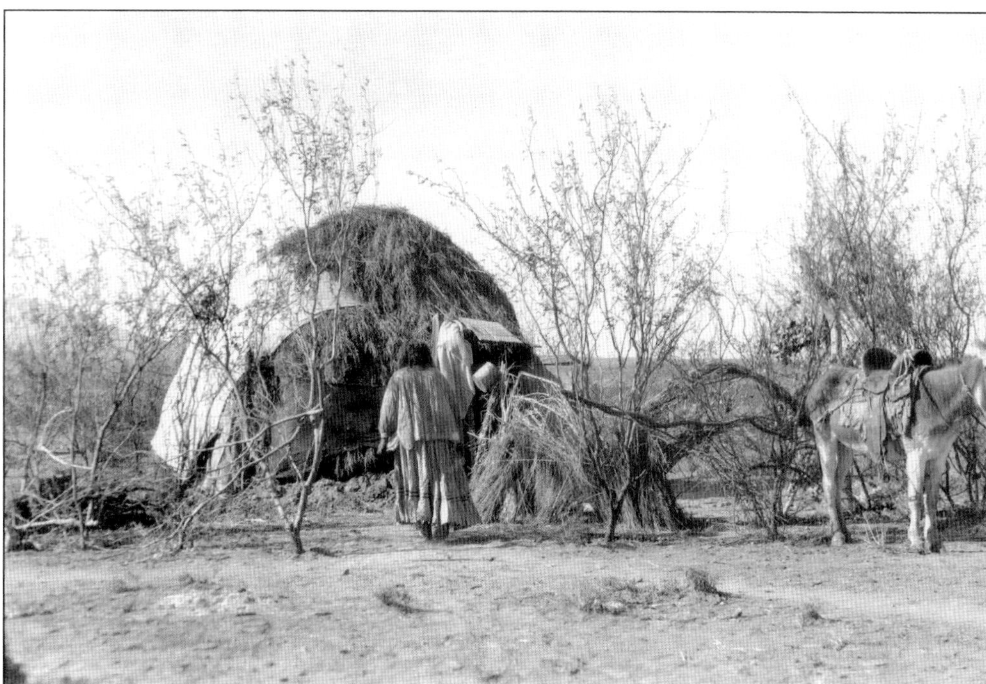

This early-1920s photograph shows a typical San Carlos Apache residence in the Bylas district. (Courtesy Diane Drobka collection; photograph by Gracie Taylor.)

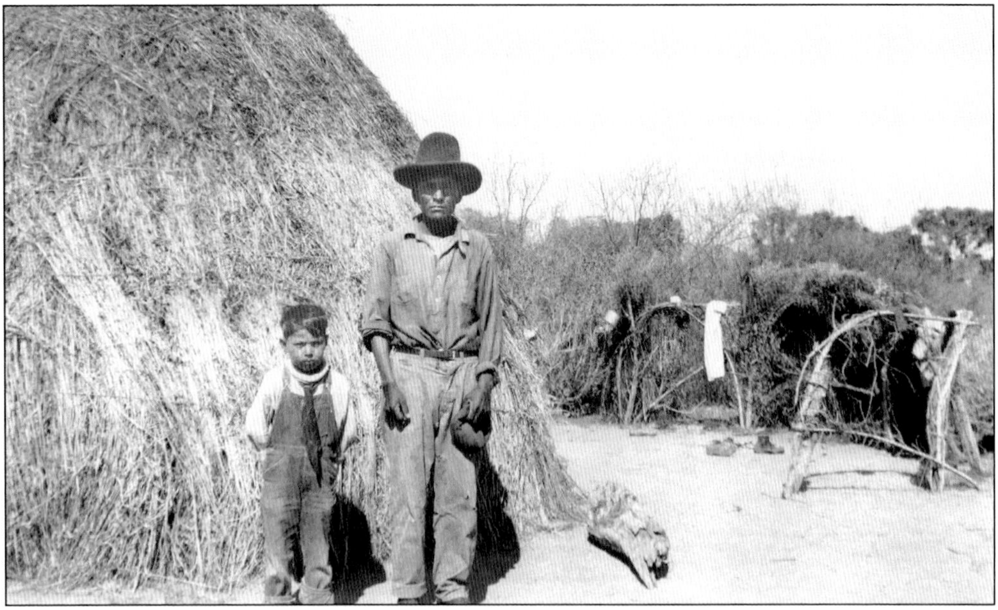

The 1924 residence of James Key and his son is seen here. Male Apaches commonly dressed in Anglo clothing while the women continued to wear the traditional camp-dress attire. (Courtesy NARA, RG 75.)

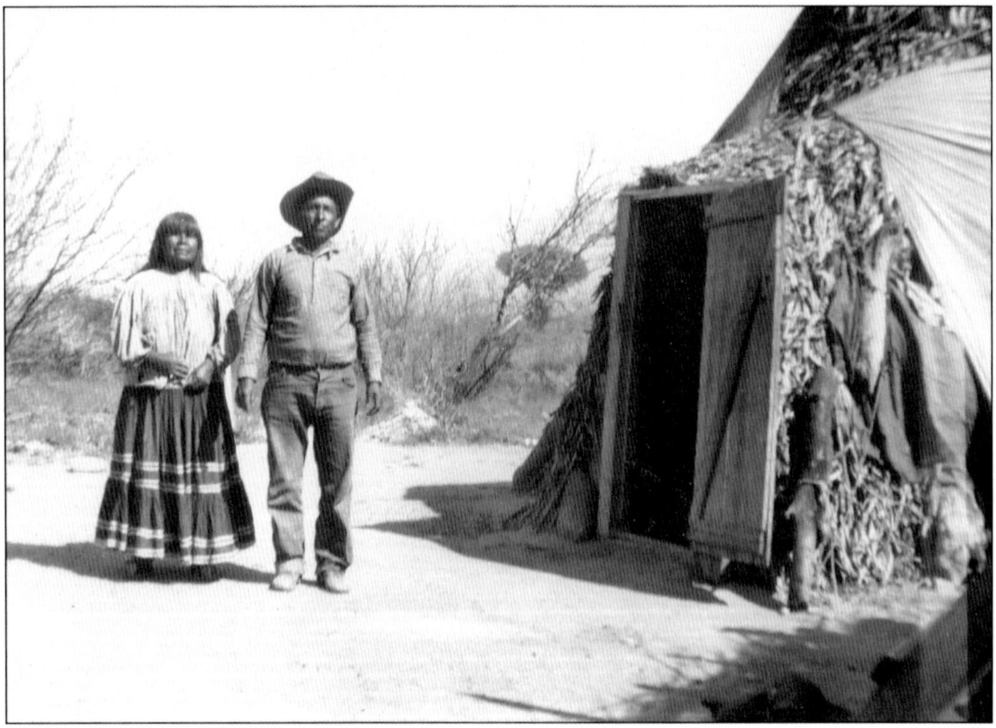

Although the wickiup structure was the preferred domicile, a concession was commonly made for a wood-framed doorway and door. Agency superintendent James Kitch hypothesized that this represented a middle stage of development on the path toward the use of frame homes. This is the home of Andrew Kidd and his wife in 1924. (Courtesy NARA, RG 75.)

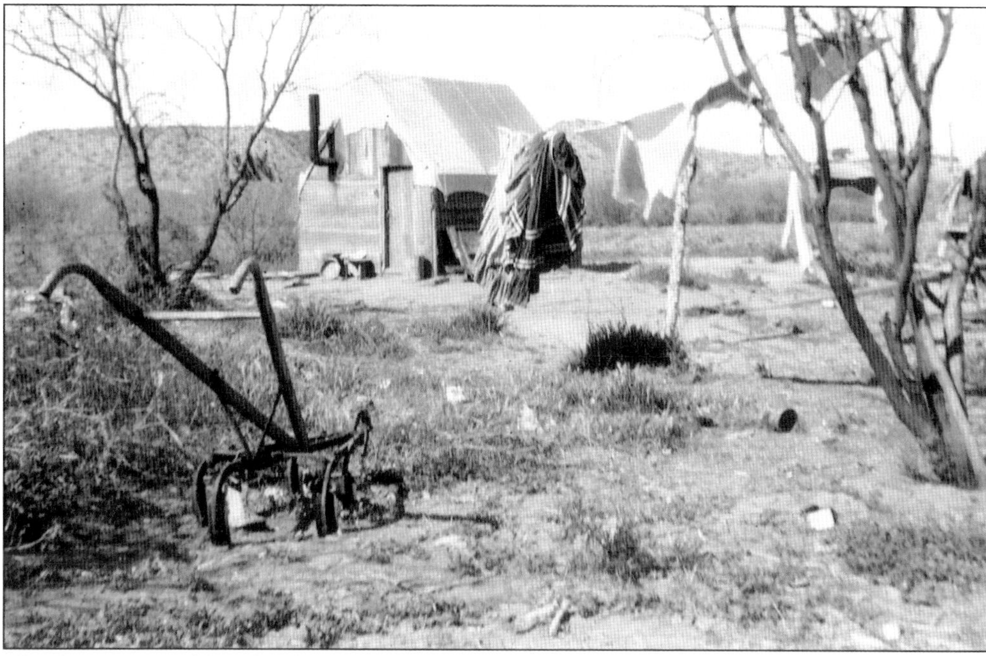

This home, owned by Claud Martin in 1924, shows an interesting combination of wickiup and frame-home architectural features, reflecting creative adaptability on the part of the Apache people to the efforts of the agents to move them into wooden houses. (Courtesy NARA, RG 75.)

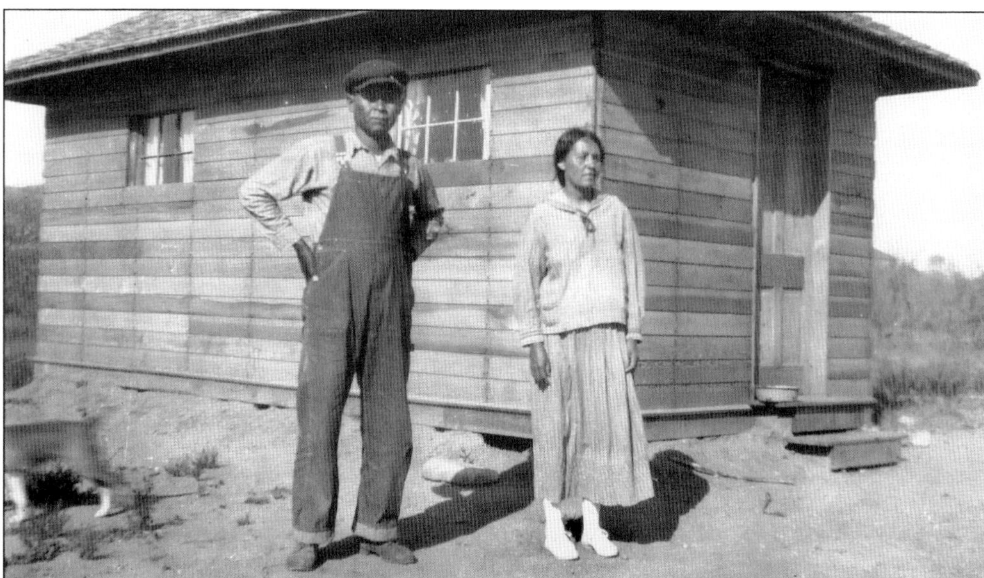

Between 1910 and 1924, there was considerable emphasis on getting Apaches into frame houses. This effort was suspended in the mid-1920s, since the homes would soon be inundated anyway. Lynn Bullis and his wife are shown with their new one-room home in 1924. (Courtesy NARA, RG 75.)

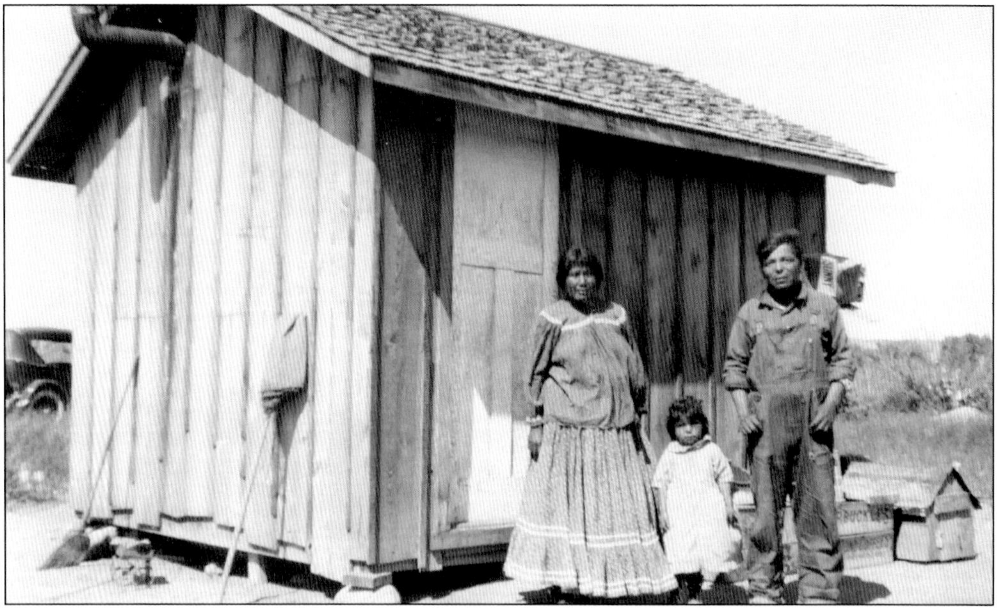

In 1929, after the relocation of the agency, superintendent James Kitch observed that Apaches continued to prefer to live in wickiups and were actually using their adjacent frame houses for storage. Joe B. Kinney and his family are pictured here in 1924 next to their new home. (Courtesy NARA, RG 75.)

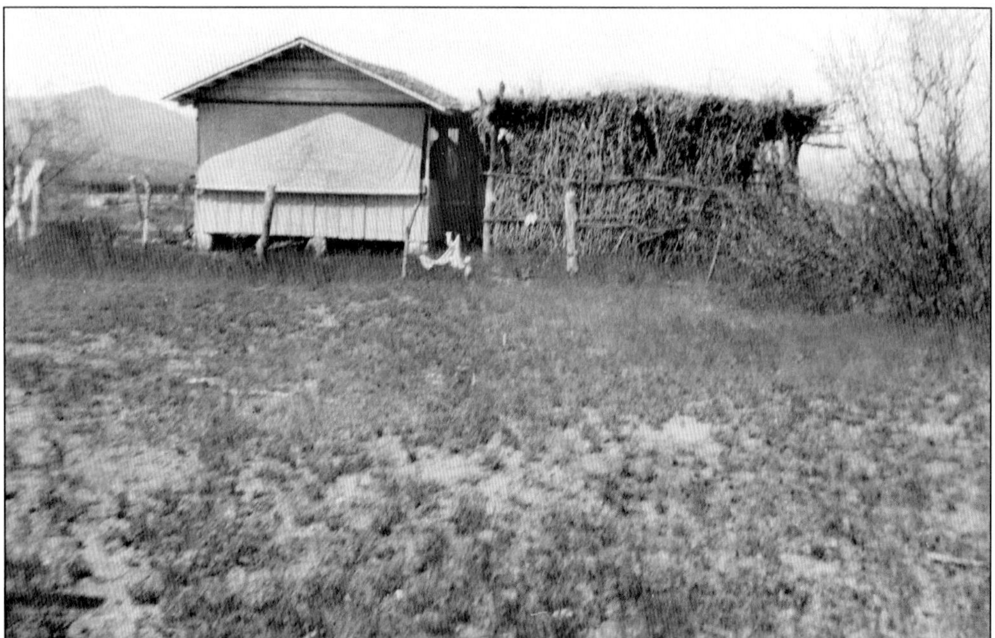

In 1910, agency superintendent Lewis M. Weaver noted that it was estimated that 40 percent of the San Carlos population was afflicted with tuberculosis. This photograph shows the home of tubercular Apache Lon Bullis with drop shades and outside brush shade. (Courtesy NARA, RG 75.)

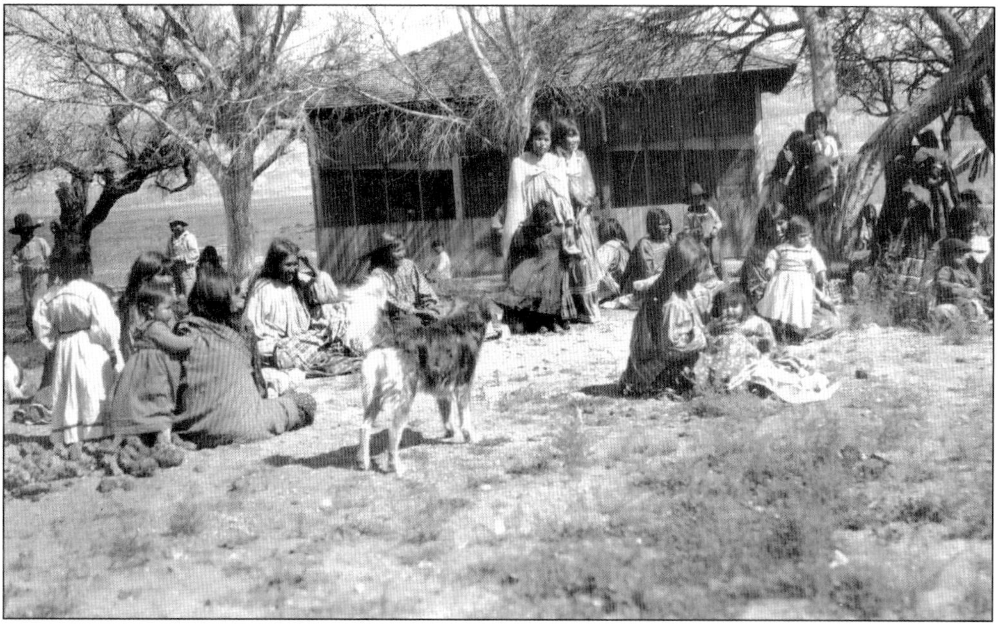

Considerable efforts were made by the San Carlos Agency medical staff in the 1920s to educate Apache mothers in methods that were considered, at least by the Anglo staff, to be necessary to improve childhood health. Here a well baby clinic for mothers and young children is being conducted in Bylas, probably by Gracie S. Taylor, the field matron there. (Courtesy Diane Drobka collection; photography probably by Gracie Taylor.)

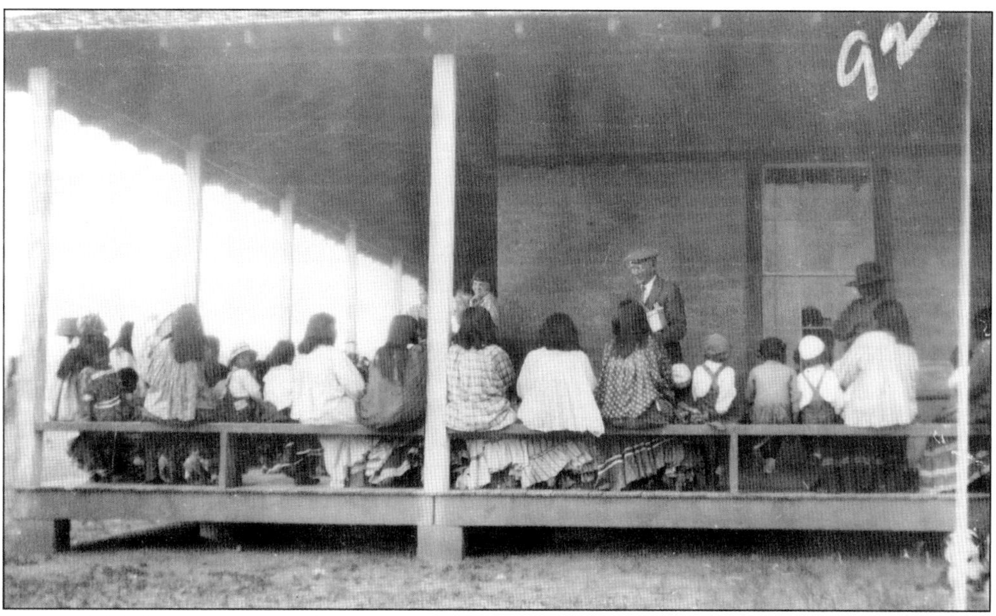

In this 1924 photograph, on what appears to be the porch of the old military hospital building at the agency, Dr. Charles F. Sawyer is giving a talk to Apache mothers. Monthly baby clinics were held in each reservation district, including judging and awarding of prizes for mothers "raising babies according to modern methods." (Courtesy NARA, RG 75.)

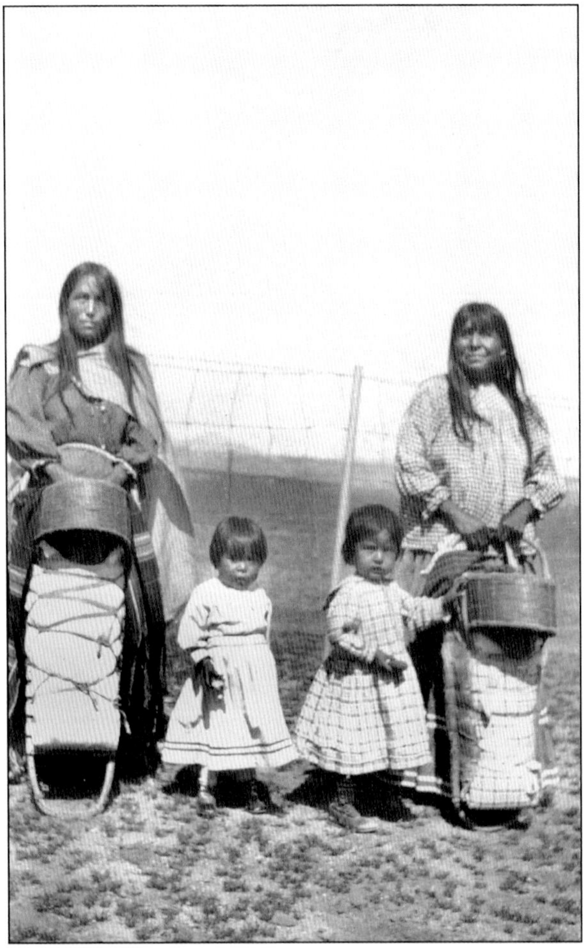

These Apache mothers and children were attendees at a monthly baby clinic at the San Carlos Agency in 1924. According to agency superintendent James Kitch's annual report for that year, "these are the old-style baby carriers which we are trying to abolish." (Courtesy NARA, RG 75.)

The San Carlos Agency nurse or field matron is with one of her students in 1924. Field matrons also visited Apache homes to assist with home economics or domestic development, along with providing basic diagnosis of ailments and needed treatments. Home care was felt to be necessary because many Apache mothers were reluctant to enter government hospitals. (Courtesy NARA, RG 75.)

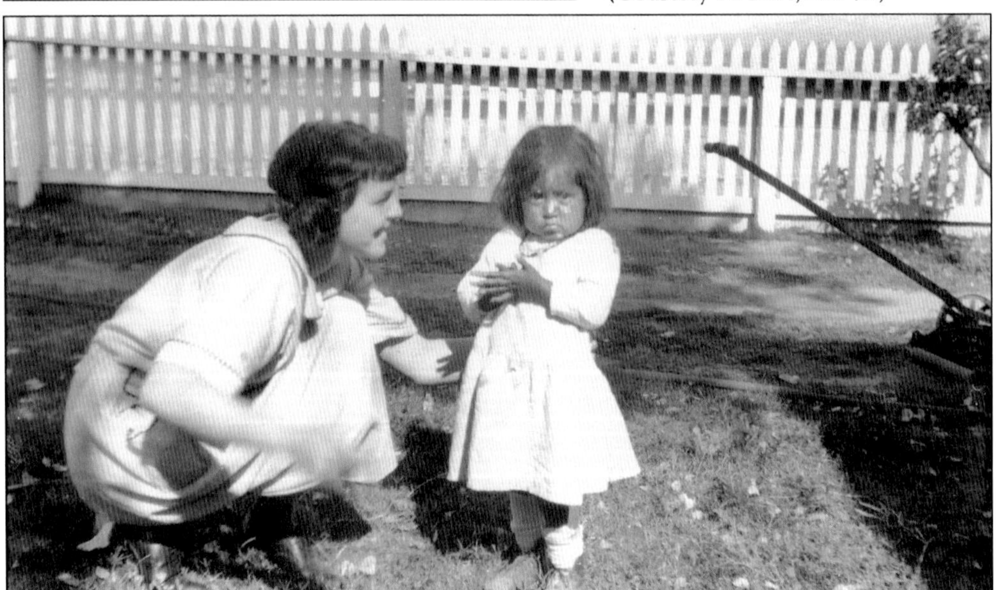

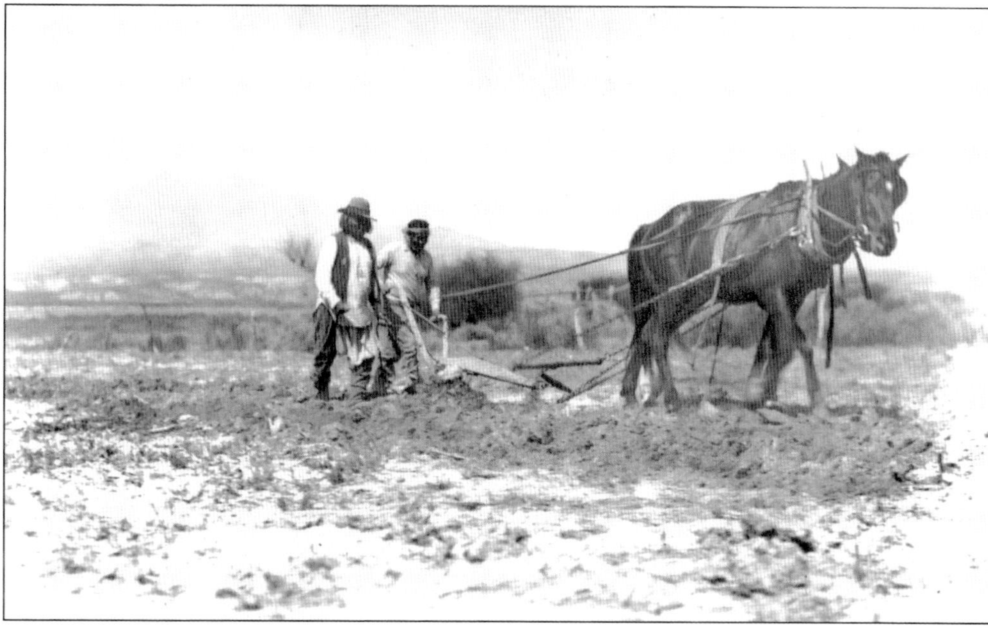

Two Apache men plow a field in 1909 at San Carlos. In 1912, two hundred and one Apaches farmed about five acres each for a total of 1,005 acres. In the mid-1920s, it was finally recognized by agent James Kitch that insufficient farmland existed on the reservation and that farming was not a profitable venture for the Apaches. (Courtesy AHF COO, No. 1097.)

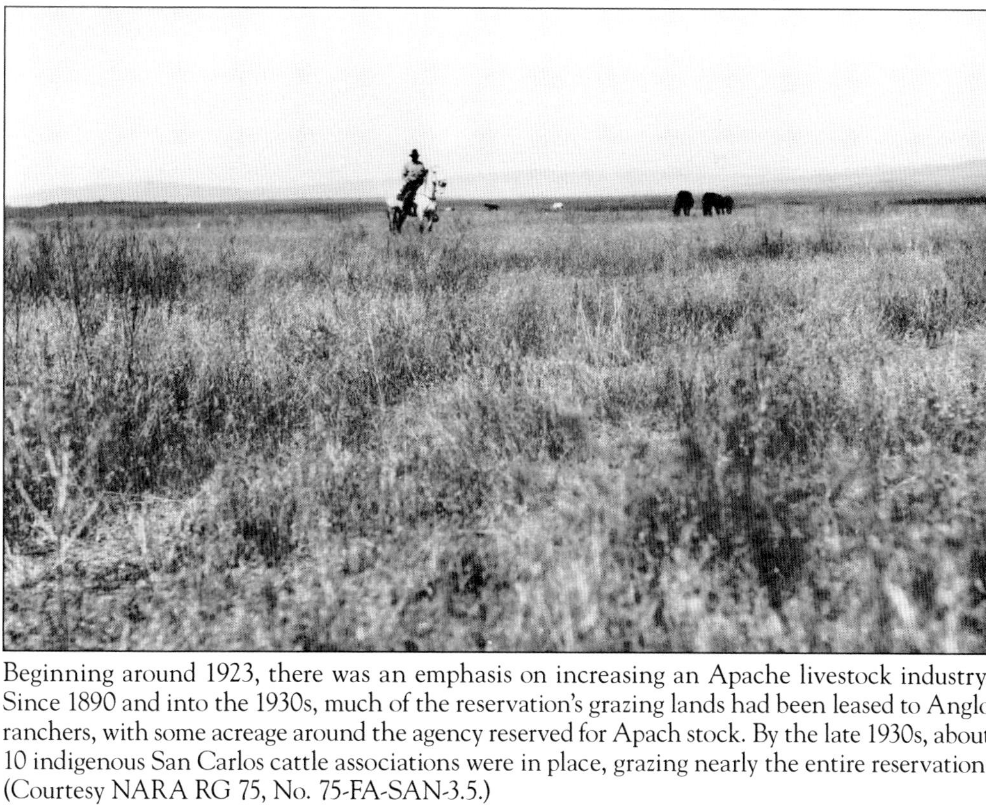

Beginning around 1923, there was an emphasis on increasing an Apache livestock industry. Since 1890 and into the 1930s, much of the reservation's grazing lands had been leased to Anglo ranchers, with some acreage around the agency reserved for Apach stock. By the late 1930s, about 10 indigenous San Carlos cattle associations were in place, grazing nearly the entire reservation. (Courtesy NARA RG 75, No. 75-FA-SAN-3.5.)

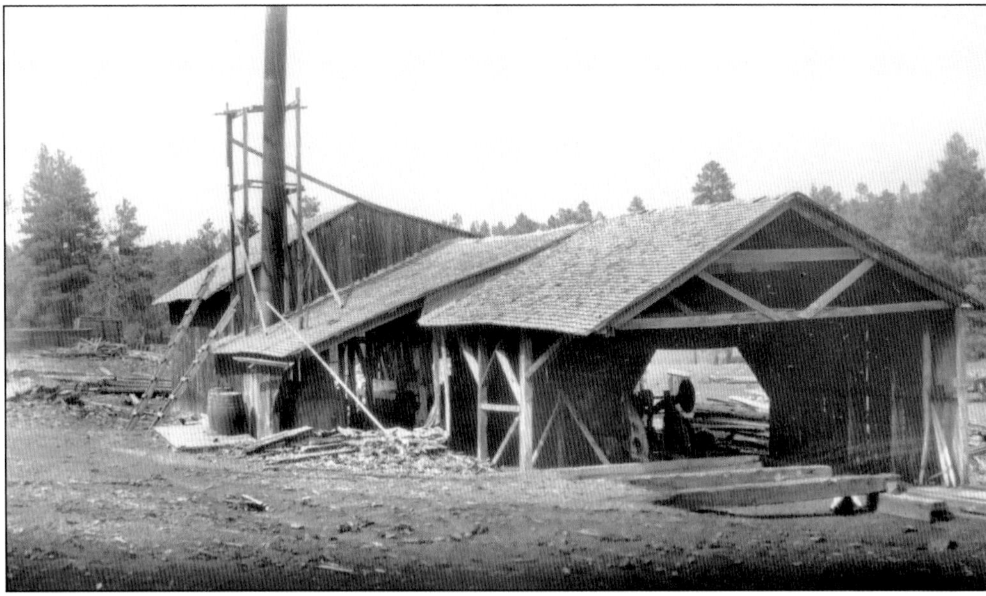

An agency sawmill was started in 1899 to provide limited employment and lumber and shingles for the agency's needs. Located about 35 miles north of the agency, it employed seven to eight Apaches and an Anglo supervisor. Pictured here in 1925, the sawmill was discontinued shortly after this photograph was taken. (Courtesy NARA RG 75, No. 75-FA-SAN-104.)

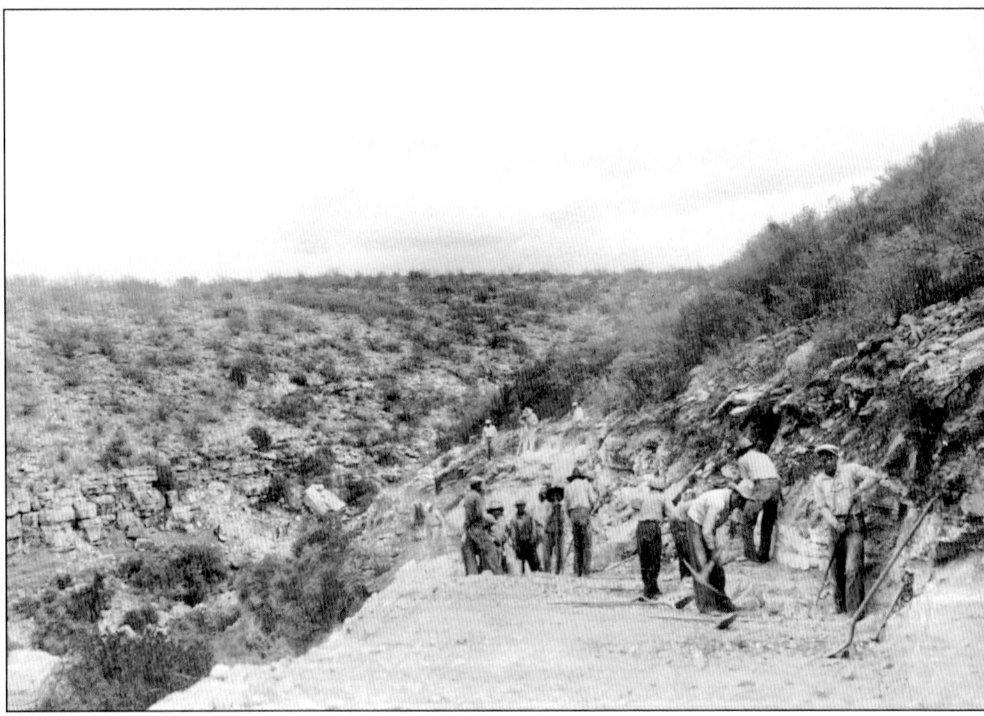

Other 1920s on-reservation employment opportunities for Apache men were provided through the construction of roads, as seen here in the Blue River Canyon area of the reserve. Adequate roads were much needed due to the increasing use of automobiles and trucks by both the agency and the Apaches themselves. (Courtesy NARA RG 75, No. 75-FA-SAN-1.8b.)

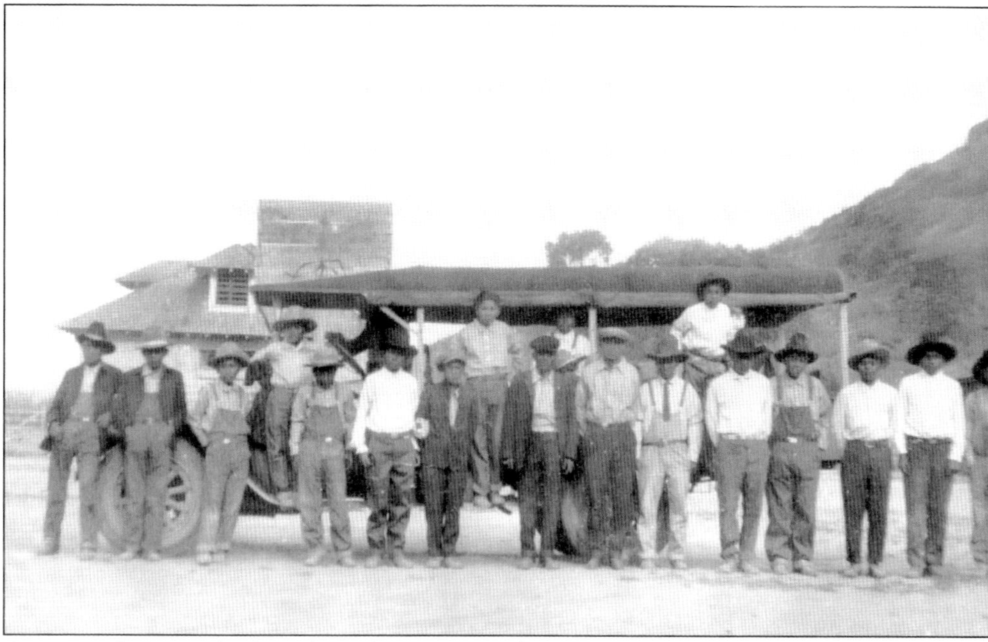

A group of 20 Apache boys from the Rice Boarding School leaves in a government truck for the beet fields of Kansas in 1924. They were employed that summer by the Garden City Sugar Company, thinning and hoeing two beet fields at $12 per acre. They returned in August having earned $1,877.53 among the group. Government expenses for the trip were put at $1,510.33. (Courtesy NARA, RG 75.)

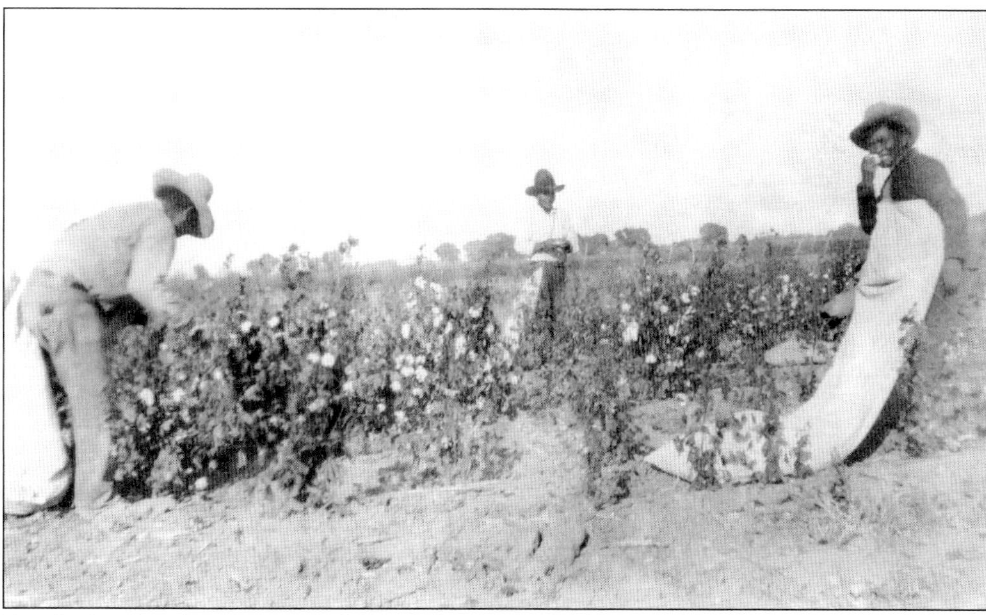

San Carlos Apache men are working in the cotton fields in the Gila River Valley near Safford in 1925. About one-half of the 8,000 acres of cotton in that area was picked by Apache men, women, and children for 1.5 to 3.5¢ per pound in August and September of that year. In all, there were more than 300 San Carlos Apaches picking cotton, earning a total of about $35,000. (Courtesy NARA, RG 75.)

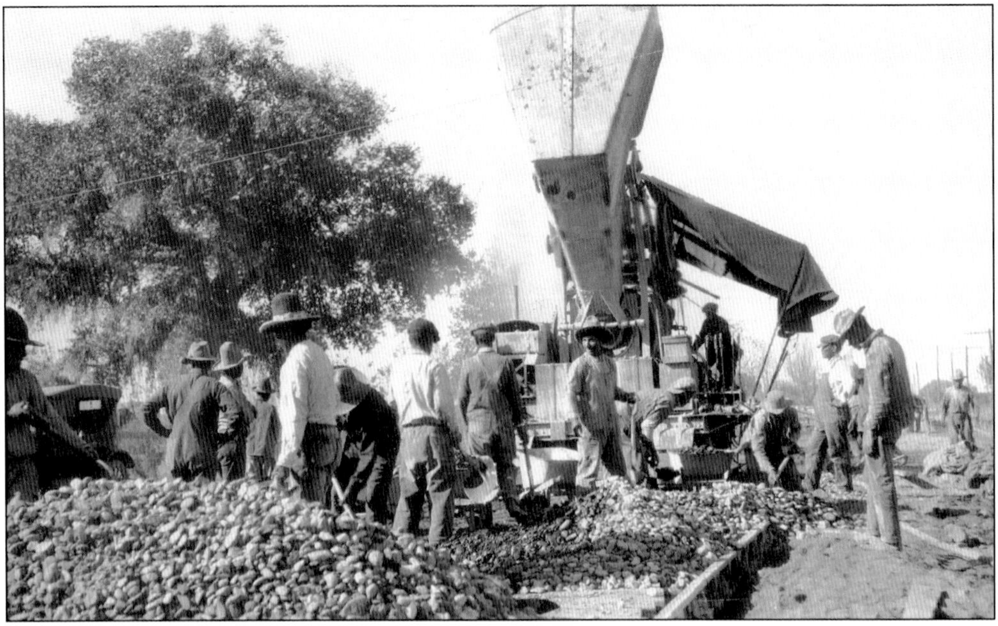

San Carlos men are working on the highway between Safford and Solomonville during the months of May and June 1925. They were employed in grading and surfacing at a rate of $3.50 a day. Tents and cots were provided by the State Highway Department, or they could stay at a boardinghouse run by the state at a cost of $1.20 per day, including three meals. (Courtesy NARA, RG 75.)

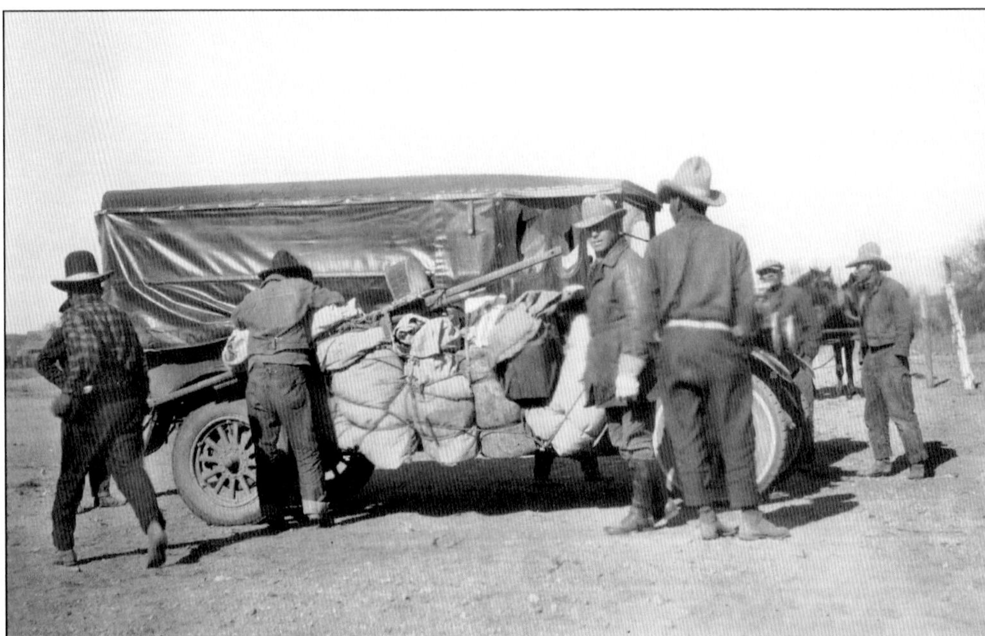

In 1925, about 500 Apaches were transported off the reservation in this Reo government truck. This group is shown leaving for the construction of the Horse Mesa Dam on the Salt River, where they were employed in road construction and building of the dam and power plant at a rate of $3 per eight-hour day. (Courtesy NARA, RG 75.)

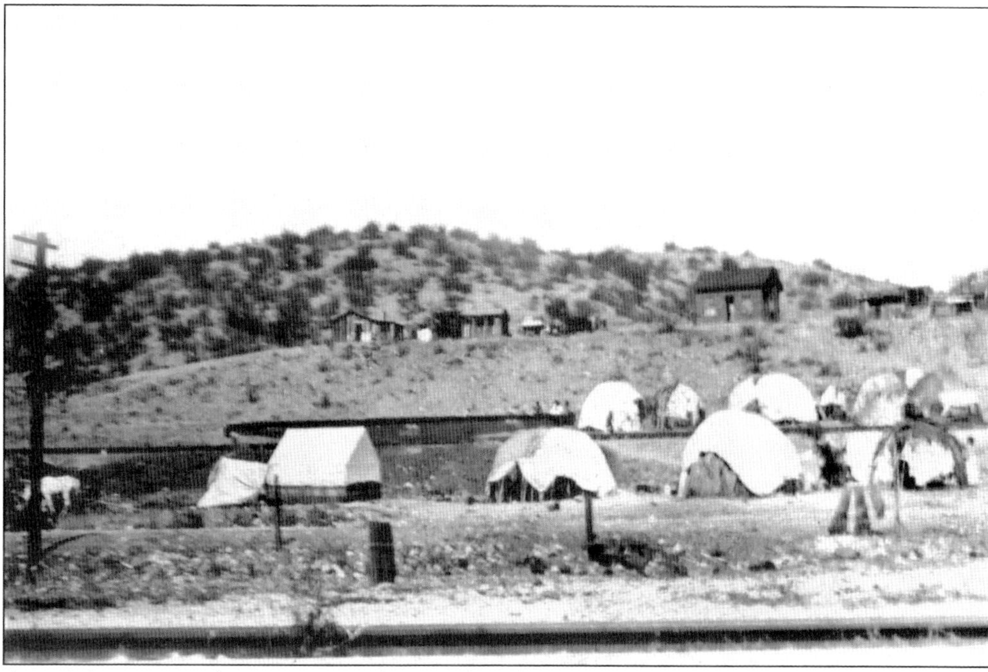

As mobility increased, many San Carlos Apaches chose to leave the reservation for employment in nearby towns. Pictured here is an Apache camp in south Globe around 1910. In 1913, about one-third (715) of San Carlos Apaches were living off the reservation. (Courtesy GCHS, GM 27-11.)

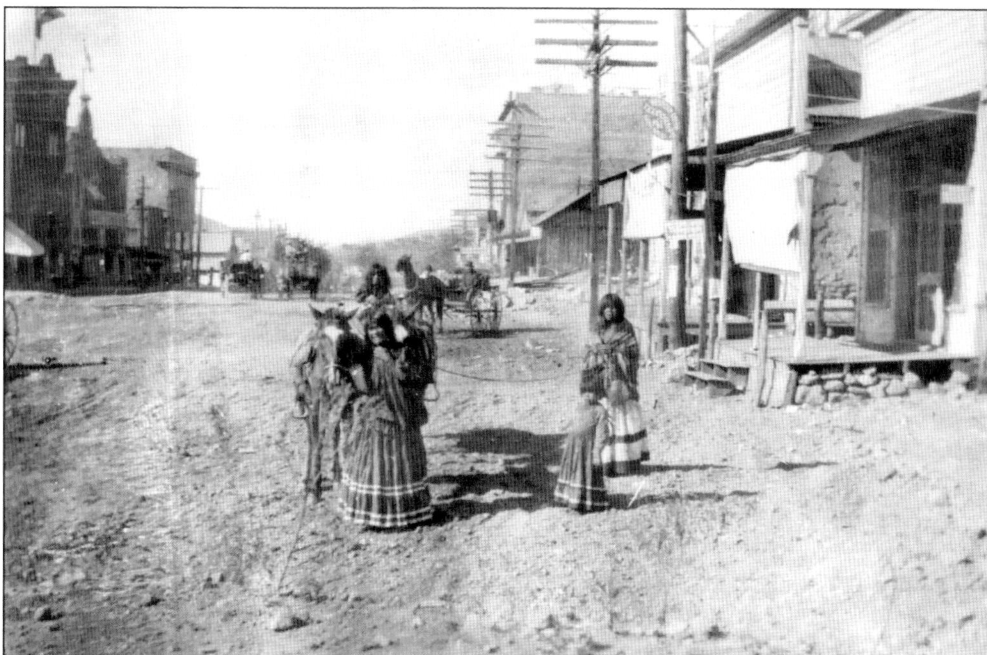

A group of Apaches in traditional dress is seen here on Broad Street in Globe about 1910. In 1927, a survey showed that there were several separate Apache camps in the towns of Globe and nearby Miami, including four camps with 42 families in the former and two camps with 23 families in the latter. (Courtesy GCHS, GM 27-122.)

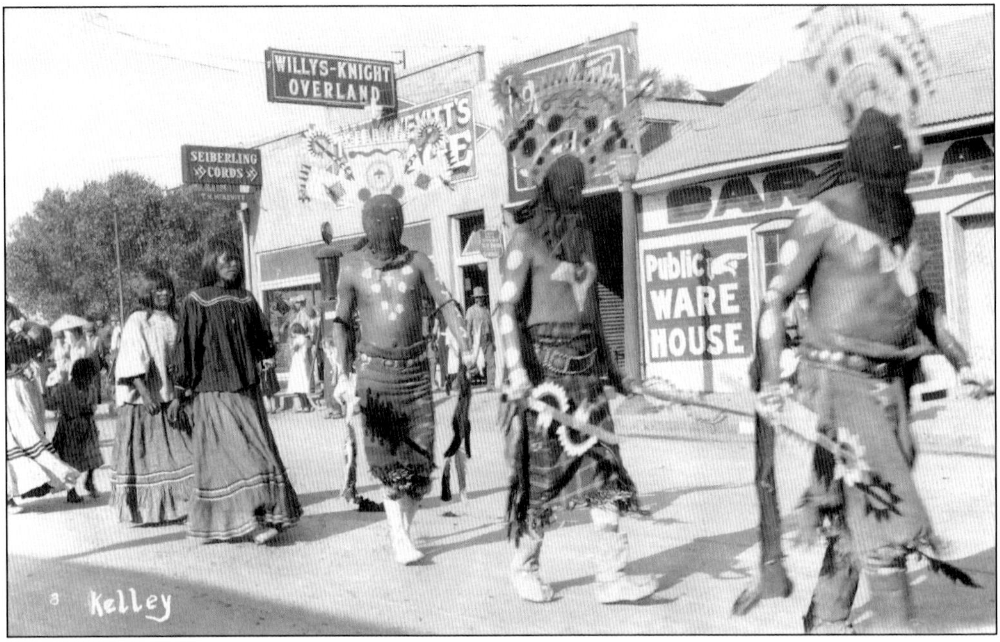

In addition to employment opportunities, San Carlos Apaches also participated in local events such as this parade in Globe in the 1920s. Pictured here are the Apache Crown Dancers that represent mountain spirits, or *gaan*. These dancers traditionally perform at various curing ceremonies or at a girl's puberty ceremony. (Courtesy GCHS, GM 27-75; photograph by Roy F. Kelley.)

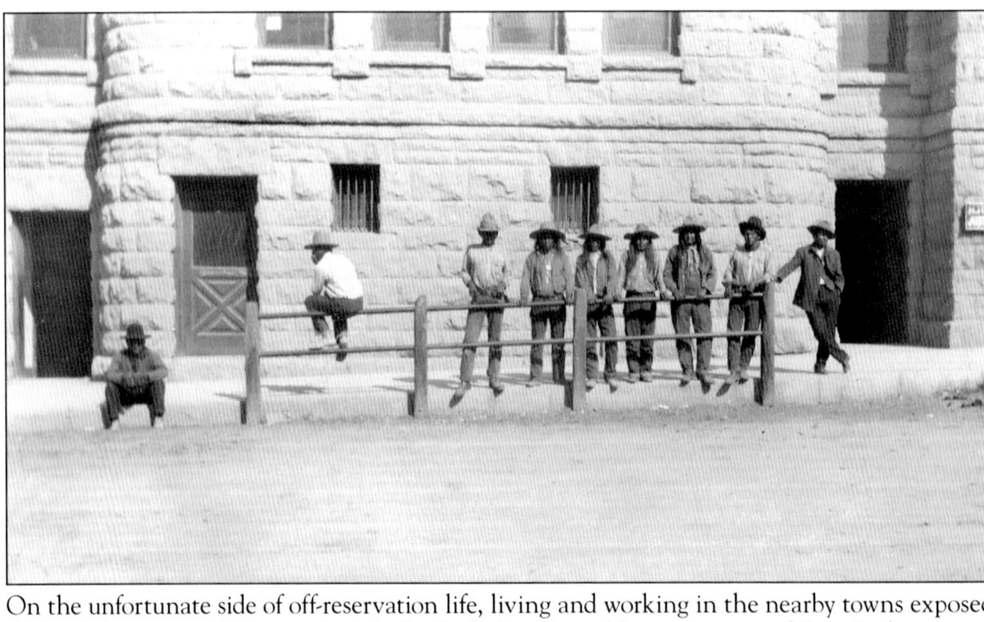
On the unfortunate side of off-reservation life, living and working in the nearby towns exposed the Apaches to local vices, particularly alcohol and gambling. A group of San Carlos men is shown outside the Globe courthouse in this 1910 image. (Courtesy GCHS, GM 36-11.)

Six

Schools and Missions

A schoolhouse was built at San Carlos in 1880, but the effort was quickly abandoned because of a renewal of hostile activities on the reservation. In fact, the building saw more use as temporary quarters for army officers stationed at the nearby camp in the early 1880s than as a school. In the absence of an on-site school, San Carlos students were sent to boarding schools in the East. In 1881, six Apache and Yavapai youngsters were sent to the Hampton Normal and Agricultural Institute in Virginia. With the opening of the Carlisle Indian Industrial School in Pennsylvania about the same time, a few Apache students were initially sent there, followed by another 52 in 1884. Additionally, about 100 Chiricahua children were sent to Carlisle from Florida after the exile of that tribe from San Carlos and Arizona. In all, some 268 Apache students attended Carlisle. Sadly, a far greater number of Apache children than those from other tribes died while at the school, tuberculosis being the culprit in nearly each instance, and are still interred there. The boarding school experience continued for San Carlos children after 1900, but they were sent to schools closer to home—the Phoenix Indian School and other schools in New Mexico, Kansas, and Nebraska.

On the reservation, a boarding school complex was reopened at the agency in the early 1890s, and classes were held regularly until the agency was moved in 1929. A boarding school opened at Rice about 1900 and smaller day schools opened at Peridot and Bylas.

The Wisconsin Synod of the Lutheran Church began missionary work in 1893, but it did not begin in earnest until about a decade later with the construction of a church and small school at Peridot. A Lutheran church was staffed at San Carlos beginning in 1918 under the leadership of Rev. Alfred Uplegger; two years later, a church was built at Bylas. Catholic churches were started at both Bylas and Rice about the same time. The Lutherans also established a mission station in the town of Globe in 1906 for San Carlos Apaches living there.

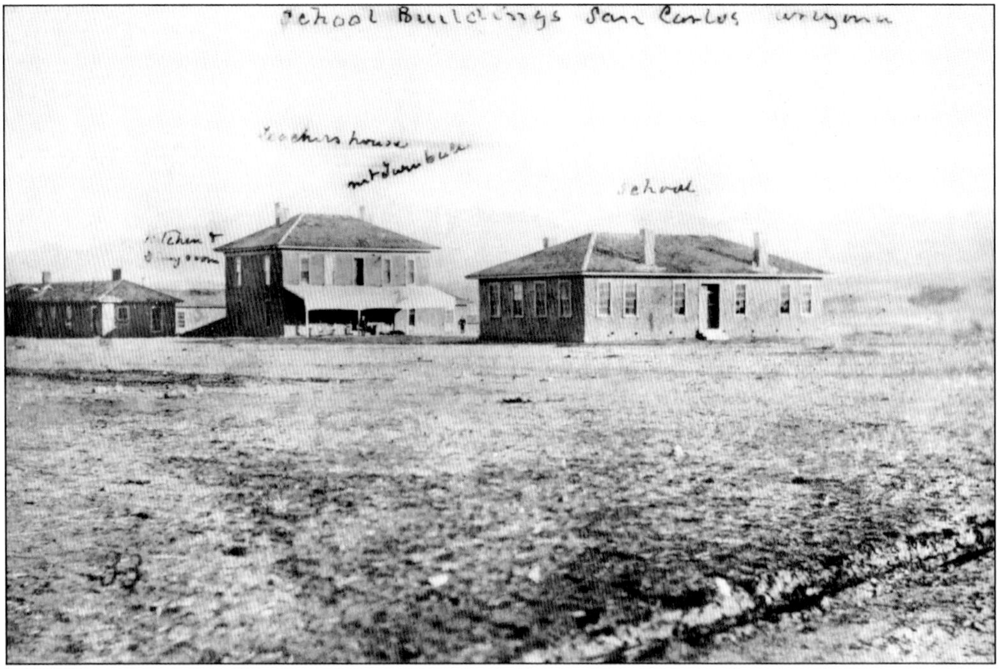

Constructed in 1880–1881, the original school buildings at San Carlos are shown in this 1880s image. The one-story classroom building at right was replaced by a two-story building in the early 1890s. The two buildings at the left burned in 1904. (Courtesy NARA, RG 75, No. 75-IP-2-2.)

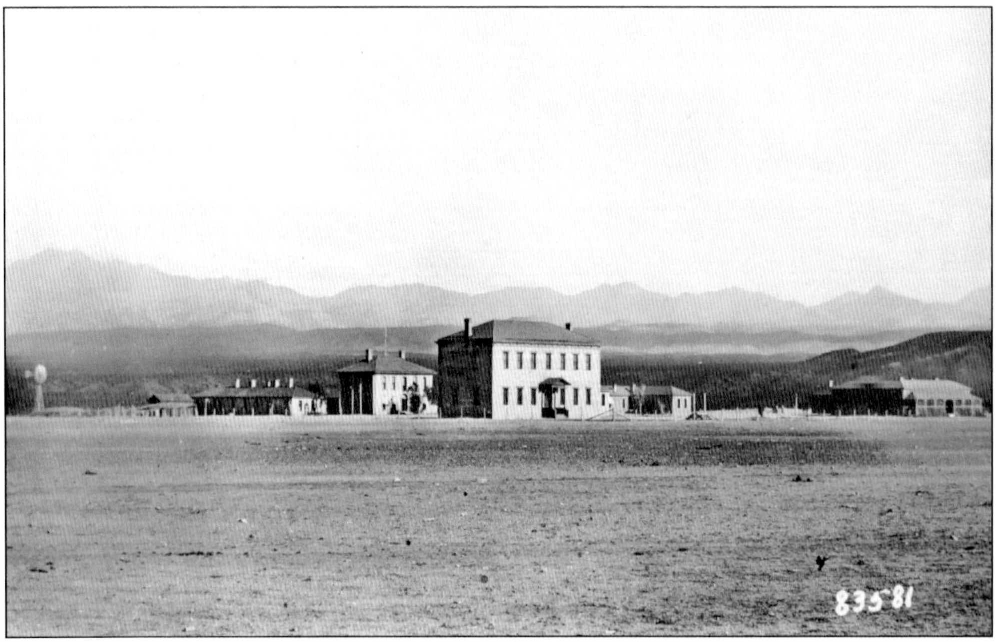

This 1895 photograph of the school buildings at the San Carlos Agency shows the replacement two-story classroom building, along with other buildings of the complex. The school operated as a boarding school until 1900 when, its function replaced by the Rice Boarding School, it became a day school until it closed in the spring of 1929. (Courtesy NARA, RG 111, Signal Corps Collection, No. 83881.)

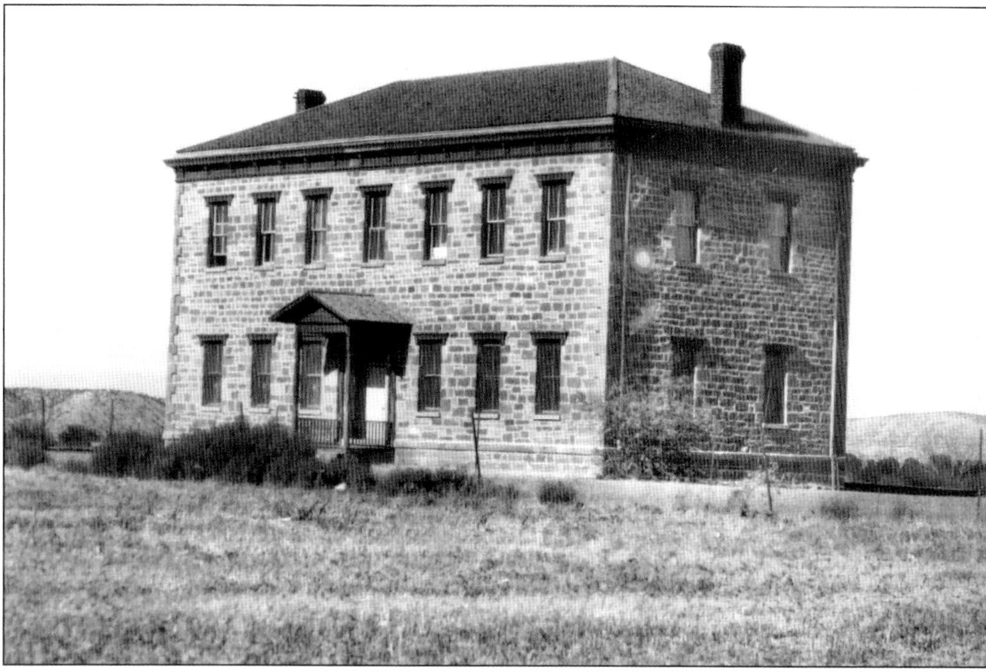

After many of the other school buildings were destroyed by a 1904 fire, the schoolhouse stands alone at San Carlos in the mid-1920s. Due to the opening of the Rice Boarding School and the imminent construction of the Coolidge Dam, the burned buildings were not replaced. This structure was dynamited in 1930. (Courtesy Diane Drobka collection.)

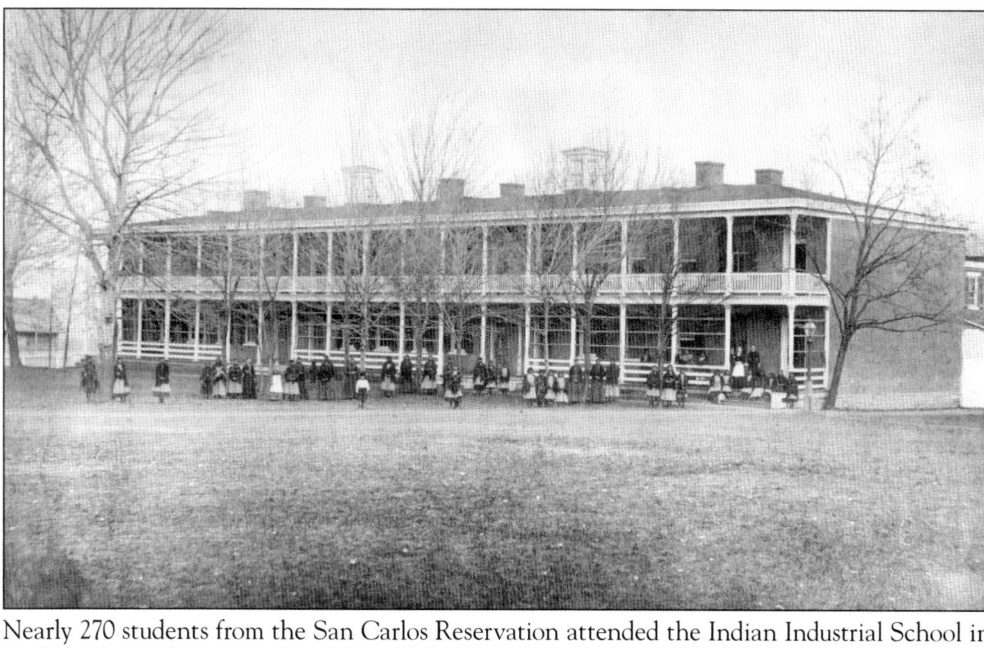

Nearly 270 students from the San Carlos Reservation attended the Indian Industrial School in Carlisle, Pennsylvania, in the 1880s and 1890s. A little over one-third of these were Chiricahua children who had been removed from San Carlos to Florida in 1886. This view from the mid-1880s shows a girls' dormitory at Carlisle. The school operated from 1879 to 1918. (Courtesy NARA, RG 75, No. 75-IP-1-2.)

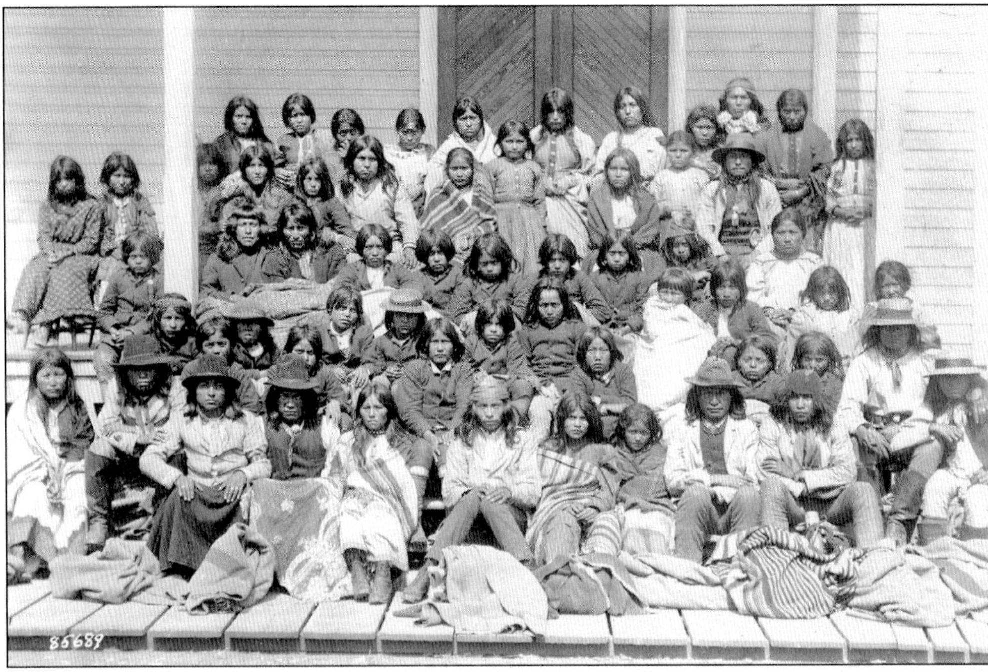

The above photograph shows a large group of Chiricahua students as they arrived at the Carlisle school from Florida in the spring of 1887. Below is how they appeared after four months of training at the school. A smaller contingent of students had arrived in November of the previous year. A total of 106 Chiricahua students were sent to the school in 1886–1887; by 1895, one hundred twelve Chiricahuas had attended the school. Of this number, 37, or one-third, died there and remain buried on the former school grounds. In nearly every instance, the cause of death was communicable tuberculosis. (Above, courtesy NARA, RG 111, Signal Corps Collection, No. 85689; below, courtesy NARA, RG 111, Signal Corps Collection, No. 86692.)

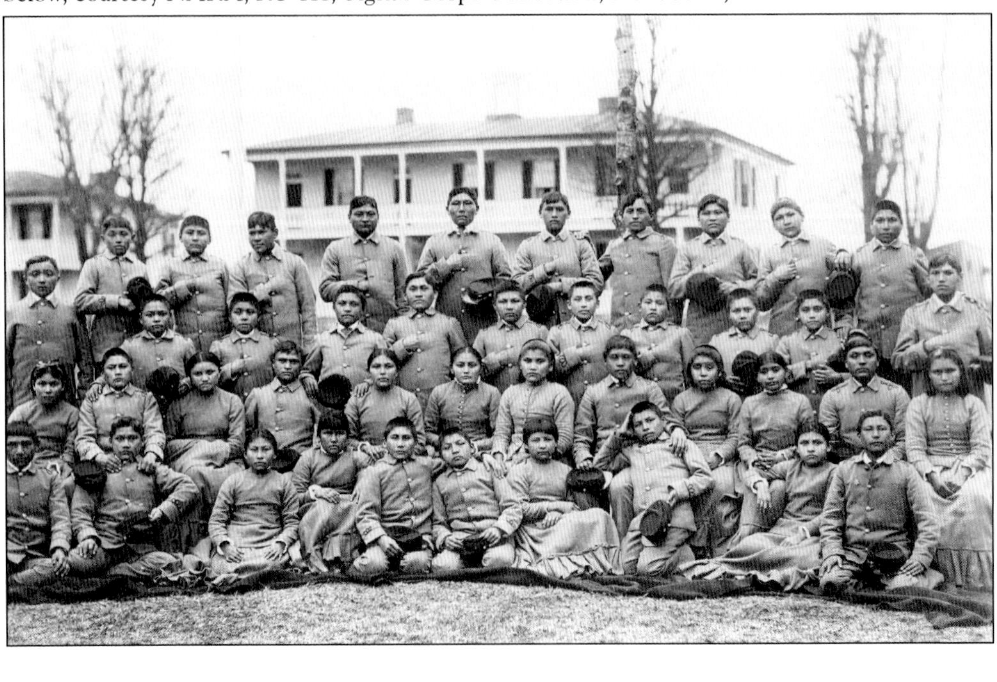

This photograph portrays two San Carlos Reservation boys, Owen Fire (Tonto Apache), left, and Festus Pelone (San Carlos Apache). Fire attended Carlisle from 1884 to 1886. He died there on June 26, 1886, and is buried in the school cemetery. Pelone was at Carlisle from 1884 to 1893. After returning to San Carlos, he was employed in 1912 as a night watchman at the Rice Boarding School. (Courtesy CCHS, No. PA CH1-066c; photograph by John N. Choate.)

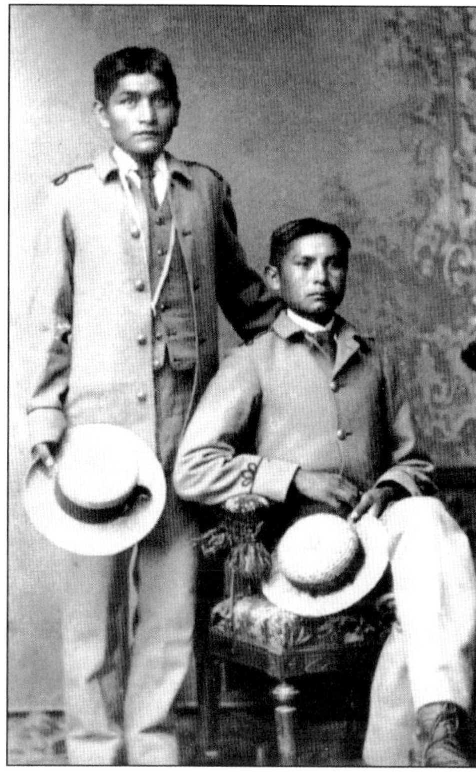

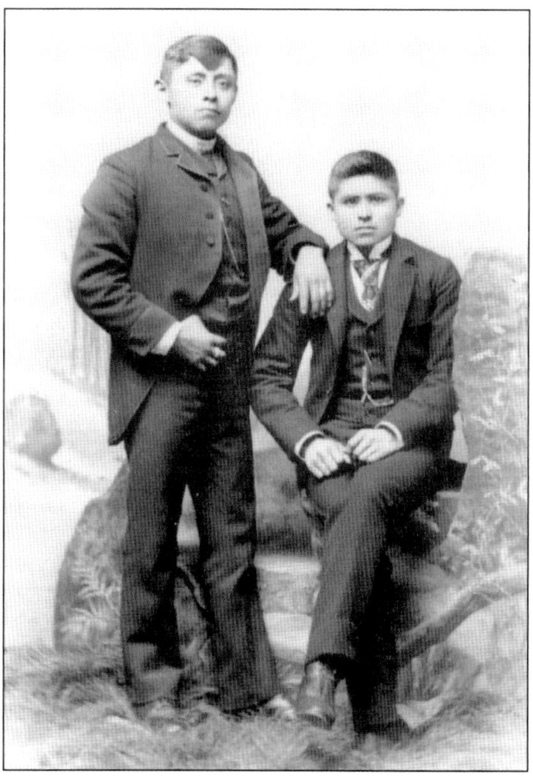

This school photograph shows Job Hunter Boy (a Tonto Apache at Carlisle, 1884–1891), left, and Norman Cassadore (Too-nas-sah, a San Carlos Apache at Carlisle, 1884–1892 and readmitted 1892–1896). Hunter Boy married a Chiricahua woman and moved to Fort Sill, Oklahoma, while Cassadore returned to San Carlos and became a farmer. Cassadore's brother Albert died at Carlisle in 1888 and is buried there. (Courtesy CCHS, CS CH No. 051; photograph by John N. Choate.)

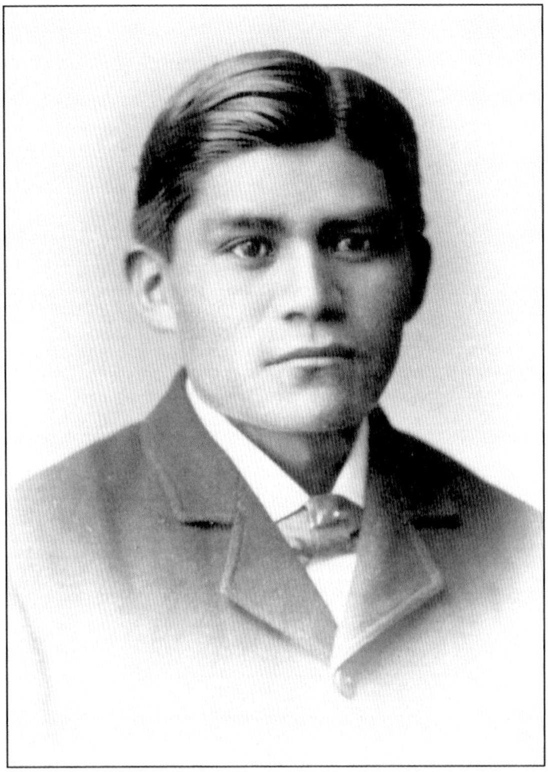

Mike Burns (Hoo-mo-thya), a Kwevkepaya Yavapai, was born around 1865. Adopted in 1872 by an Anglo army officer, Capt. James Burns, Mike attended Carlisle from 1880 to 1884. Returning to San Carlos, he worked as a scout and interpreter until 1894. After 1900, he spent his years at the Fort McDowell Reservation writing a lengthy history of his people before passing away in 1934. (Courtesy CCHS, No. PA CH1-073d; photograph by John N. Choate.)

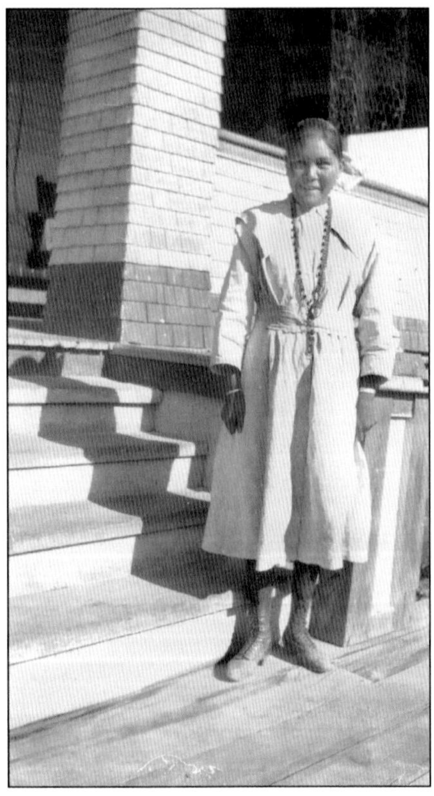

A San Carlos Apache student is shown in this 1924 photograph returning from an off-reservation school. The agency superintendent observed at the time that practically all the returning girls reverted to a traditional way of life, while returning boys took up industrial lines of work. (Courtesy NARA, RG 75.)

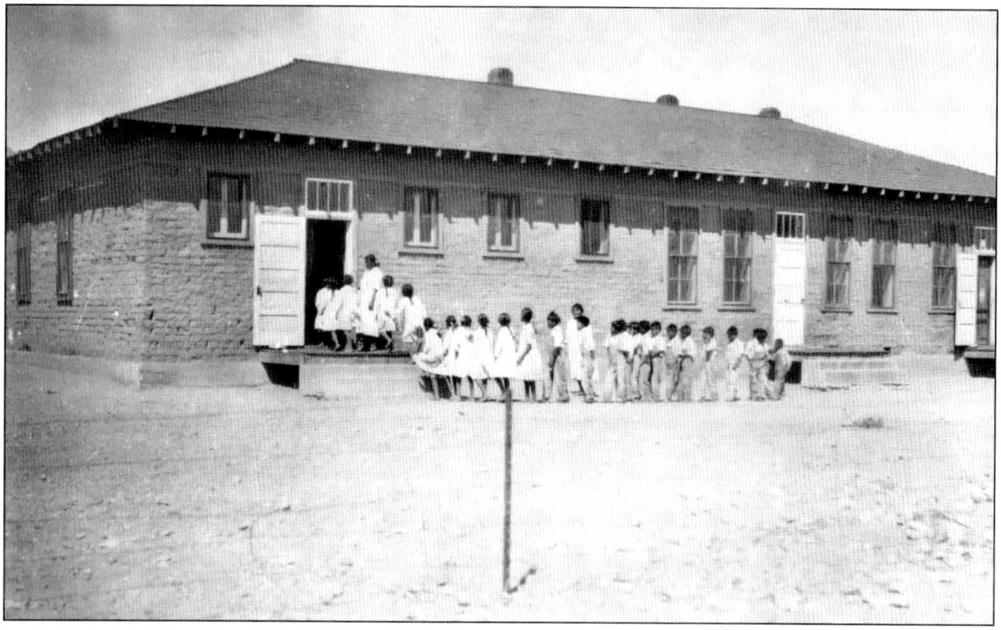

In 1913, Apaches living in the Bylas area petitioned for a day school. The following year, a schoolhouse with a 50-student capacity, a laundry, and a teacher's cottage were constructed. The school operated until 1925, when it closed and was taken over and run by the Lutheran Church. (Courtesy Diane Drobka collection; photograph probably by Gracie Taylor.)

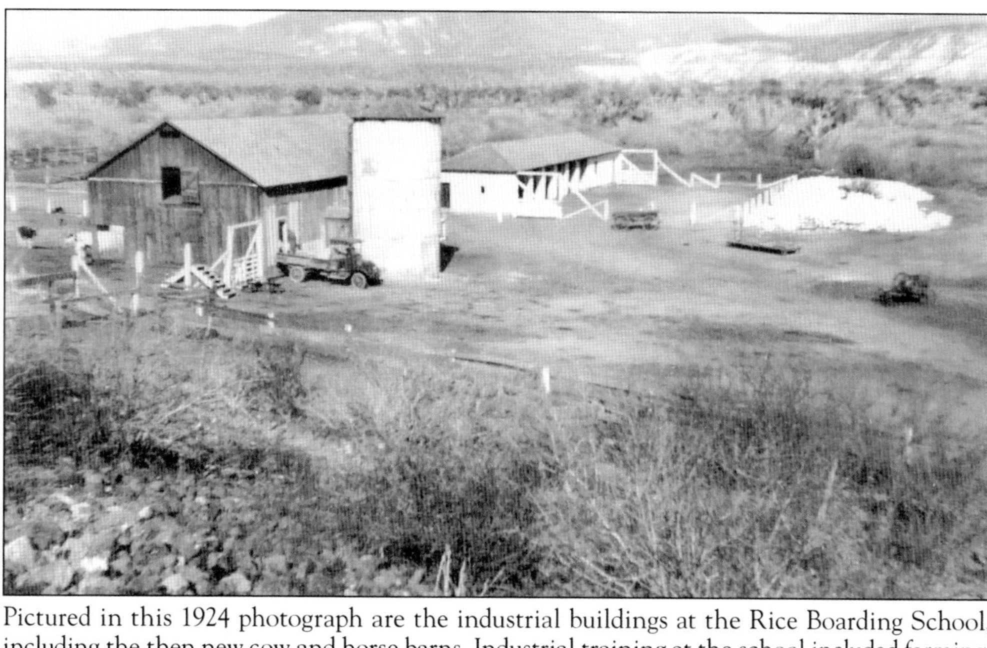

Pictured in this 1924 photograph are the industrial buildings at the Rice Boarding School, including the then new cow and horse barns. Industrial training at the school included farming, dairying, and mechanical trades. Male students also assisted in the upkeep of the school and repair work. (Courtesy NARA, RG 75.)

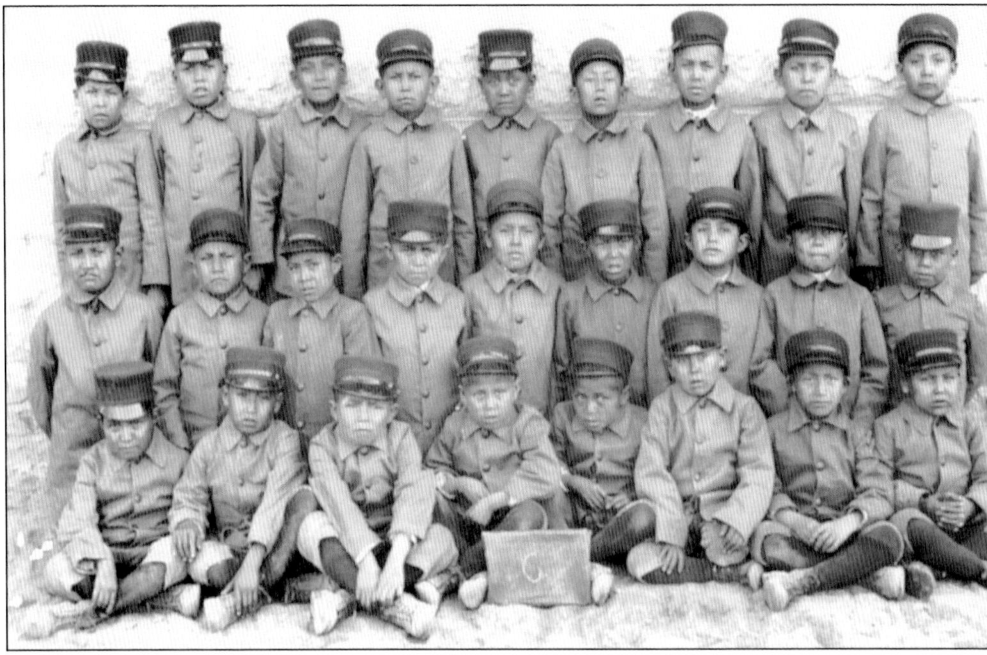

The Rice Boarding School, located at Talklai, opened in 1900. The school was situated about three-quarters of a mile from the Gila Valley, Globe, and Northern Railroad depot, and was named for Lt. Sedgwick Rice, acting Indian agent at San Carlos in 1898, who helped negotiate the agreement for the crossing of the reservation by the rail line. By 1906, the school was filled to capacity with 216 Apache students. The physical layout included two large dormitories, one for boys and one for girls; a school building with four classrooms; and a chapel. The school farm consisted of 60 irrigated acres, where all the hay for the school was raised, along with large crops of fruit and vegetables. Two uniformed Rice Boarding School classes are shown in these photographs, probably from the early 1920s. (Above, courtesy ASUL, Francis J. Uplegger Collection, CPSPC 187.14; below, courtesy ASUL, Francis J. Uplegger Collection, CPSPC 187.89.)

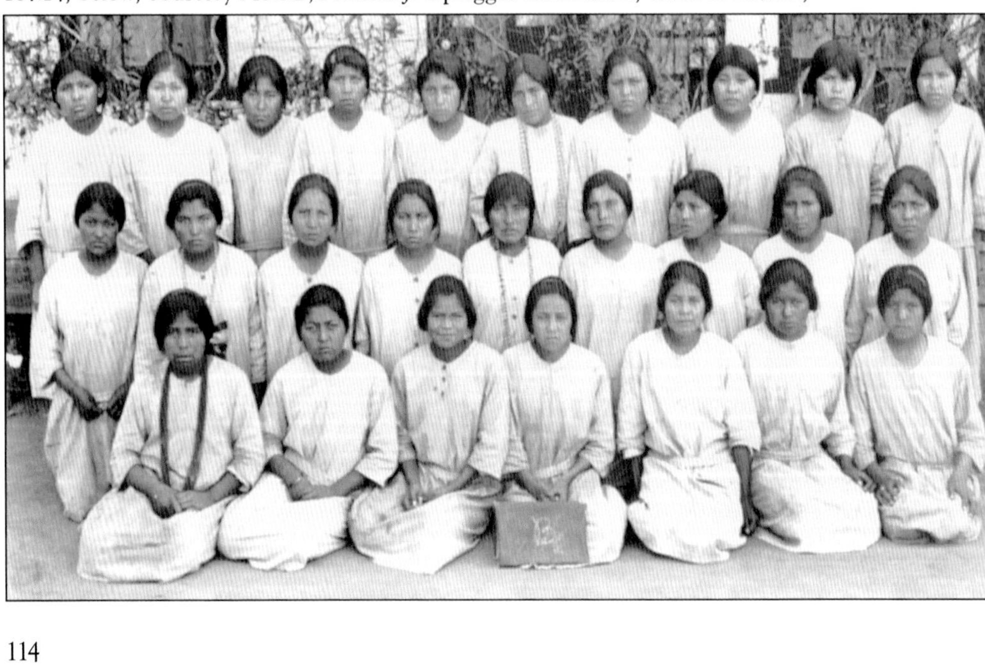

After 1915, the Lutheran mission work at San Carlos was in the hands of the Uplegger family. Pictured here at Peridot, probably in 1941, are, from left to right, Henry E. Rosin and his wife, Johanna (Uplegger) Rosin; Dr. Francis J. Uplegger; Dorthea Uplegger; and Alfred M. Uplegger. Alfred was pastor of the church at Old San Carlos. (Courtesy ASUL, Francis J. Uplegger Collection, CPSPC 187.25.)

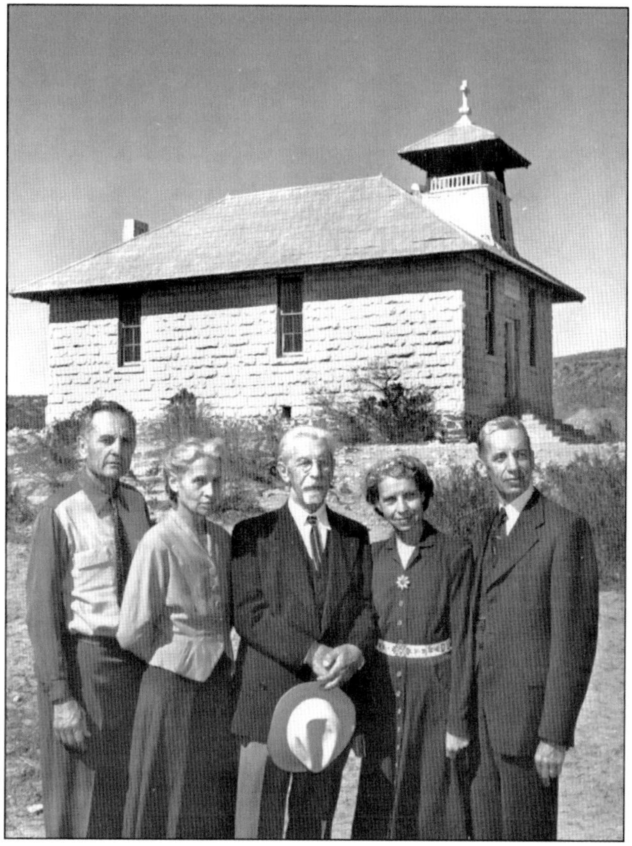

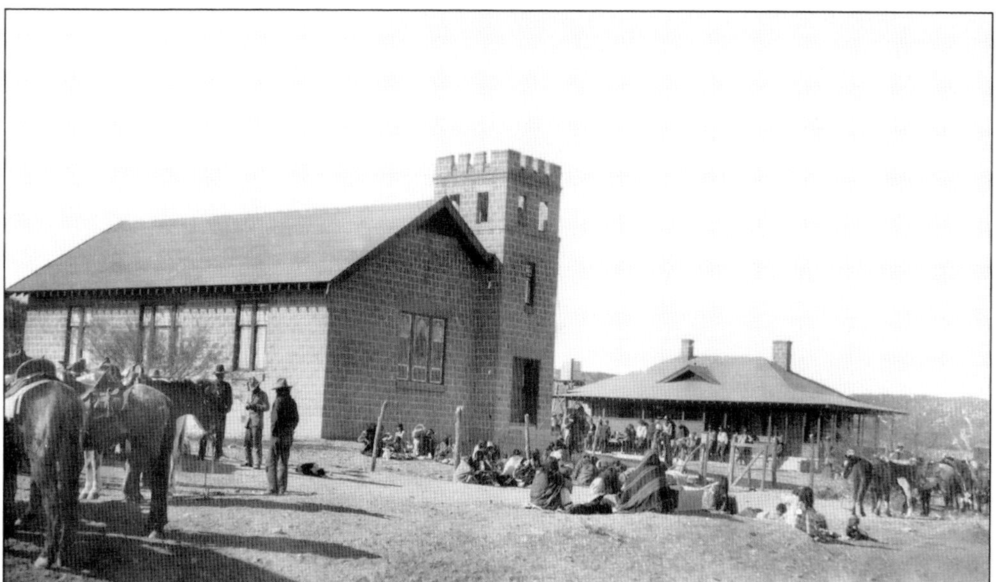

This photograph was taken at the dedication of the Lutheran church at Bylas in 1922, following completion of the church and house buildings. Rev. Gustav Schlegel was the pastor. (Courtesy Diane Drobka collection.)

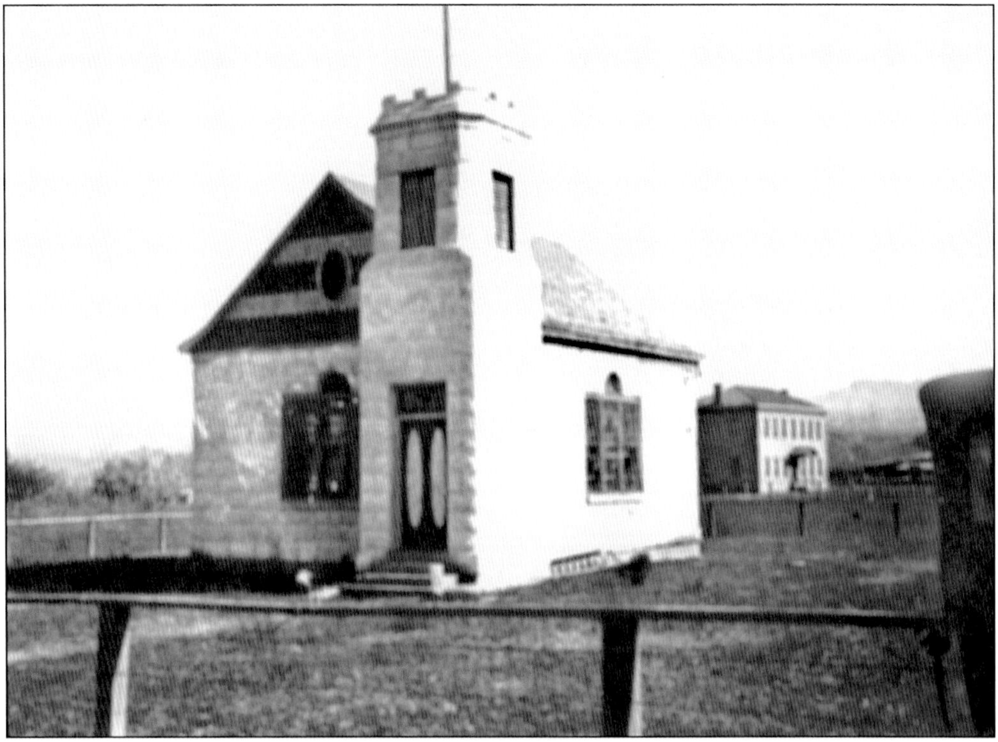

In 1910, four acres at the agency were reserved for the Lutherans. The chapel was built in 1911, apparently at government expense since it was used for services accommodating Apache students at the San Carlos school, which can be seen in the background at right. The church was quickly turned over to the Lutherans and, initially, was served by pastors from Peridot Station. (Courtesy ASUL, Francis J. Uplegger Collection, CPSPC 187.3.18.)

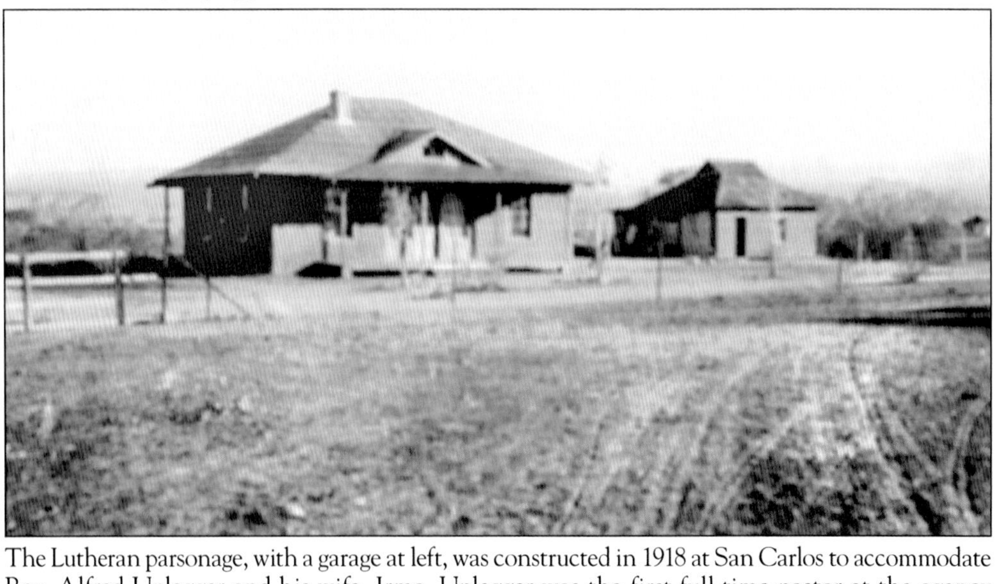

The Lutheran parsonage, with a garage at left, was constructed in 1918 at San Carlos to accommodate Rev. Alfred Uplegger and his wife, Irma. Uplegger was the first full-time pastor at the agency locale, even though the Lutherans had been conducting services there for several years. (Courtesy ASUL, Francis J. Uplegger Collection, CPSPC 187.3.17.)

Seven

The End of Old San Carlos

The plight of the Pima tribe living on the Gila River Reservation just southeast of Phoenix had been acutely recognized since the 1880s. For centuries, their economy had been heavily dependent on a farming subsistence base. By the end of the 19th century, it had become precarious because the Gila River flow had been greatly diminished by Anglo farming developments east of the San Carlos Reservation. Studies by the U.S. Geological Survey to identify potential reservoir sites around 1900 pointed to the most suitable spot for a dam—at a rocky constriction of the Gila River, located about seven miles below the San Carlos Agency. Over the strong objections of the San Carlos Apaches, site characterization studies continued, and in 1924, the U.S. Congress appropriated about 22,000 acres of San Carlos tribal land for the dam and reservoir.

Aside from the loss of significant tribal acreage and much of the arable land, which was in short supply on the reservation, the greatest resentment perhaps was over the fact that the agency itself and many Apache homes and farmsteads would be inundated. In truth, the agency and its environs were never a hospitable setting, but for some 55 years, it was the only homeland that most had known, and there were hundreds of ancestors buried in the agency cemeteries and along the adjoining washes and draws.

Coolidge Dam was completed in October 1928 after offering temporary employment to several hundred San Carlos men. The agency was moved to Rice the following spring. Some of the stone buildings were dismantled and moved to the new location; the remaining ones, particularly the large stone warehouses—the place of hundreds of ration days—and the two-story school building, were dynamited on February 16, 1930. Negotiations between the Apaches and the federal government resulted in nearly 200 of the Apache graves being moved to a cemetery at Peridot. Following the wishes of Apache elders, a large cemetery containing approximately 300 graves was covered in place with a concrete slab of about one and a half acres. It contained 500 cubic yards of grout.

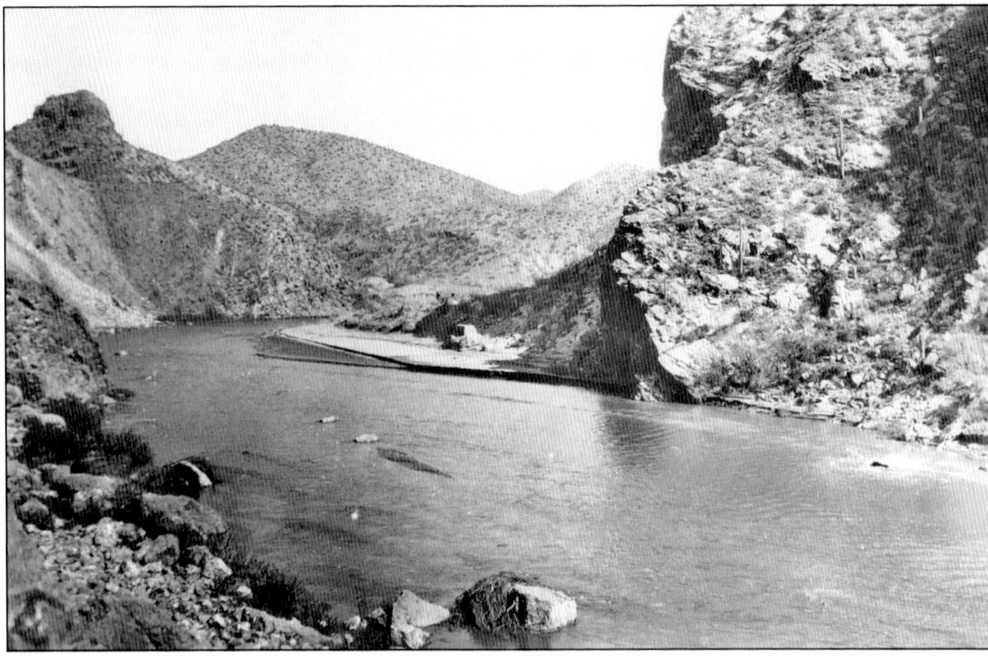

Studies began in 1896 to find a storage reservoir locale on the middle Gila River reach. The site finally selected was located about seven miles below the mouth of the San Carlos River where the Gila enters the San Carlos Box Canyon, the upper end of which was the dam site. (Courtesy Diane Drobka collection.)

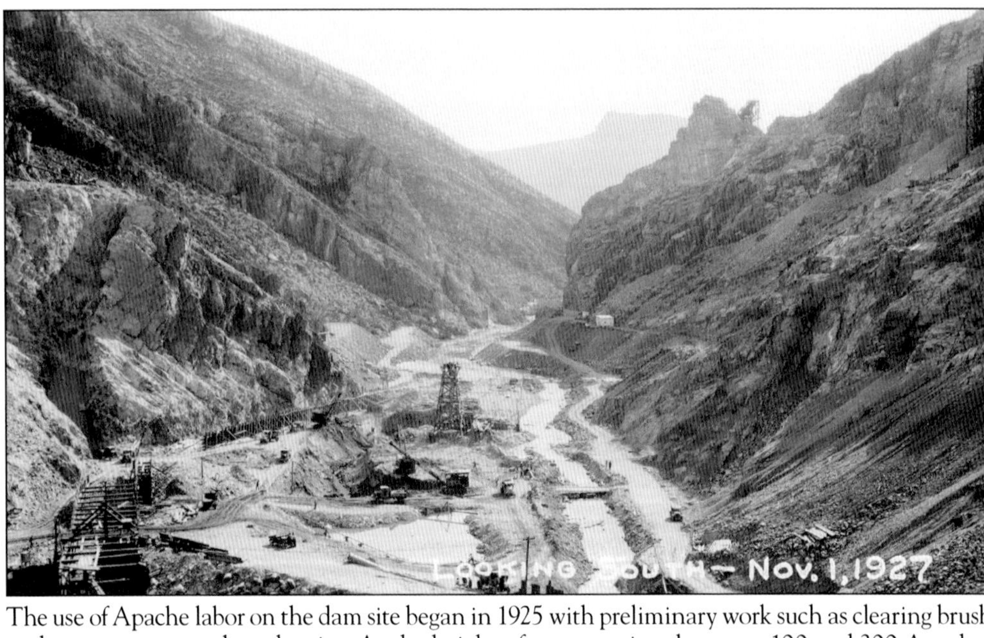

The use of Apache labor on the dam site began in 1925 with preliminary work such as clearing brush and as carpenters and mechanics. At the height of construction, between 100 and 300 Apaches were employed, performing unskilled to highly skilled labor. (Courtesy NARA, RG 75.)

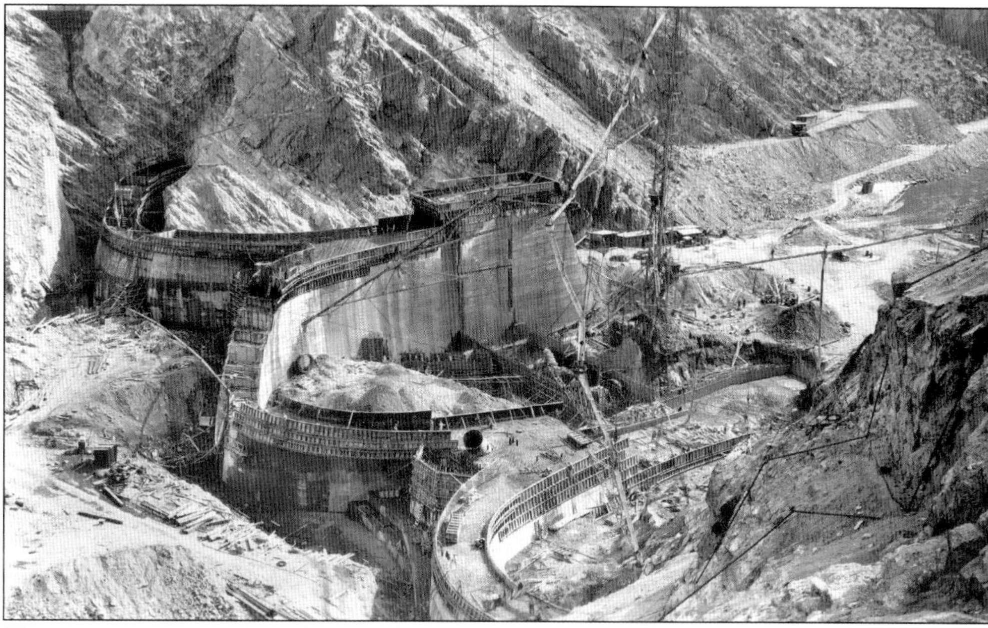

This construction-progress photograph from February 1928 shows concrete being placed at the downstream end of the west main buttress of the Coolidge Dam. (Courtesy NARA, RG 75.)

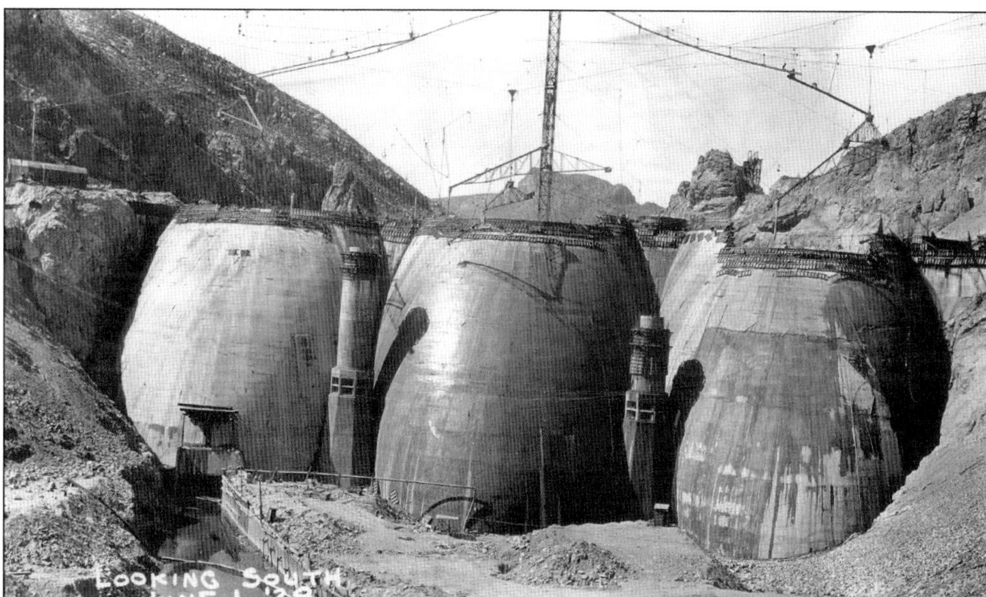

By June 1, 1928, construction of the three domes was reaching completion, as shown in this upstream view of the structure looking south, or downriver. (Courtesy NARA, RG 75.)

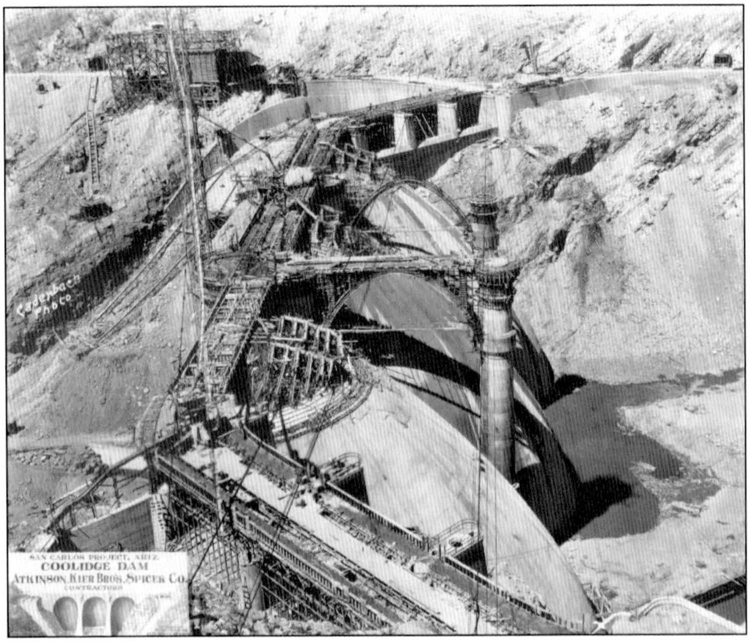

In this construction-sequence photograph looking west across the dam as it nears completion, the twin tower intakes can be seen to the right of the dam, and construction is progressing on the west spillway at the upper left. (Courtesy GCHS, GM 33-13.)

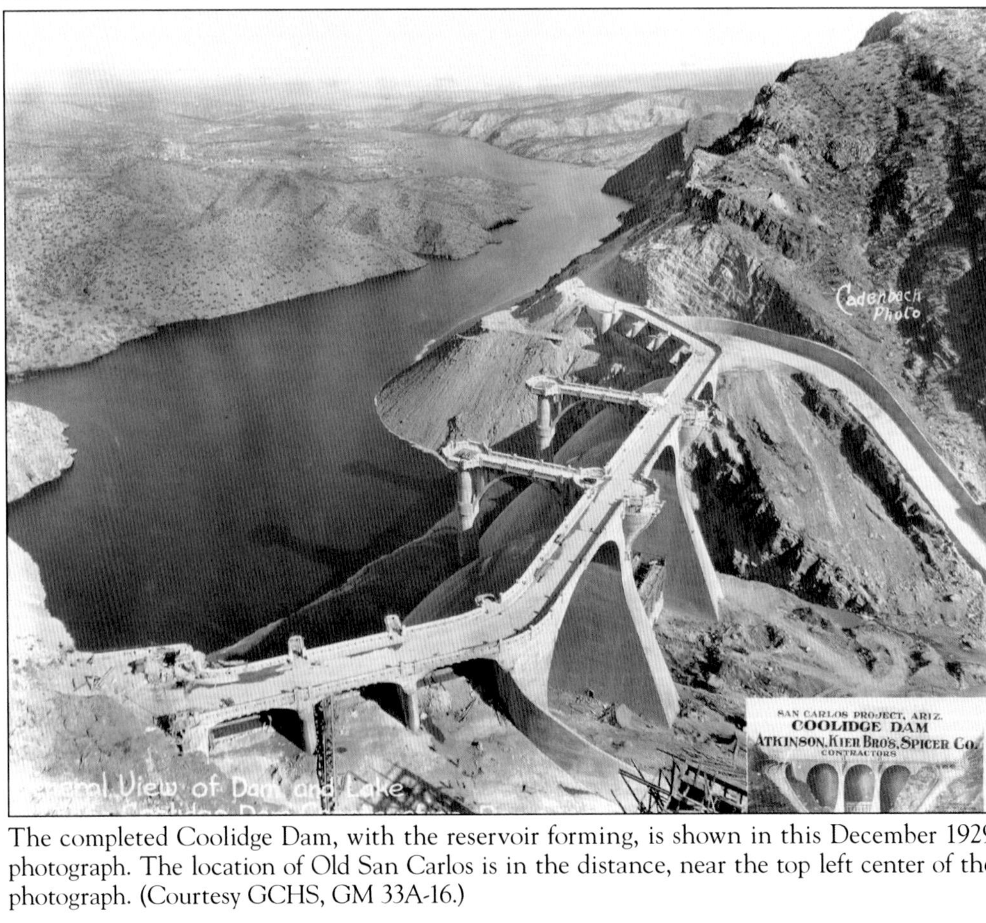

The completed Coolidge Dam, with the reservoir forming, is shown in this December 1929 photograph. The location of Old San Carlos is in the distance, near the top left center of the photograph. (Courtesy GCHS, GM 33A-16.)

When completed, Coolidge Dam included 205,000 cubic yards of concrete and 3,500 tons of reinforcing steel. The reservoir, when full, would be 23 miles long and would contain 1,200,000 acre feet of water, which would be used to irrigate some 100,000 acres of land downriver. (Courtesy GCHS, GM 33A-8.)

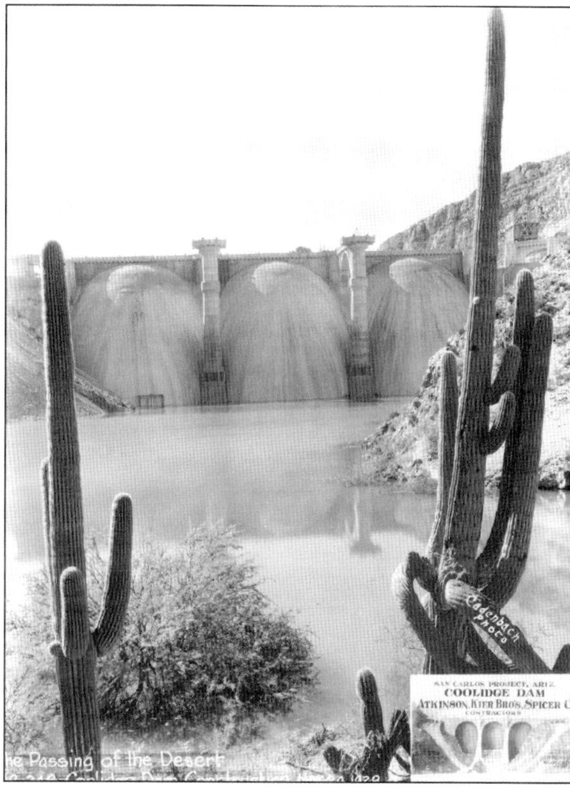

The dedication of Coolidge Dam was held on March 4, 1930, and was attended by former U.S. president Calvin Coolidge, Arizona governor John Phillips, and satirist Will Rogers. In addition to the compulsory speeches, 3,000 attendees also witnessed a ceremonial smoking of the peace pipe by members of the Pima and San Carlos Apache tribes. (Courtesy GCHS, GM 33-53.)

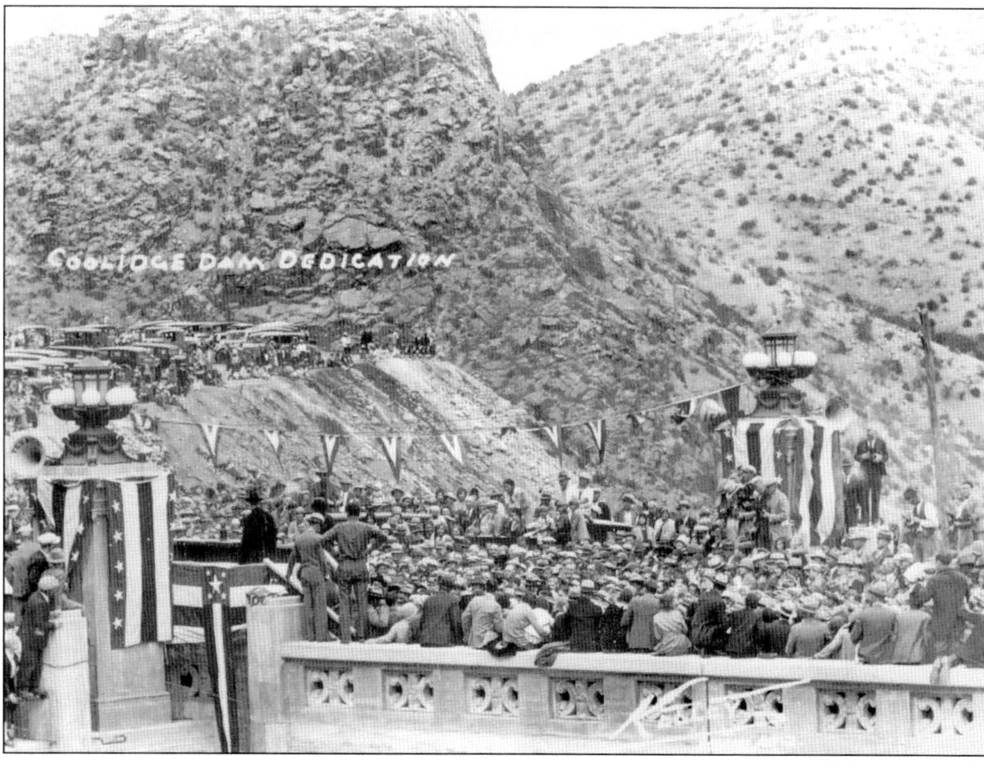

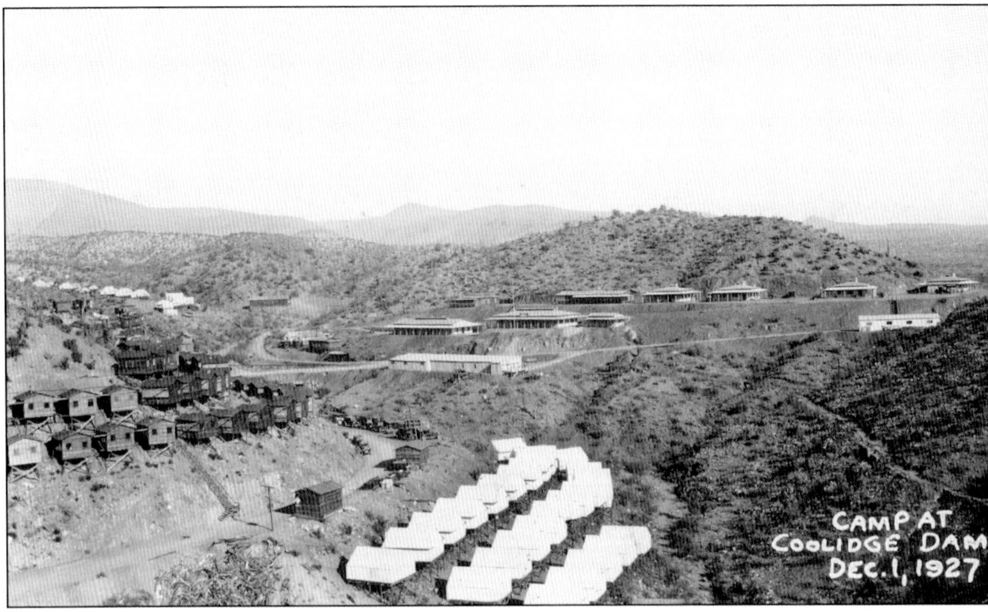

The construction camp, built in 1927, included 50 wood-frame family dwellings with running water and electricity. Single men were housed in bunkhouses and tent houses. A number of the frame houses were purchased by the Indian Service in 1929 to be sold to Apache families and placed on their new farms after relocation. (Courtesy GCHS, GM 33-19.)

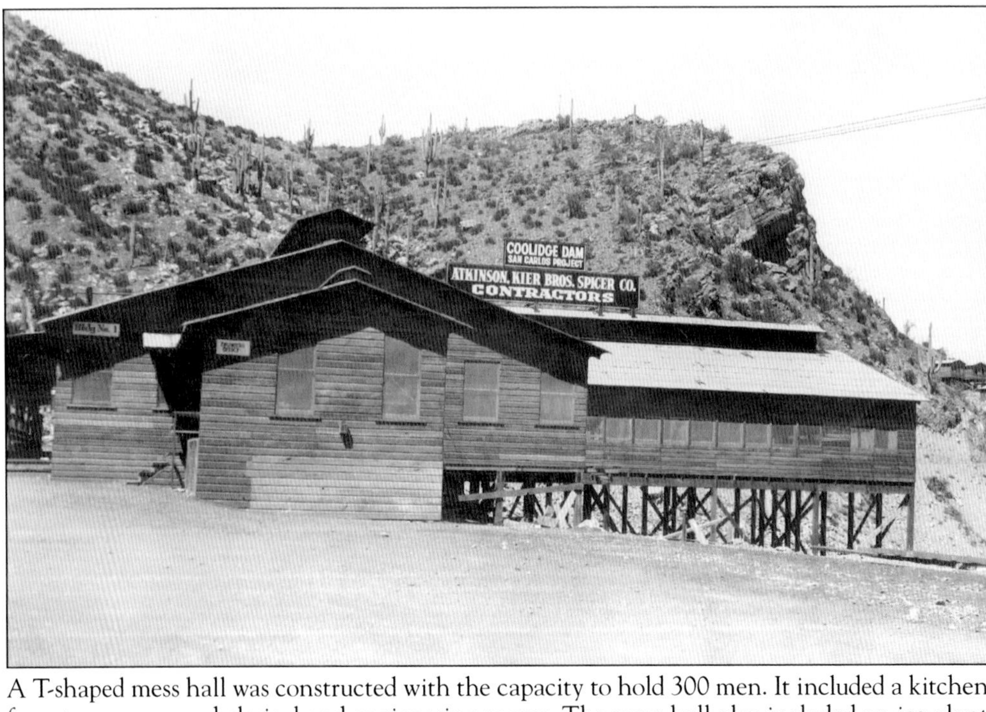

A T-shaped mess hall was constructed with the capacity to hold 300 men. It included a kitchen, four storerooms, and clerical and engineering rooms. The mess hall also included an ice plant, which had a daily capacity of 8,000 pounds. (Courtesy Diane Drobka collection.)

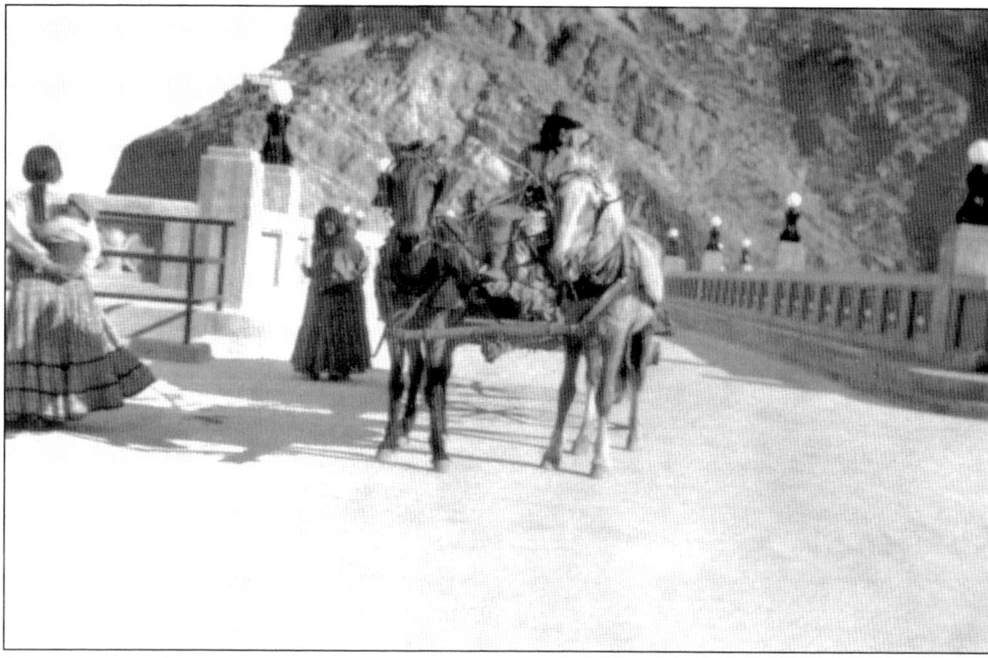

Unfortunately, the San Carlos Apaches gained little positive long-term value from the constructed dam, save for a new place and manner for crossing the Gila River, as seen in this 1929 photograph. Since the 1960s, the tribe has developed recreational facilities and opportunities at the San Carlos Lake. (GCHS, GM 33-75A.)

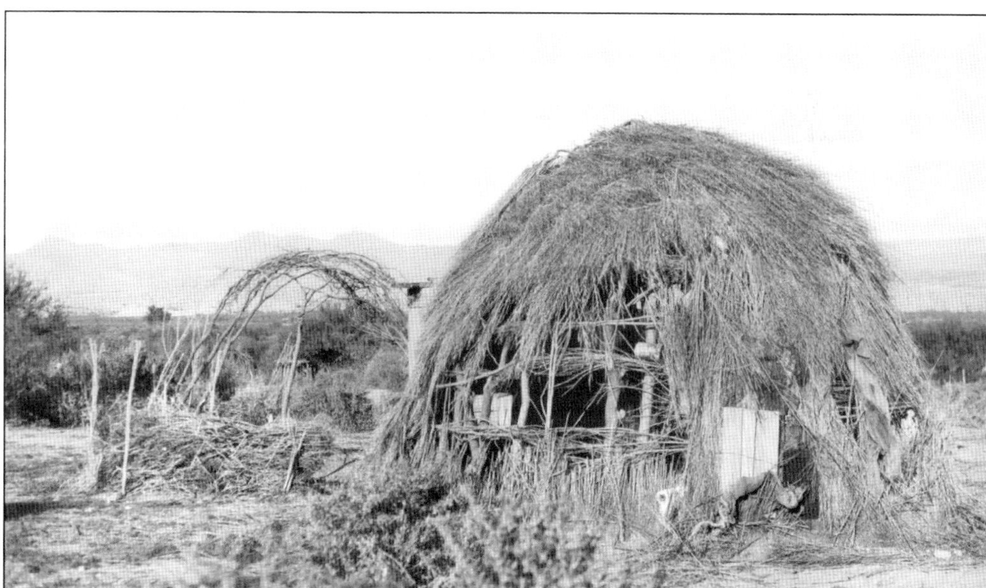

Government estimates of the damages to the San Carlos Apaches from the reservoir included 190 homes, 645 Apache people directly affected, and the loss of 564 acres of farmed land and 2,013 acres of grazing land. Wickiups to be abandoned were assessed a value of $20; frame houses from $100 to $250. (Courtesy Diane Drobka collection.)

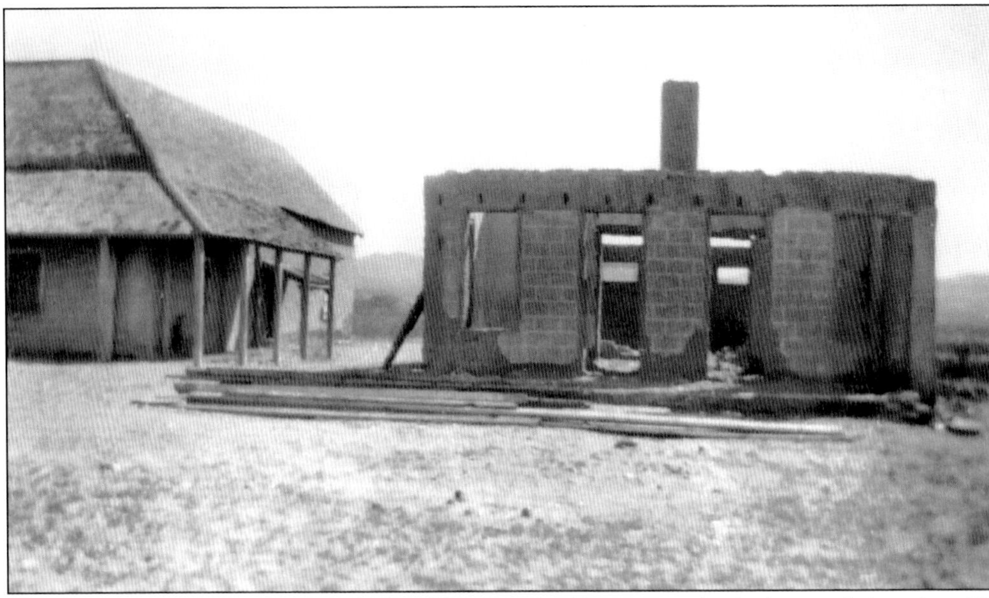

As the dam was being constructed, the old agency buildings were slowly dismantled, and usable architectural features were removed for the new agency. Buildings that could not be easily moved were left behind to be destroyed prior to inundation. (Courtesy GCHS, GM 27-19.)

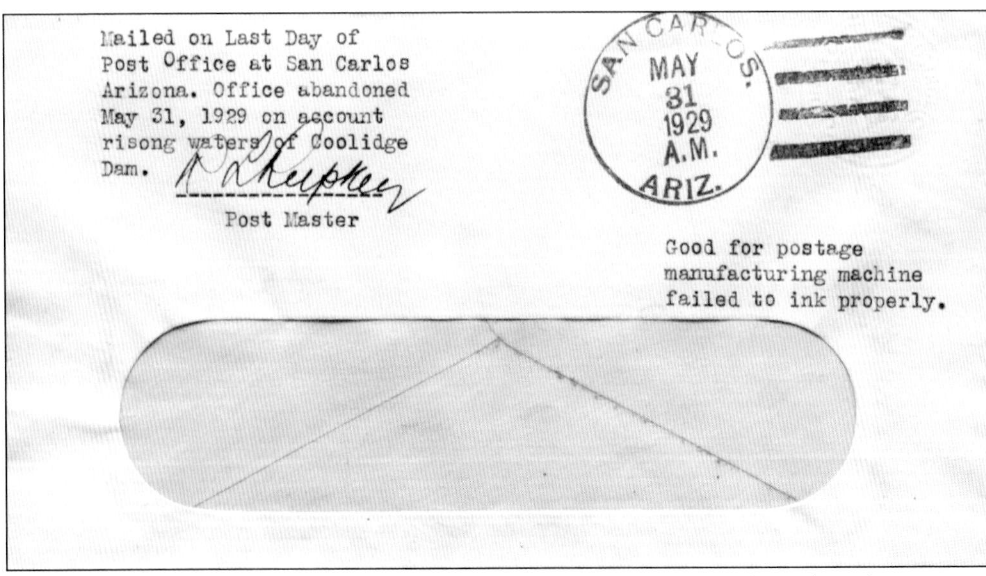

The Old San Carlos Post Office formally closed on May 31, 1929, as indicated on this image of an envelope mailed by postmaster R. L. Rupkey as part of his last official duties. For a time, there was a fear that the name "San Carlos" would be appropriated by an Anglo community several miles away, but it was taken to the new agency location. (Courtesy authors' collection.)

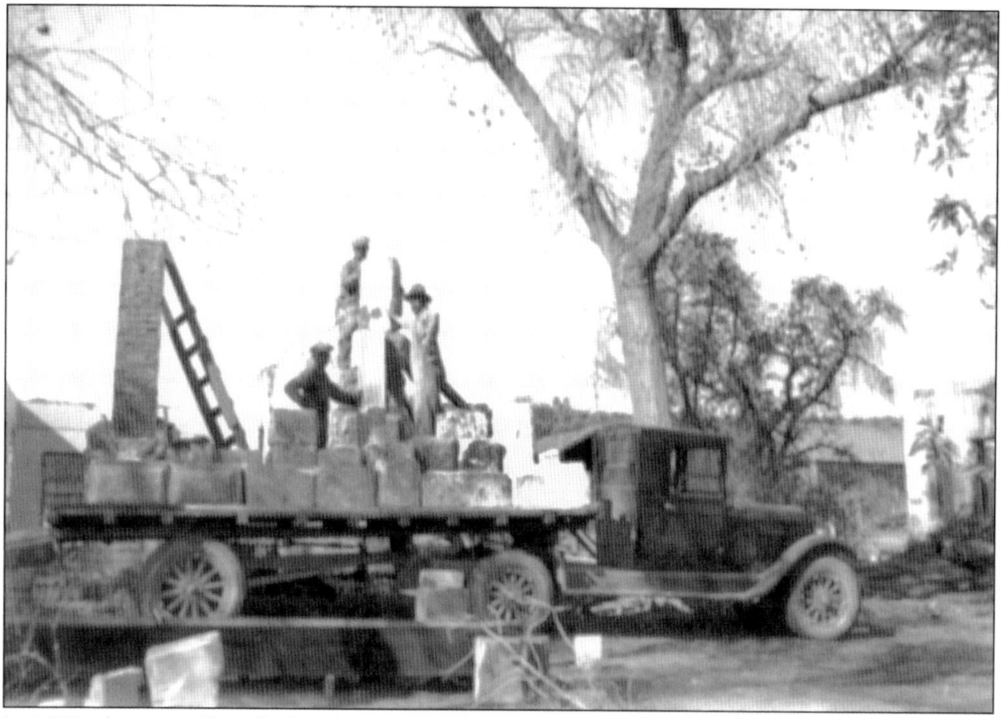

In 1929, the stone San Carlos Agency employees' houses (the former officers' dwellings) were dismantled and reconstructed at the new agency location. (Courtesy ASUL, Forrest Doucette Collection, SPC 94:4.211.)

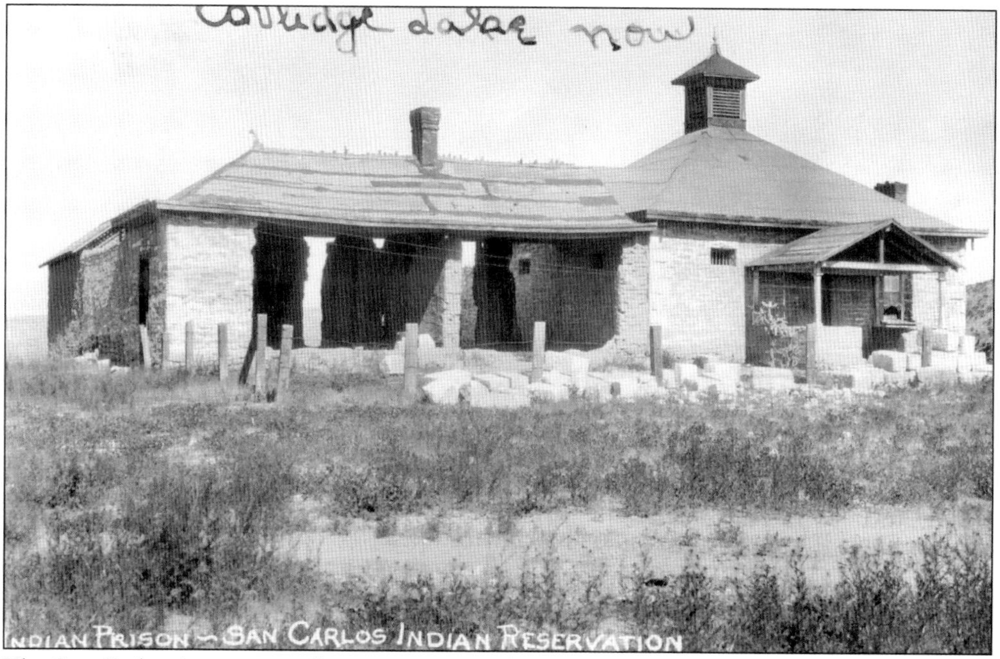

The San Carlos Agency guardhouse, constructed in the early 1890s to replace the former adobe structure that had held Geronimo and many others in the 1870s and 1880s, was left behind. It was among the structures dynamited on February 16, 1930. (Courtesy GCHS, GM 27-56.)

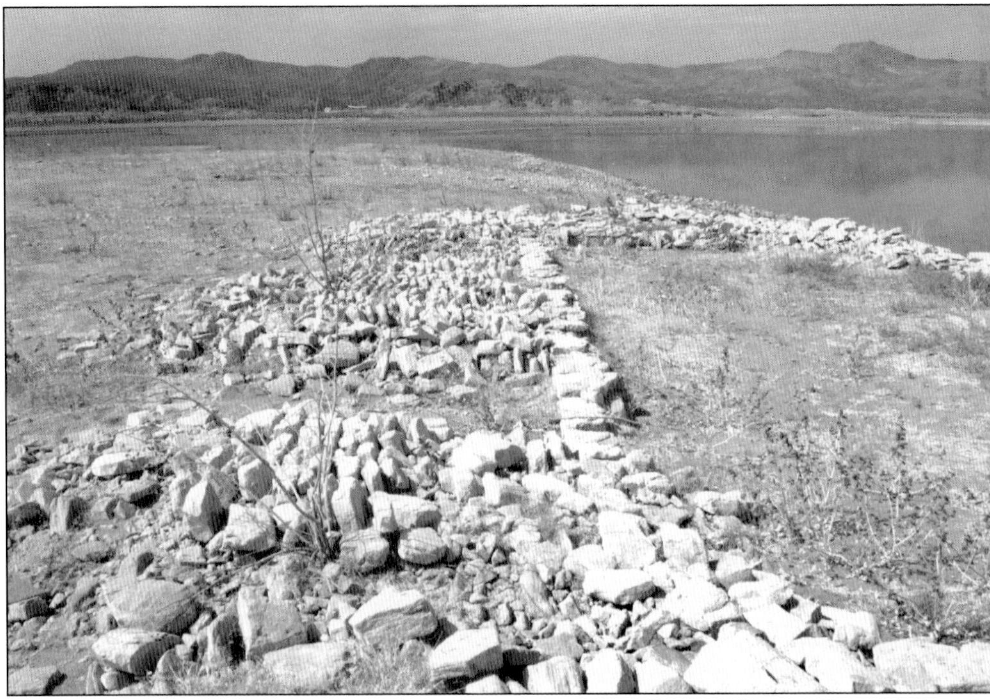

When razed in 1930, the Old San Carlos Indian Agency guardhouse's front walls toppled to the left, as shown in the photograph, retaining the original masonry courses. Note the doorway in the center of the wall. (Courtesy authors' collection; photograph by Paul Nickens, 2001.)

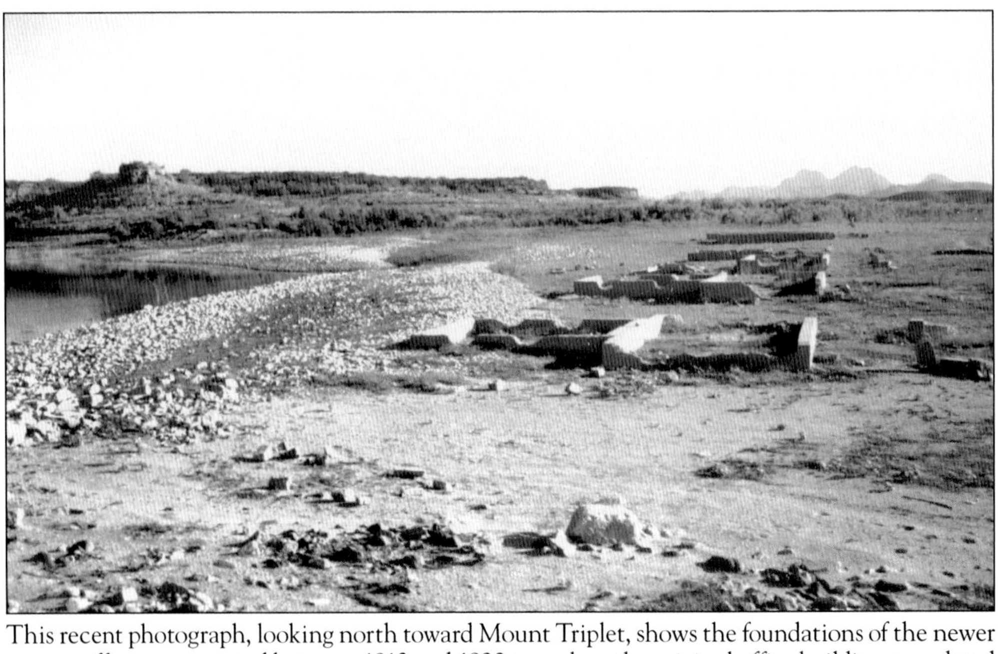

This recent photograph, looking north toward Mount Triplet, shows the foundations of the newer agency offices constructed between 1913 and 1920 to replace the original office building completed in 1876. (Courtesy authors' collection; photograph by Paul Nickens, 2001.)

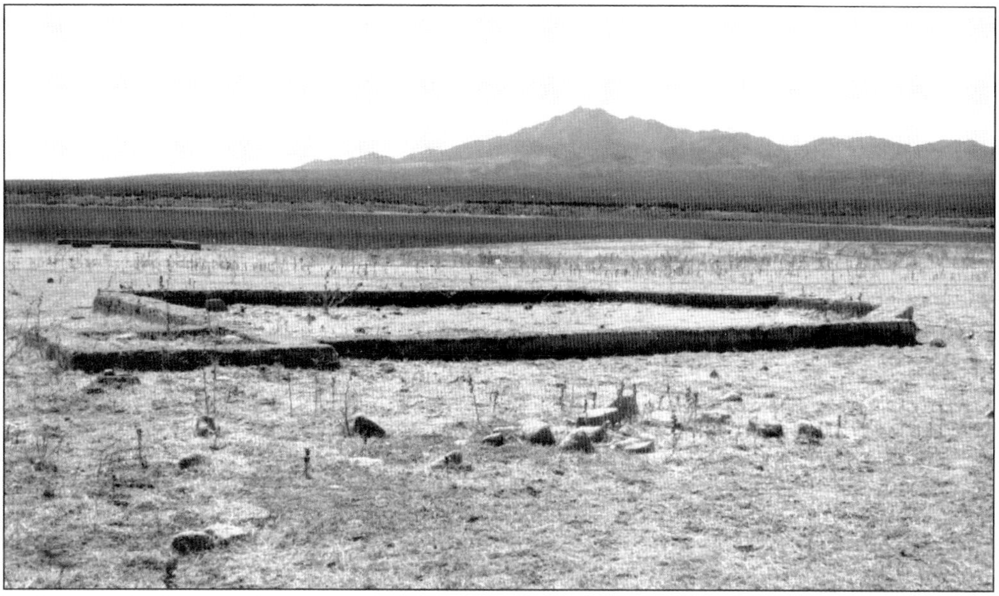

In this view looking southeast toward Mount Turnbull, the foundation of the Lutheran chapel at Old San Carlos is evident. Built about 1911, the church was dismantled in 1929 by the Lutherans, and the building stones were used to construct a schoolhouse at Peridot. (Courtesy authors' collection; photograph by Paul Nickens, 2001.)

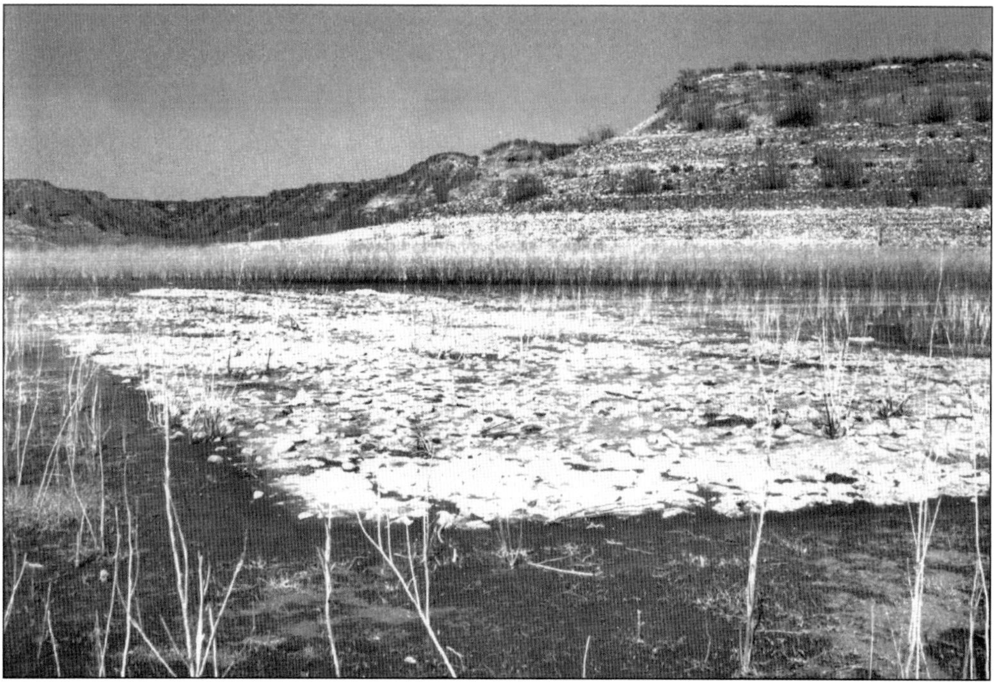

Per the wishes of Apache elders, a concrete cover was placed over a large cemetery at Old San Carlos containing about 300 ancestors' graves. As can be seen in this recent photograph, repeated inundation over the years has not disturbed this important place. The consequences of fluctuating water levels and waves can be seen on the slopes above the protected cemetery. (Courtesy authors' collection; photograph by Paul Nickens, 2001.)